Apple Pro Training Series

OS X Lion
Server Essentials

Arek Dreyer and Ben Greisler

Apple
Certified

Apple Pro Training Series: OS X Lion Server Essentials
Arek Dreyer and Ben Greisler
Copyright © 2012 by Peachpit Press

Published by Peachpit Press. For information on Peachpit Press books, contact:

Peachpit Press
1249 Eighth Street
Berkeley, CA 94710
(510) 524-2178
www.peachpit.com
To report errors, please send a note to errata@peachpit.com.
Peachpit Press is a division of Pearson Education.

Apple Series Editor: Lisa McClain
Production Coordinator: Kim Elmore, Happenstance Type-O-Rama
Technical Editor: Andrina Kelly
Apple Reviewer: John Signa
Apple Project Manager: Judy Lawrence
Copy Editor: Jessica Grogan
Proofreader: Jessica Grogan
Compositor: Chris Gillespie, Happenstance Type-O-Rama
Indexer: Jack Lewis
Cover Illustration: Kent Oberheu
Cover Production: Chris Gillespie, Happenstance Type-O-Rama

ISBN 13: 978-0-321-77508-5   ISBN 10: 0-321-77508-2
9 8 7 6 5 4 3 2 1 Printed and bound in the United States of America

Acknowledgments We extend a big thank you to all the people at Apple for getting Lion and Lion Server out the door, and of course to Steve Jobs, for inspiring us all.

Thanks to the Mac sysadmin community for always striving to better serve your users.

Thanks to Lisa McClain for gently making sure these materials made it into your hands, and to Jessica Grogan and Kim Elmore for working their editorial and production magic.

Thank you, also, to the following people. Without your help, this book would be much less than what it is: David Colville, Gordon Davisson, John DeTroye, Andre LaBranche, Charles Edge, Matthias Fricke, Allen Hancock, Aaron Hix, Eric Hemmeter, Jason Johnson, Adam Karneboge, Andrina Kelly, Ian Kelly, Bob Kite, Judy Lawrence, Chad Lawson, Woody Lidstone, David Long, Tip Lovingood, Duane Maas, Andrew MacKenzie, Jussi-Pekka Mantere, Steve Markwith, Kim Mitchell, Nader Nafissi, Tim Perfitt, Mike Reed, Schoun Regan, Jeremy Robb, John Signa, Chris Silvertooth, David Starr, Kevin White, Simon Wheatley, and Josh Wisenbaker.

Arek Dreyer Thanks to my lovely wife, Heather Jagman, for her love and support.

Ben Greisler My love and appreciation to my wife, Ronit, and my children, Galee and Noam, for supporting me through this project.

Contents at a Glance

Table of Contents

Getting Started

This book is based on the same criteria used for Apple's official training course, Lion 201: OS X Server Essentials 10.7, which provides an in-depth exploration of Lion Server. This book serves as a self-paced tour of the breadth of functionality of Lion Server and the best methods for effectively supporting users of Lion Server systems.

The primary goal of this book is to prepare technical coordinators and entry-level system administrators for the tasks demanded of them by Lion Server; you will learn how to install and configure Lion Server to provide network-based services, such as configuration profile distribution and management, file sharing, authentication, and collaboration services. To become truly proficient, you'll need to learn the theory behind the tools you will use. For example, not only will you learn how to use the Server app—the tool for managing services and accounts— but you will also learn about the ideas behind profile management, how to think about access to and control of resources, and how to set up and distribute profiles to support your environment.

You will learn to develop processes to help you understand and work with the complexity of your system as it grows. Even a single Lion Server computer can grow into a very complicated system, and creating documentation and charts can help you develop processes so that additions and modifications can integrate harmoniously with your existing system.

This book assumes that you have some knowledge of OS X Lion, because Lion Server is built on top of Lion. Therefore, basic navigation, troubleshooting, and networking are all similar regardless of whether the operating system is Lion or Lion Server. This book concentrates on the features that are unique to Lion Server. When working through this book, a basic understanding and knowledge of Lion is preferred, including knowledge of how to troubleshoot the operating system. Refer to *Apple Pro Training Series: OS X Lion Support Essentials* from Peachpit Press if you need to develop a solid working knowledge of Lion.

Unless otherwise specified, all references to Lion and Lion Server refer to version 10.7.2, which was the most current version available at the time of writing. Due to subsequent upgrades, some screen shots, features, and procedures may be slightly different from those presented on these pages.

Learning Methodology

This book is based on lectures and exercises provided to students attending Lion 201: OS X Server Essentials 10.7, a three-day, hands-on course designed to give technical coordinators and entry-level system administrators the skills, tools, and knowledge to implement and maintain a network that uses Lion Server. For consistency, this book follows the basic structure of the course material, but you may complete it at your own pace.

The exercises contained within this book are designed to let you explore and learn the tools necessary to manage Lion Server. They move along in a predictable fashion, starting with the installation and setup of Lion Server and moving to more advanced topics such as performing multiprotocol file sharing, using access control lists, and permitting Lion Server to manage network accounts. If you already have a Lion Server set up, you can skip ahead to some of the later exercises in the book, provided you understand the change in IP addressing from the examples to your server and are not running your server as a production server.

This book serves as an introduction to Lion Server and is not meant to be a definitive reference. Because Lion and Lion Server contain several open source initiatives, it is impossible to include all the possibilities and permutations here. First-time users of Lion Server and users of other server operating systems who are migrating to Lion Server have the most to gain from this book; still, others who are upgrading from previous versions of Lion Server will also find this book a valuable resource.

Lion Server is by no means difficult to set up and configure, but how you use Lion Server should be planned out in advance. Accordingly, this book is divided into eight chapters:

► Chapter 1 covers planning, installation, and initial configuration of Lion Server. It contains an introduction to the various administration tools, and has a focus on SSL (Secure Socket Layer) certificates.

► Chapters 2 and 3 define authentication and authorization, various types of access control, and Open Directory and the vast functionality it can provide.

► Chapter 4 covers managing accounts with the new Profile Manager service.

► Chapter 5 introduces deployment services, including NetBoot and the System Image Utility.

► Chapter 6 introduces the concept of sharing files, associating share points with users and groups, and controlling access to files with Access Control Lists.

► Chapter 7 teaches you how to use the Server app to configure how your server offers web sites.

► Chapter 8 focuses on setting up collaboration services such as mail, web, wiki, calendaring, and instant messaging.

Chapter Structure

Each chapter begins by listing the learning goals for the chapter and providing an estimate of time needed to complete the chapter. The explanatory material is augmented with hands-on exercises essential to developing your skills. If you lack the equipment necessary to complete a given exercise, you are still encouraged to read the step-by-step instructions and examine the screen shots to understand the procedures demonstrated.

WARNING ▶ The initial exercise in this book requires you to reformat a volume on which you will install Lion Server. All data on this volume will be erased. Once past that point, the majority of the exercises in the book are designed to be non-destructive if followed correctly. However, some of the exercises are disruptive; for example, they may turn off or on certain network services. Other exercises, if performed incorrectly, could result in data loss or corruption to some basic services, possibly even erasing a disk or volume of a computer connected to the network on which Lion Server resides. Thus, it is recommended that you run through the exercises on a Lion Server computer that is not critical to your work or connected to a production network. This is also true of the Lion computer you will use in these exercises. Please back up all your data if you choose to use a production computer for either the Lion Server and/or the Lion computers. Instructions are given for restoring your services to their preset state, but reasonable caution is recommended. Apple, Inc. and Peachpit Press are not responsible for any data loss or any damage to equipment that occurs as a direct or indirect result of following the procedures described in this book.

You'll also find resources that provide ancillary information throughout the chapters. These resources are merely for your edification, and are not essential for the coursework or certification.

Each chapter closes with a list of relevant Apple Knowledge Base articles and recommended documents related to the topic of the chapter. Lion Server documentation (http://www.apple.com/macosx/server/resources/) and Knowledge Base articles (http://www.apple.com/support) are free resources that contain the very latest technical information on all of Apple's hardware and software products. We strongly encourage you to read the suggested documents and search the Knowledge Base for answers to any problems you encounter.

Finally, at the end of each chapter is a short chapter review that recaps the material you've learned. You can refer to various Apple resources, such as the Knowledge Base, and Lion Server documentation, as well as the chapters themselves, to help you answer these questions.

System Requirements

This book assumes a basic level of familiarity with Lion. All references to Lion and Lion Server refer to v10.7.2, unless otherwise stated.

Here's what you will need to complete the lessons in the book:

▶ Two Macintosh computers, one with Lion installed and one on which you will install Lion Server

▶ An Ethernet switch to keep the two computers connected via a small private local network

▶ Two Ethernet network cables for connecting both computers to the switch

▶ A router (preferably an AirPort base station) to connect the small private network to the Internet, so you can obtain Apple Push Notification service (APNs) certificates for the Profile Manager service

▶ Optionally, a wireless access point (preferably an AirPort base station) to provide wireless access for iOS devices to your private network

▶ Optionally, three additional Macintosh computers on which to install Lion Server and configure as: an Open Directory replica; a member server; and a bound server on which to import users.

Apple Certification

After reading this book, you may wish to take the OS X Server Essentials 10.7 Exam. Passing both this exam and the OS X Support Essentials 10.7 Exam earns Apple Certified Technical Coordinator 10.7 (ACTC) certification. This is the second level of Apple's certification program for Mac professionals, which includes:

▶ Apple Certified Support Professional 10.7 (ACSP)—Ideal for help desk personnel, service technicians, technical coordinators, and others who support OS X Lion customers over the phone or who perform Mac troubleshooting and support in schools and businesses. This certification verifies an understanding of Lion's core functionality and an ability to configure key services, perform basic troubleshooting, and assist end users with essential Mac capabilities. To receive this certification, you must pass the OS X Support Essentials 10.7 Exam. This book is designed to provide you with the knowledge and skills to pass that exam.

▶ Apple Certified Technical Coordinator 10.7 (ACTC)—This certification is intended for Lion technical coordinators and entry-level system administrators tasked with maintaining a modest network of computers using Lion Server. Since the ACTC certification addresses both the support of Mac clients and the core functionality and use of Lion Server, the learning curve is correspondingly longer and more intensive than that for the ACSP certification, which addresses solely Mac client support. This certification requires passing both the OS X Support Essentials 10.7 Exam and OS X Server Essentials 10.7 Exam.

NOTE ▶ Although all of the questions in the OS X Server Essentials 10.7 Exam are based on material in this book, simply reading it will not adequately prepare you for the exam. Apple recommends that before taking the exam you spend time setting up, configuring, and troubleshooting Lion Server.

Apple hardware service technician certifications are ideal for people interested in becoming Macintosh repair technicians, but also worthwhile for help desk personnel at schools and businesses, and for Macintosh consultants and others needing an in-depth understanding of how Apple systems operate.

▶ Apple Certified Macintosh Technician (ACMT)—This certification verifies the ability to perform basic troubleshooting and repair of both desktop and portable Macintosh systems, such as iMac and MacBook Pro. ACMT certification requires passing the Apple Macintosh Service Exam and the Lion Troubleshooting Exam. To learn more about hardware certification, visit http://training.apple.com/certification/acmt.

About the Apple Training Series

Apple Pro Training Series: OS X Lion Server Essentials is part of the official training series for Apple products developed by experts in the field and certified by Apple. The chapters are designed to let you learn at your own pace. You can progress through the book from beginning to end, or dive right into the chapters that interest you most.

For those who prefer to learn in an instructor-led setting, training courses are offered at Apple Authorized Training Centers worldwide. These courses are taught by Apple Certified Trainers, and they balance concepts and lectures with hands-on labs and exercises. Apple Authorized Training Centers have been carefully selected and have met Apple's highest standards in all areas, including facilities, instructors, course delivery, and infrastructure. The goal of the program is to offer Apple customers, from beginners to the most seasoned professionals, the highest-quality training experience.

To find an Authorized Training Center near you, please visit http://training.apple.com.

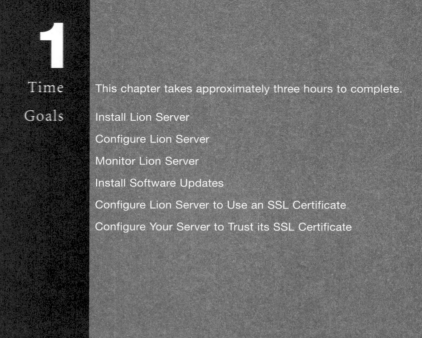

1

Time

This chapter takes approximately three hours to complete.

Goals

Install Lion Server

Configure Lion Server

Monitor Lion Server

Install Software Updates

Configure Lion Server to Use an SSL Certificate

Configure Your Server to Trust its SSL Certificate

Installing and Configuring OS X Lion Server

OS X Lion Server helps your users collaborate, communicate, share information, and access the resources they need to get their work done, whether in business or education. You can divide working with Lion Server into four phases:

1. Planning and installation: Plan how the server will be set up, verify and configure the hardware, and install the Lion Server software.

2. Configuration: Use the Server app to configure your Lion Server.

3. Monitoring: Use tools such as the Server app, Server Admin, and the Server Status widget to Monitor the status of your Lion Server, and optionally to specify an email address to receive notifications of specific alerts.

4. Ongoing Maintenance: Use tools such as the Server app, Server Admin, and Workgroup Manager to perform ongoing server and account maintenance and monitoring.

This chapter begins with planning, installation, configuration, and monitoring, and then introduces the tools that you will use throughout the rest of this book to manage your Lion Server.

You will also learn how to configure your Lion Server to use an SSL certificate to help users verify your server's identity, and encrypt communications with your server.

Evaluating Lion Server Requirements

Before you install the software, take the time to evaluate the server needs of your organization and the Lion Server hardware requirements.

You can install the Lion Server software on any Mac computer, provided it meets the following requirements.

Minimum Hardware Requirements

The basic installation requirements for Lion Server are as follows:

- ► A Mac computer with an Intel Core 2 Duo, Core i3, Core i5, Core i7, or Xeon processor
- ► 2 GB of RAM
- ► At least 10 GB of available disk space

You do not need a keyboard or display. As you'll see later in this chapter, you can install Lion Server using an administrator computer or another server.

To upgrade to Lion Server, your Mac must be running at least OS X 10.6.6 or later (version 10.6.8 is recommended).

Some features require an Apple ID, and some features require a compatible Internet service provider.

Additional Hardware Considerations

Typical considerations when choosing server systems include network and system performance, disk space, and RAM.

Networking

Be sure to consider the speed of the network interface when making a server hardware decision. Many of Apple's products support Gigabit Ethernet. If a Mac ships with a built-in Ethernet port, that port supports Gigabit Ethernet. If you consider installing Lion Server on a MacBook Air in a learning and testing scenario, the Apple USB Ethernet Adapter for MacBook Air, which does not have an Ethernet port, supports 10/100 Base-T Ethernet. You can combine two Ethernet interfaces to act as one, to aggregate network throughput for services such as Apple file sharing.

> **NOTE** ► Ethernet is required to provide NetBoot service. See Chapter 5, "Implementing Deployment Solutions," for more information.

Availability

In order to help ensure that Lion Server stays up and running, you can enable two Energy Saver system preference settings:

▶   Start up automatically after a power failure

▶   Restart automatically if the computer "freezes" (not available on all Macs)

Installing Lion Server

It is possible to purchase a Mac with Lion Server pre-installed. However, you may find yourself upgrading an existing Mac with OS X Snow Leopard, Snow Leopard Server, or Lion to Lion Server. Before you purchase Lion Server on the Mac App Store, confirm that your Mac is indeed eligible to run Lion Server.

Verifying System Requirements

Before you install Lion Server, confirm that your system meets the hardware requirements. You can find this information on the label attached to the box of every Mac sold, or you can find it with the About This Mac and System Information applications.

To check if a Mac that is already running Lion can run Lion Server, you can start with the About This Mac application, then move on to System Information, which contains all the information you need in a single application.

1   From the Apple menu, choose About This Mac.

Confirm that the Processor meets the requirements for Lion Server.

Confirm that there is at least 2 GB listed for Memory.

2   Click More Info.

The Overview pane displays information about your computer.

If you plan to perform a remote configuration of your Lion Server, you will authenticate with the hardware serial number, so make a note of it now.

3   To confirm that you have enough disk space, click Storage.

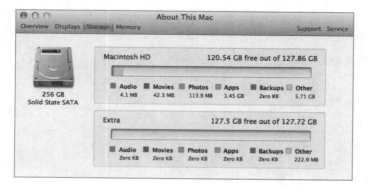

Confirm that you have at least 10 GB of free disk space available.

Preparing to Configure Remotely

You can perform an initial configuration of Lion Server locally on a Mac, using its keyboard and a display, but you can also do this remotely, for instance, if the Mac is in a server room that is not very comfortable to be in. In order to perform a remote configuration, you need to gather information from your target server. You'll use this information to:

▶   identify and locate the target server—with the MAC address.

▶   authenticate to the server—with the hardware serial number.

To find the MAC address of the primary Ethernet interface, you can use the System Report from System Information.

1   If you already have System Information open from the previous section, click System Report from the Overview pane.

Otherwise, hold the Option key, click the Apple menu, and choose System Information.

2   Click Network in the System Information sidebar.

3   In the list of Active Services, click the primary interface you will use for your Lion Server.

4   In the details section, locate the MAC Address. It is highlighted in the figure below.

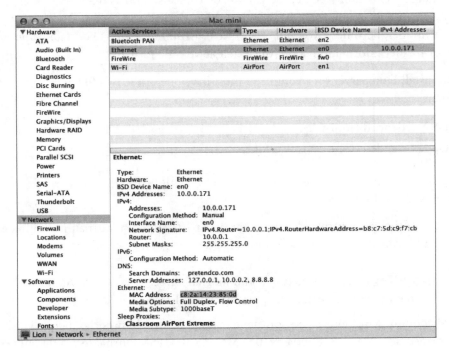

Formatting/Partitioning Drives

After you have confirmed that your computer meets the hardware requirements, you can simply install Lion Server on your existing hard disk, or you can install Lion Server on another disk. You can also begin making decisions surrounding the devices and subsequent formatting of those devices prior to actually installing the software.

Disk Utility is located in the Utilities folder, which is in the Applications folder. Using this utility, you can divide a hard disk into one or more partitions. Doing so allows you to first choose a partition scheme for your disk. Your choices are as follows:

▶ GUID Partition Table—Used to start up Intel-based Mac computers

▶ Apple Partition Map—Used to start up PowerPC-based Mac computers

▶ Master Boot Record—Used to start up DOS and Windows-based computers

> **NOTE** ▶ In order to install Lion Server on a volume, that volume's disk must be formatted with the GUID Partition Table. You can examine a disk's partition scheme with the Disk Utility application, which lists this information as the "Partition Map Scheme," and with the System Information application, which lists this information as "Partition Map Type."

Once you choose a partition scheme, you can divide your disk into as many as 16 logical drives, each with its own format. Each logical drive is called a partition. Once you format a partition, it becomes a volume. See *Apple Pro Training Series: OS X Lion Support Essentials* for further information about the available volume formats.

In order to install Lion Server on a volume, it must have one of the two following journaled formats:

▶ Mac OS X Extended (Journaled)

▶ Mac OS X Extended (Case-Sensitive/Journaled)

Unless you have a compelling reason to use Case-Sensitive/Journaled format, use Mac OS X Extended (Journaled).

You can use the other, nonjournaled formats for data partitions, but journaling eliminates the need for a lengthy disk check on a volume after a power outage or other failure.

> **MORE INFO** ▶ For more information about journaling, see "Mac OS X: About file system journaling" at http://support.apple.com/kb/HT2355.

> To read about moving your HFS+ journal to a separate disk in order to increase disk performance, see "Mac OS X Server v10.6: Moving an HFS+ Journal to a different volume" at http://support.apple.com/kb/HT3790.

By using separate partitions, you can segregate your data from the operating system. You may decide to store user data on a separate volume. Having the operating system on its own volume conserves space by keeping user files and data from filling up the boot volume. In case you need to perform a clean install of Lion Server at a later time, you can erase the entire boot volume and install the operating system without touching the data on the other volumes.

> **NOTE** ▶ Lion Server stores data for many of its services in /Library/Server on the boot volume by default, but as you will see later in this chapter, you can use the Server app to change the Service Data location. In any event, make sure you have a good backup of your server before erasing your Lion Server boot volume.

To create multiple partitions on a single hard disk, simply select your hard disk, choose the number of partitions from the Partition Layout menu, and choose the following for each partition:

▶ Name of partition—Using lowercase alphanumeric characters and removing spaces in volume names may help reduce troubleshooting of share points later down the road.

▶ Format of partition—See the previous list for various acceptable Lion Server partition formats.

▶ Size of partition—Again, Lion Server requires at least 10 GB of available disk space for installation.

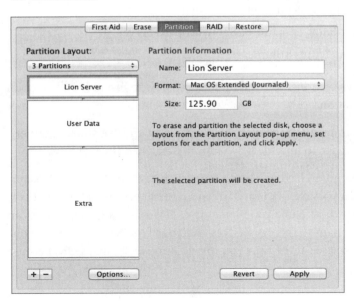

Before you click the Apply button, remember: *All previous data on the disk may be erased!*

Having multiple *partitions* does not increase speed, but installing multiple *drives* may increase server performance. Installing the operating system on one drive and installing additional drives to store user data can reduce connection times to the operating system and to data. If you add the second drive on a separate bus, the server can read and write to each of those buses independently.

RAID (Redundant Array of Independent Disks)

In order to provide increased availability or performance, you can install Lion Server on a RAID volume, but you cannot create a Recovery HD on a RAID Volume. See *Apple Pro Training Series: OS X Lion Support Essentials* for further information about Recovery HD.

Filevault Full Disk Encryption

For Lion Server, full disk encryption isn't recommended for the startup disk or any disk that stores service data, because full disk encryption requires a user to enter an encryption password after the computer starts up.

Installing Lion Server

There are three possible scenarios for installing Lion Server on your Mac:

▶ Install Lion Server components on Lion

▶ Install Lion Server over Snow Leopard or Snow Leopard Server

▶ Install Lion Server on an empty volume

After reading the next three sections, you will understand how to install Lion Server on your Mac for all three situations.

For all situations, it's best to manually assign your Lion Server an IPv4 address, rather than to rely on a DHCP service to provide a dynamically-assigned IPv4 address.

Because some services depend on having a host name (such as server17.pretendco.com), it is recommended that you provide DNS forward and reverse records so that the IPv4 address you use matches the host name you plan to use. This way, other computers can use your Lion Server's host name to access services that your Lion Server offers. If you don't have DNS records available at the time you install Lion Server, that's OK, because

Lion Server will provide DNS records for itself. However, if the DNS service for all the devices on your network does not provide DNS records for your Lion Server, other computers and devices will not be able to access services on your Lion Server by its host name.

Installing Server Components on Lion

You can install Lion Server on your Mac running Lion. This includes any Mac that shipped with Lion, and any Mac that was upgraded to Lion. It's recommended that before you install Lion Server, you configure your Mac to have a manually assigned IPv4 address so that your Lion Server's host name matches its IPv4 address.

During the installation of Lion Server, the Lion Server installer downloads a server software package, so you must be able to connect to the Apple Software Update server on port 80, or to a local Software Update Server which is connected to the Internet. See "Lion Server: Installation requires Internet access" at http://support.apple.com/kb/HT4770 for more information.

There are three main steps, which are covered in more detail immediately after this list:

▶ Configure your Mac with Lion to use a manually-assigned IPv4 address.

▶ Confirm that DNS records are available to associate the IPv4 address with a host name (like server17.pretendco.com).

▶ Install the Lion Server app on Lion.

Configuring your Mac with a Manual IPv4 Address

1 Choose System Preferences from the Apple menu.

2 Click Network.

3 If the lock icon is locked, click the lock and provide local administrator credentials.

4 In the list of interfaces on the left, select an Ethernet interface.

5 Click the pop-up menu for Configure IPv4 and choose Manually.

6 Specify the IPv4 network information with the settings you will use for your Lion Server.

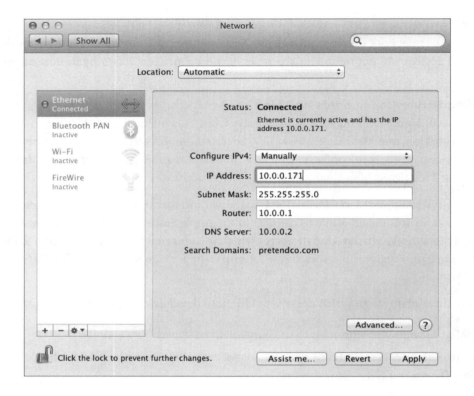

7 Click Apply.

Checking that Your Network's DNS Service Provides Forward and Reverse DNS Records
Computers and devices on your network can contact your Lion Server by its host name
only if the DNS service available on your network provides a DNS record.

1 Click Launchpad in the Dock.

2 Click the Utilities folder.

3 Click Network Utility.

4 Click Lookup.

5 Type the host name you will assign your Lion Server, and click Lookup.

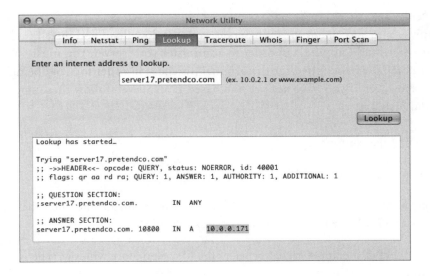

If there is a forward DNS record available for the host name, it will be in the answer section , as highlighted in the figure above.

6   In the "Enter an internet address to lookup" field, enter the IPv4 address you assigned your Lion computer and click Lookup.

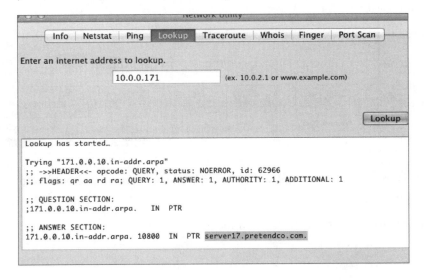

If there is a pointer record available for the IPv4 address, it will be in the answer section.

7   Quit Network Utility.

Installing the Server app

As stated in the license agreement for Lion Server, you can download and install the Server app on other Mac computers in order to administer your server. You must use the same Apple ID you supplied for the original purchase in order to avoid being charged again. However, if you have not yet purchased Lion Server, follow these steps to purchase and install it:

1 Log in to your Lion computer.

2 Click the App Store in the Dock.

3 If you aren't already signed in, choose Sign In from the Store menu, and enter the Apple ID that you will use to purchase the Server application.

4 In the search field in the upper-right corner of the Mac App Store window, type Server, and then press Return.

5 Select the "OS X Lion Server" application.

6 Click the price of the Server application ($49.99 in the U.S.).

7 Click Buy App (or Install).

You may need to provide your Apple ID credentials again.

The Mac App Store starts the download, and then opens Launchpad.

After "OS X Lion Server" has completed downloading, the Server app should automatically open.

8 In the Welcome to Server pane, click Continue.

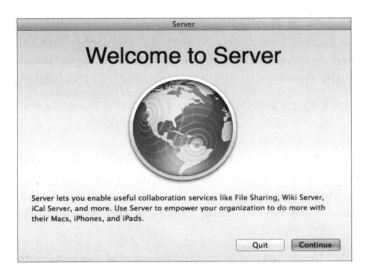

9 Agree to the license agreement.

10 In the Install Software pane, click Continue.

11 Provide administrator credentials, and then click Continue.

Wait while additional components are downloaded.

Installing Server Components on Snow Leopard Server

If you have an existing Snow Leopard Server, you can upgrade to Lion Server. Purchase and install Lion and Lion Server separately from the Mac App Store, and open "Install Mac OS X Lion" to perform the upgrade.

It is always best practice to back up any existing setup prior to running the upgrade so you can restore should anything go wrong.

> **NOTE** ▶ Updating the server software should be a planned event. Always run updates on a test system before rolling out into production. In some cases, third-party solutions have not continued to operate smoothly with the new software. You should pre-flight the update in isolation first and roll out the update once you have tested your implementation.

See the document "Lion Server Upgrading and Migrating" for detailed instructions; the URL is in the References section at the end of this chapter.

Installing Lion Server on an empty volume

If you purchase a Mac mini Server or a Mac Pro Server with Lion Server, the computer comes with a copy of Lion Server already installed; you don't have to install Lion Server, you can turn on the new computer and start configuring it.

It is also possible to install Lion Server on an empty volume; see the article http://support.apple.com/kb/HT4766, "Lion Server: Installing Lion Server on a blank volume" for detailed instructions on making sure the "Install Mac OS X Lion" and the "Server" applications are available in the same folder before running "Install Mac OS X Lion," selecting a blank volume, clicking Customize, and selecting the Server Software package.

NOTE ► It is possible to create a NetRestore image of this new volume that has an unconfigured Lion Server. See Chapter 5, "Implementing Deployment Solutions," as well as this document: http://support.apple.com/kb/HT4746, "Lion Server: Mass deployment strategies."

Configuring an Administrator Computer

You can configure, monitor, and manage a Lion Server from another computer (referred to as an administrator computer), simply by installing the Server app on that administrator computer. Additionally, you can download and install the Server Administration Tools.

NOTE ► Use only Macs with Lion or Lion Server to administer Lion Server. Do not use earlier versions of Mac OS X or Mac OS X Server.

There are two ways to obtain the Server app. You can:

► Copy the Server app from a computer that's already configured as a server; or you can:

► Install "OS X Lion Server" from the Mac App Store.

After you purchase Lion Server from the Mac App Store on your server, you can, free of charge, download and install it on another Mac you want to use to administer your Lion Server. Of course, you need to purchase a copy of Lion Server for each Mac computer that you will run as a Lion Server.

Configuring your Test Network for Exercises

The exercises in this book assume a private network with:

► Internet access

► DHCP service available

► Router at 10.0.0.1

► Subnet mask of 255.255.255.0

► DNS service available at 10.0.0.1

One way of providing this scenario is to use an Apple AirPort device such as AirPort Extreme or Time Capsule. In the exercises, the AirPort Extreme is configured to share its public address, as shown in the figure below:

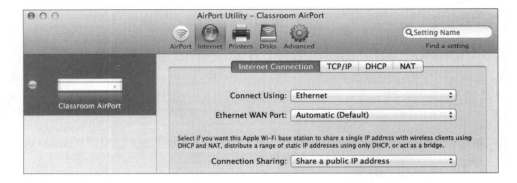

The DHCP range is 10.0.0.210 through 10.0.0.254, as shown in the figure below:

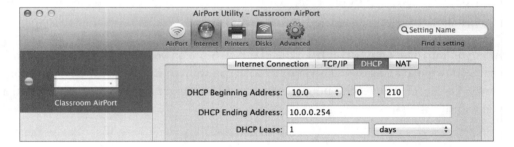

It is outside the scope of this book, however, to provide step-by-step instructions on configuring your network infrastructure to match the assumptions for the exercises.

Configuring your Administrator Computer for Exercises

If you're following the exercises in this book, you'll want to set a network location for the chapters in this book, so you can quickly refer back to them from any other network location. You will also be changing your computer name to make it easier to follow the examples in this book. Make sure your Lion computer is on the same subnet as your Lion Server (your Lion Server must use an Ethernet port, but your administrator computer can use Wi-Fi or Ethernet).

In order to download software updates from Apple, as well as the Mac App Store, your network should have DNS service available. However, if the DNS service on your network does not yet have DNS records set up for the host name that you assign to your Lion Server, you should configure your administrator computer to include, in its list of DNS Servers, the IP address that you will assign to your Lion Server, so that you can connect to your Lion Server using its host name.

The exercises in this book use 10.0.0.171 as the IP address for the Lion Server, and the server at 10.0.0.1 provides DNS records for other Internet hosts; you can use the same IP address scheme if you like, or adapt the information to your particular situation.

In the following steps, you will:

▶ create a network location for the exercises, so you can switch between using your administrator computer for exercises and for regular productivity.

▶ configure your administrator computer to use the IP address of your Lion Server for DNS service.

▶ configure your administrator computer to also use your network's regular DNS service.

▶ download or copy the Server app to your administrator computer.

1 If you're not already logged in, log in to your Lion computer and open System Preferences.

2 Click the Sharing preferences pane and change the computer name to Administrator Computer. You can change it back anytime you want.

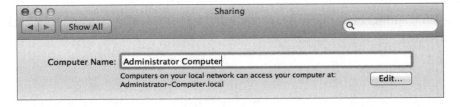

3 Click Show All, and click the Network preferences pane.

4 Choose Edit Locations from the Locations pop-up menu.

5 Click the Add (+) button to create a new location, and name it Lion Server Essentials Book.

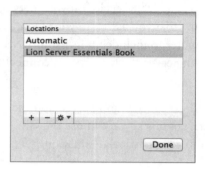

6 Click Done to dismiss the Locations pane.

7 For each network interface you're not using for the exercises: Select the interface in the left column, click the Services Action pop-up menu (labeled with a gear and a down arrow), and choose Make Service Inactive.

8 Click Apply.

9 In the left column, select the interface you will use for these exercises, and then click Advanced.

10 Click the TCP/IP tab.

11 Click the pop-up menu for Configure IPv4 and choose Using DHCP, if it is not already set to Using DHCP.

12 Click the DNS tab.

13 In the DNS Servers column, click the Add (+) button and add the IP address that you will use for your Lion Server, so you can reach it by its DNS host name by using its DNS service, if necessary.

This chapter assumes that you have only one client and one administrator computer, and your Lion Server will provide DNS service, so enter the IP address that you will assign to your server: 10.0.0.171.

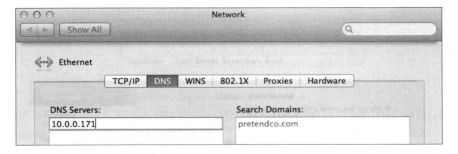

14 Click OK to dismiss the DNS pane, and then click Apply to apply the Network changes.

15 Click Show All, and click Users & Groups.

16 Select Login Options and choose Off from the "Automatic login" pop-up menu, select "Name and password" for "Display login window as," and select the checkbox labeled "Show fast user switching menu as: Full Name."

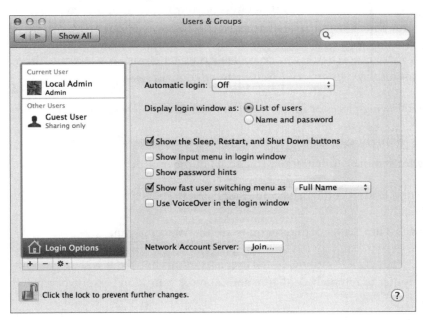

17 For these chapters, you may also want to change your Energy Saver preferences to have your Lion computer never go to sleep.

18 Close the System Preferences window, which quits System Preferences.

19 Open the Mac App Store and download the Server app, or copy the Server app from another computer if you already downloaded it.

Initial Lion Server Configuration

If you install Lion Server on a Mac that's already been configured, there's not much initial configuration; Lion Server uses the same local administrator user name and password, as well the same network settings, as before.

Starting Remote Configuration

You will be doing a remote configuration in this chapter, as if the server were in a server room or network closet down the hall from you without a video monitor to rely on.

The Server app will search for and display all the computers on the local subnet that are running Lion Server, whether or not they are configured. If more than one Lion Server is displayed, you need to know the MAC address of your target computer to be able to choose it from the list.

> **NOTE** ▸ If there is no DHCP service available on the network you're using, the Server app will not display a Lion Server waiting to be configured.

You need the following pieces of information in order to remotely configure Lion Server:

▸ IP address, Bonjour name, or DNS name of the Mac

▸ Password for remote configuration: (the serial number of the Mac)

Follow these steps to start configuring your Lion Server remotely:

1 Turn on your Lion Server computer on to see the Welcome pane.

> **NOTE** ▸ Do not click Continue. In the exercises in this book you will use an administrator computer to remotely configure and monitor your Lion Server when possible.

2 On your administrator computer, click Launchpad in your Dock.

3 Click the Server app. You may need to swipe to the next page in Launchpad to see the Server app (hold down the Command key and press the Right Arrow key, or if you have a trackpad, swipe to the left with two fingers to get to the next page in Launchpad).

> **NOTE ▶** Do not click Continue! If you do, you will be on the path to installing Lion Server. If you accidentally click Install, that's OK, you'll see the License agreement, and you can click Disagree to go back. Only use the Server app on your administrator computer to configure and manage your Lion Server.

4 From the Manage menu, choose Connect to Server.

5 At the Choose a Mac window, select your server from the list, and then click Continue.

The Server app displays all the servers on your local subnet, not just Lion Servers that have not yet been configured. You can identify your server by its MAC address; the Server app lists any Lion Server that has not yet been configured with its Bonjour name, which consists of its computer model and its MAC address.

6   Enter your server's complete hardware serial number (the serial number is case-sensitive), and click Continue.

NOTE ▸ Unlike previous versions of Mac OS X Server, you must use the complete serial number.

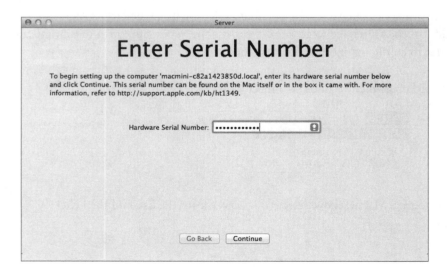

As soon as your administrator computer successfully authenticates to your Lion Server, your server's screen will indicate that it's being set up by displaying a "Remote Setup In Progress" message in the Welcome pane.

Making Configuration Decisions

When you perform an initial configuration of Lion Server, you interact with the Server Assistant. The following information should help you decide how to choose various options that the Server Assistant offers.

Region Pane

7   In the Region pane, make an appropriate selection, and then click Continue.

Keyboard Pane

8   In the Keyboard pane, select an appropriate layout and click Continue.

Transferring an Existing Server Pane

You can transfer data and settings from a Time Machine backup or another volume with Lion Server installed.

> **NOTE** ▶ This feature allows a lateral migration from one Lion Server to another Lion Server, a new feature with Lion Server.

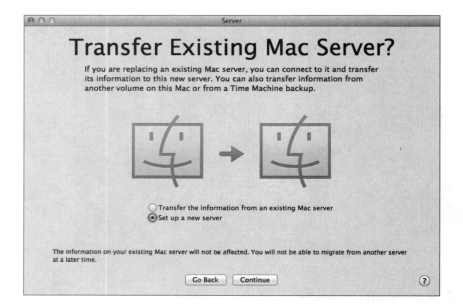

9   Select Set up a new server, and click Continue.

Apple ID Pane

If you supply your Apple ID, the Server Assistant will automatically generate Apple Push Notification Service (APNs) certificates for your server and send you an email notification that they have been successfully generated. See Chapter 4, "Managing Accounts," for more information about APNs and the Profile Manager.

10   For the purpose of the exercises in this book, leave the fields empty and click Continue.

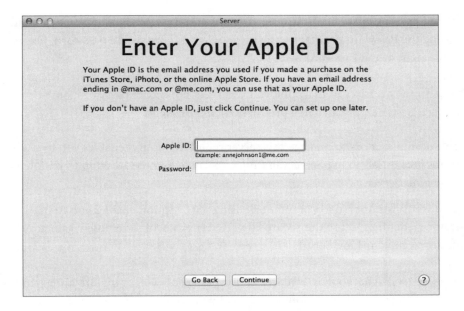

License Agreement pane

You must have a valid license for each copy of Lion Server that you run. Of course, you can use the Server app on as many Lion computers as you like for the purpose of remotely configuring, managing, and monitoring Lion Server.

11 Agree to the License.

Registration Information pane

If you provided an Apple ID, Server Assistant uses this to populate the fields in the Registration pane.

12 For the purpose of the exercises in this book, leave the fields empty and click Continue.

Administrator Account pane

If you provided an Apple ID, Server Assistant suggests using your name, however you may want to use a more general administrator name, like Local Admin.

You must configure an initial administrator user account. In a production environment, consider using the Password Assistant to help you select a more secure password; just click the key at the right of the Password field.

> **NOTE ▶** In the exercises in this book you will use a nonsecure password, but you should use a secure password in a production environment.

The "Enable administrators to manage this server remotely" option enables you to use administrator credentials to use Screen Sharing and Apple Remote Desktop to remotely control your Lion Server.

The "Enable administrators to log in remotely using SSH" option enables you to use administrator credentials to use the Secure Shell (SSH) protocol to remotely gain command-line access to your Lion Server.

> **NOTE ▶** The SSH checkbox is available at this point only with a remote initial configuration. When you configure Lion Server locally instead of remotely, the SSH service is not enabled, but you can later use the Server app to enable remote login using SSH.

13 For the purpose of the exercises in this book, enter the following information:

Name: Local Admin

Short Name: ladmin

Password: ladminpw

Verify: ladminpw

14 Leave selected the checkbox labeled "Enable administrators to manage this server remotely."

15 Leave deselected the checkbox labeled "Enable administrators to log in remotely using SSH."

16 Click Continue.

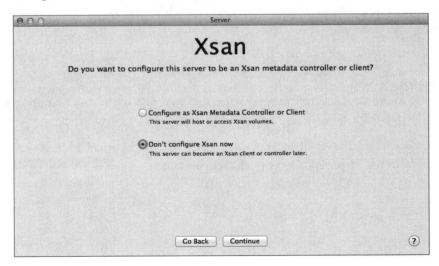

Xsan Pane

If your server has a Fibre Channel card installed, you will be presented with an Xsan configuration pane. This book does not cover configuring Xsan. Unless you understand the implications of configuring Xsan at this point, click "Do not install Xsan."

17 For the purpose of the exercises in this book, if you see the Xsan pane, click "Don't configure Xsan now" and then click Continue.

Multiple Networks Detected pane

If your server is connected to more than one active Ethernet network, you will see the Multiple Networks Detected pane. Choose the primary network connection from the pop-up menu, and Server Assistant uses that network connection to determine your server's host name.

18 For the purpose of the exercises in this book, you should have only one active network connection. If you see the Multiple Networks Detected pane, choose the appropriate network connection and click Continue.

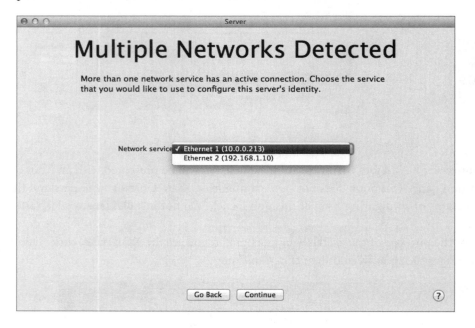

Organization pane

If you provided an Apple ID at the Apple ID pane, the Server Assistant uses that information to populate the fields here.

The Server Assistant uses the email address you provide here as the email address that receives alerts from the Server app. You can change this later.

The Server Assistant will use this information if you later use the Server app to create a self-signed SSL certificate. See the section Understanding SSL Certificates for more information.

19 For the purpose of the exercises in this book, enter the following information:

Organization Name: Pretendco

Admin Email Address: student17@pretendco.com

20 Click Continue.

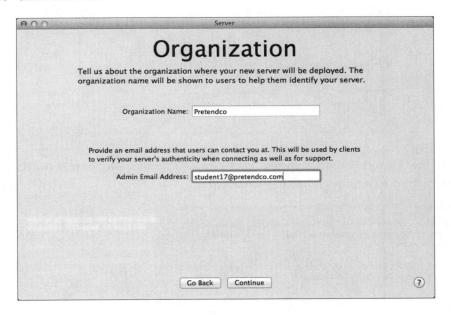

Time Zone pane

You are asked to specify the time zone where the server will be located and to choose whether or not this server will use another server running the Network Time Protocol (NTP). It is important to note that if you are planning to handle authentication through Kerberos or are connecting this server to another server running Kerberos, synchronizing time to avoid time drift is paramount. This is because by default, a Kerberos authentication scheme does not permit time skew greater than five minutes between itself and computers requesting authentication.

21 Select the time zone appropriate for your location.

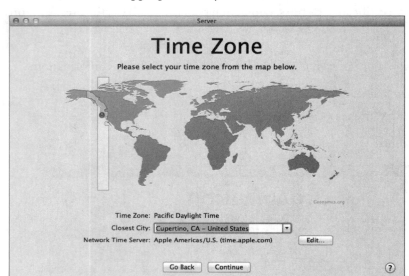

22 Next to the Network Time Server field, click Edit, choose an appropriate network time server from the pop-up menu, and click OK.

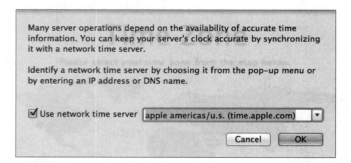

Host Name pane

You have three choices. If you want computers and devices that are not on your organization's internal network to be able to access services offered by your Lion Server, select "Host name for Internet." The second option, "Host name for private network" might be appropriate if you install Lion Server with a private IPv4 address on a network that allows computers and devices to use a Virtual Private Network (VPN) to gain access to that network. However, if your Lion Server does not need to ever be accessed by anyone outside of your local private network, you could select "Host name for local network."

23 For the purpose of the exercises in this book, select "Host name for Internet" and click Continue.

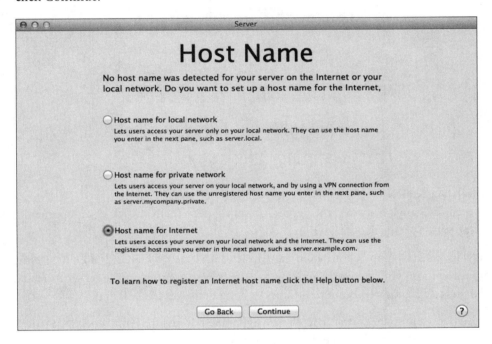

Connecting to Your Mac pane

This pane allows you to set your Computer Name, Host Name, and offers a shortcut to the Network system preference.

In the figure below, the Server Assistant automatically provided a Computer Name based on the Organization Name you provided at the Organization pane. The Host Name is blank, because your server acquired an IPv4 address via DHCP, and there is no DNS record for that IPv4 address. In the next step you will change the IPv4 address.

The Network Address

If you click Change Network, the Server Assistant opens the Network system preference so you can modify your network setup.

A new instance of Lion Server will obtain an IPv4 address via DHCP. If a DHCP server is not present on your network, and you use the Server Assistant at the server instead of remotely, a self-allocated Bonjour address starting with 169.254 will appear.

It is highly recommended that you choose a manual address for your servers, because dynamic addressing will reduce the number of services you can offer, and most services require a statically assigned address.

Apple servers can use multiple interfaces for network access. Examples include computers with Wi-Fi cards installed and Mac Pro computers with dual Gigabit Ethernet ports.

The Network system preference displays any interfaces it finds, so you can select whether TCP/IP should be enabled for each interface. You are prompted for detailed configuration information for each selected interface on subsequent panes.

The figure below shows how each Ethernet interface is displayed for configuration. Each interface has its own IP settings—for hosting different server services or dividing the amount of traffic supported over any one interface, including the ability to disable IPv6 and set your Ethernet interface to match the speed of your switch, should the need arise. You can also manually configure multiple interfaces or reconfigure network information later using the Network preferences.

If the DNS Server you specify in the DNS Server field of the Network preferences does not supply forward and reverse DNS records for the address you specify in the IP Address field, then the Server app automatically configures and starts the DNS service on your server, and updates the DNS Server field to use its own DNS service in addition to the DNS service you specify.

24 Click Change Network.

25 For each network interface you're not using for the exercise: Select the interface in the left column, click the Services Action pop-up menu (labeled with a gear and a down arrow), and choose Make Service Inactive.

26 Configure your primary network interface with the following information:

Configure IPv4: Manually

IP Address: 10.0.0.171

Subnet Mask: 255.255.255.0

Router: 10.0.0.1

DNS Server: 10.0.0.1

Search Domains: pretendco.com

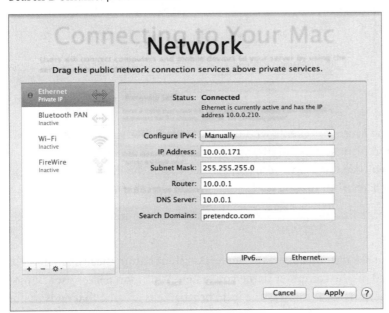

27 Click Apply.

NOTE ▶ In the Network preferences, you can also create multiple settings for a single interface. (To do so, select the interface and click the Duplicate button.) This option is useful for assigning multiple IP addresses to the same Ethernet interface. One use of this is to host multiple websites, with unique IP addresses and unique webpages, from a single server with only one Ethernet interface. This configuration may require modifying DNS entries.

After you click Apply, you see the Connecting to Your Mac pane again, with the Network Address updated, as shown in the figure below.

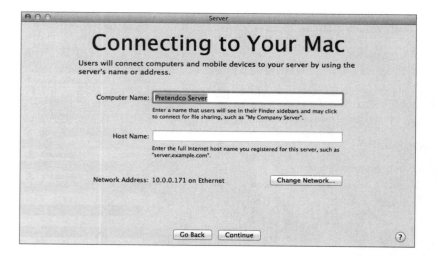

The Computer Name

The Computer Name is used by clients who use the Apple Filing Protocol (AFP) to access AFP share points and print services on the server. The Computer Name can contain spaces. OS X users will see this name in the Shared section of the Finder sidebar if your server offers file- or screen-sharing services.

If you specified an organization name, Server Assistant uses that information to suggest a computer name.

Although you do not see it in this pane, the Server Assistant automatically generates a local hostname based on the computer name you assign. Your Lion Server uses Bonjour to advertise its services on its local subnet. The local hostname is a name that ends in .local and follows the rules for DNS names. Server Assistant automatically removes any special characters and replaces any space character with a dash in the local hostname.

28 Replace the default contents of the Computer Name field with the text server17.

After the server is done being configured, its computer name appears in the Finder window sidebar of other mac computers on your server's subnet.

The Host Name

The host name, or the primary DNS host name, is a unique name for your Lion Server, historically referred to as the fully qualified domain name, or FQDN. Some services on Lion Server either require a working FQDN or will work better if one is available. Computers and devices can access services on your Lion Server by using your Lion Server's DNS host name, even if they are not on the same local subnet.

When you configure Lion Server, be sure to have an active network connection, even if it is only to a network switch that doesn't have anything else connected to it. The Host Name gets automatically updated if you edit the Network Address (see the following section), so you may want to update your network address before specifying your host name.

If there is a DNS record that resolves the IPv4 address that your Lion Server uses (whether this was manually assigned on Lion before you upgraded to Lion Server, or assigned by DHCP) with a DNS host name, you will see that Server Assistant automatically entered the DNS host name in the Host Name field.

If the Server Assistant does not detect the DNS name you specify here from a DNS service, the Server Assistant automatically:

► configures the DNS service on your server to provide a forward DNS record for your primary DNS name and a reverse DNS record for your IPv4 address.

► starts the DNS service.

► configures your server's primary network interface to use 127.0.0.1 (the loopback address which always points back to the computer itself) as the primary DNS service.

This ensures that your server will always be able to resolve its host name to its IPv4 address, and its IPv4 address to its host name.

29 Enter server17.pretendco.com in the Host Name field.

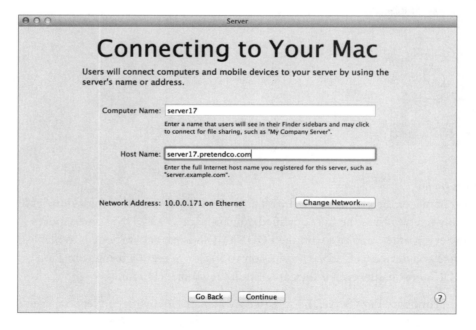

30 Click Continue.

AirPort Management pane

If your local network has an Apple AirPort device such as an AirPort Extreme or a Time Capsule, you can allow Server Admin to update that AirPort's configuration when you enable certain services, such as Address Book or Mail. This is a powerful feature that allows the Server app to modify the Network Address Translation (NAT) port mappings so that certain services are available to the public, even if your Lion Server has a private IPv4 address.

> **NOTE** ▶ Deselect the checkbox if you do not want to allow your Lion Server to manage the AirPort base station, otherwise the Server app will continually ask you for the password to the Airport base station.

31 If necessary, deselect the checkbox so that your server is not allowed to manage the AirPort and click Continue.

Review pane

This is a last chance to make any changes before you commit to the configuration choices.

32 Click Set Up.

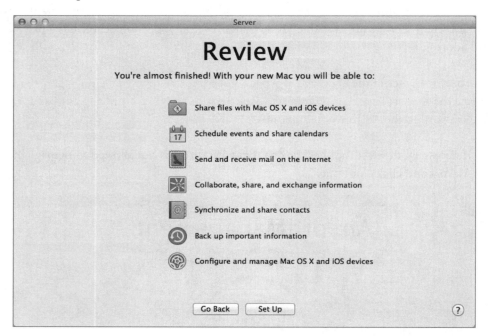

Thank You pane

If you use Server Assistant to perform a remote configuration of Lion Server, you see two options: Configure and Share Screen.

If you click Configure, the Server app connects to the remote Lion Server so you can use the Server app to continue to configure, manage, and monitor your Lion Server.

If you click Share Screen, the Server app opens the Screen Sharing application so you can remotely access your Lion Server as if you were using a keyboard and mouse right at the Lion Server itself.

If you configured Lion Server using that Lion Server (rather than remotely), the Thank You pane has a simple button to start using Lion Server.

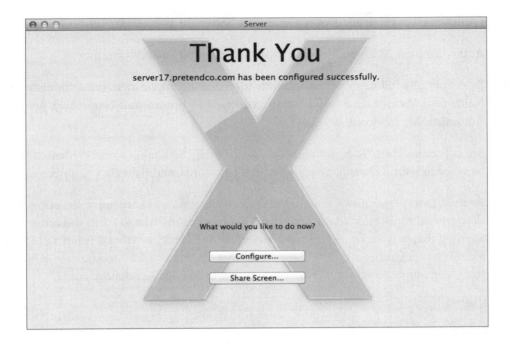

33 At this point, choose Manage > Close.

Using Tools for Monitoring

You will now learn about the tools you can use to monitor your Lion Server. Later chapters in this book address configuring the various services on your Lion Server.

This section covers using the Server app, Server Admin, and the Server Status widget.

Connecting to a Lion Server with the Server App on an Administrator Computer

If you use the Server app from an administrator computer, you need to specify a Lion Server to connect to, as well as administrator credentials. Additionally, you need to trust the SSL certificate, but you need to do that only the first time you connect to a specific Lion Server.

1 If necessary, open the Server app.

Do not click Continue, as this is the start of installing Lion Server. You will use the Server app to remotely administer and monitor your Lion Server.

2   From the Manage menu, choose Connect to Server (or press Command-N).

3   At the Choose a Mac window, select your server and then click Continue.

4   By default, the full name of the currently logged-in user appears in the Administrator Name field. Provide the administrator credentials (Administrator Name: Local Admin; Administrator Password: ladminpw).

5   Select the checkbox "Remember this password in my keychain," so the credentials will be saved in your Keychain, a secure store of passwords, and then click Connect.

6   Because Lion Server uses a self-signed SSL certificate named com.apple.servermgrd that your administrator computer has not yet been configured to trust, you see a warning that you are connecting to a server whose identity certificate is not valid. Just for this test environment, click Show Certificate, then select the checkbox for "Always trust "com.apple.servermgrd" when connecting to "server17.pretendco.com.""

7   Click Continue.

8   In order to make the changes to your certificate trust settings, when prompted, provide your administrator credentials (Name: Local Admin; Password: ladminpw) and click Update Settings.

Using the Server App to Monitor your Lion Server

Once you're connected to a Lion Server, either locally, while logged in on your Lion Server, or remotely, using an administrator computer, you can start using the Server app.

You can use the Server app to configure your Lion Server to send an email alert when any of the following conditions occur:

► A disk is low on available space.

► A software update is available.

► An SSL certificate is about to expire.

► An email message has a virus.

► The network configuration has changed.

To configure the email address that is the recipient of Alerts from the Server app:

1 In the Server app sidebar, click Alerts.

2 Click the Action pop-up menu (looks like a gear), and choose Configure Email Address.

3 Enter the email address that should receive alerts, and click OK.

It's a good idea to use the Server app to pro-actively monitor your Lion Server, so you can address any issues that crop up, rather than reacting to an alert in a crisis situation.

One of the alerts is for low disk space; instead of waiting for an alert, you should regularly use the Server app to display information about available disk space.

1 Select your server in the Server app sidebar.

2   Click Storage (your server may appear different than the figure below).

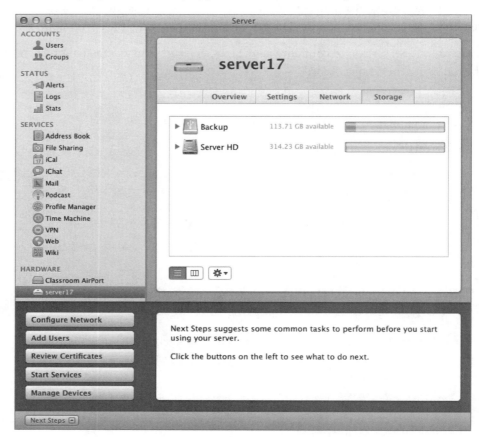

Although there is no alert for an abnormally high amount of processor usage, memory usage, or network traffic, it's still a good idea to monitor these occasionally. The Server app displays a graph of the following categories of information:

▶ Processor Usage (including System CPU and User CPU)

▶ Memory Usage

▶ Network Traffic (including Outbound Traffic and Inbound Traffic)

You can change the time frame of each graph, from as small a span as 1 hour, to as long as 7 days.

To use the Server app to display the available graphs:

1   In the Server app sidebar, click Stats.

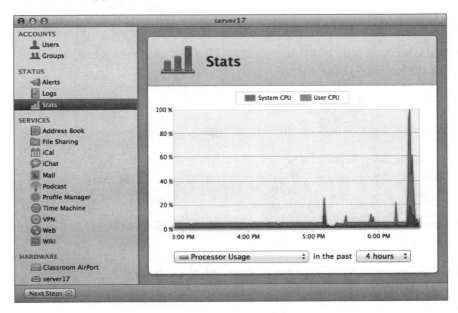

2   Click the pop-up menu on the left to choose Processor Usage, Memory Usage, or Network Traffic.

3   Click the menu on the right to choose the duration of time to include for the graph.

Installing Server Admin Tools on Lion and on Lion Server

Although the Server app should meet most of your needs as a Lion Server administrator, there are other tools you will use in this book, including Server Admin and Workgroup Manager. In order to install these tools, you need to download the Server Admin Tools 10.7 (it is available from http://support.apple.com/downloads) and install the package.

In general, the Server Admin tools are not required to run Lion Server, but they are required for the exercises in this book.

To install the Lion Server Admin Tools on your administrator computer:

1   Search for "Server Admin Tools 10.7" from http://support.apple.com/downloads/.

2   Download the latest version of Server Admin Tools appropriate for the version of Lion Server that you are using. This book was written using the "Server Admin Tools 10.7.2" disk image.

3   After the download has completed, click your Downloads folder in your Dock, and open the disk image you just downloaded.

4   In the Finder, in the disk image you just opened, open the package named ServerAdminTools.pkg, which automatically opens the Installer application.

5   Follow the directions in the Installer to install the package.

6   When the installation has completed, close the Installer window.

7   Eject the Server Admin Tools disk image by selecting it in the Finder and choosing File > Eject.

8   Locate the Server Admin Tools by clicking Launchpad in the Dock, then clicking the Server folder.

> **NOTE ▸** The Server folder is installed in your Applications folder.

After you install Server Admin Tools 10.7, the following tools are installed:

► Podcast Composer
► Server Admin
► Server Monitor
► System Image Utility
► Workgroup Manager
► Xgrid Admin

NOTE ▶ If you have the Server Admin Tools 10.6 installed on Snow Leopard or Snow Leopard Server, and upgrade or migrate to Lion or Lion Server, the 10.6 Tools will be removed because they are not compatible with Lion.

NOTE ▶ Although you should generally match the version of the Server Admin Tools with the version of OS X Server, you can use Server Admin Tools 10.7 to administer Snow Leopard Server computers.

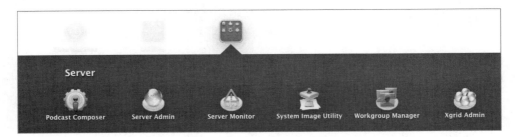

After you configure Lion Server, you can follow the same procedure on your server to install the Server Admin Tools on your server, but you may find that you do not need to do so, because you will use your administrator computer to configure, manage, and monitor your Lion Server.

Using Server Admin to Monitor your Lion Server

With Server Admin, you can configure and monitor services running on your Lion Server systems.

NOTE ▶ This chapter covers Server Admin only briefly; it is covered in greater detail throughout the book.

Connect to your server with Server Admin.

1 Click Launchpad in the Dock.

2 Click the Server folder.

3 Click Server Admin.

4 In the Address field, enter the DNS host name (or IP address or local host name if the network is not set up for DNS) of the server. In this case, use the DNS name server17.pretendco.com.

5   Authenticate as your local administrator. In this case, enter the user name (ladmin) and password (ladminpw).

6   Click Connect.

You see a Server Admin window with a general overview of your Lion Server.

7   Click the word Servers in the upper-left corner of Server Admin.

The Servers list contains a list of available servers (discovered via Bonjour services discovery), any servers ready for install, any servers ready for setup, and all the servers you're connected to (in this case, just your server at the moment). To add a server to the list, click the Add (+) pop-up menu in the lower-left corner of window, choose Add Server, and authenticate to the server. To remove a server from the list, select it, click the Action pop-up menu (labeled with a gear and a down arrow), and choose Remove Server.

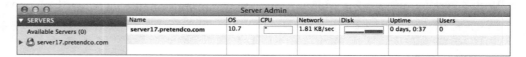

If you select your server from the list on the left, you will be able to interact with your server directly. If, however, you click directly on the word *Servers* in the window, you will be able to view statistics on all the connected servers, such as the name, operating-system version, CPU usage, network throughput, disk usage, uptime, and number of connected users.

Display the percentage of free disk space on attached volumes:

1   Click Servers in the upper-left corner of Server Admin.

2   Double-click the disk usage icon in the entry for your server.

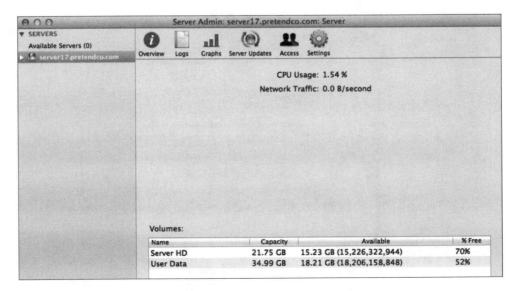

Note that this gives you detailed information, including an exact amount of space available for each volume.

Working with General Settings in Server Admin

1   To work with the general settings for a server, select the server in the Servers list and use the buttons at the top of the window.

2   Click Overview to view information about the server. You can view hardware information, server software version information, services running, and in the Status section, the number of connected users, uptime, and graphs for CPU use, network throughput, and available disk space.

   NOTE ▶ If Server Admin does not have enough room to display graphs, you must resize the Server Admin window to make room for graphs. You could use the Displays system preference to increase your screen resolution, or choose Dock > Turn Hiding On from the Apple menu to make more room for the Server Admin window. In either case, your next step is to drag the bottom of the Server Admin window toward the bottom of your screen, in order for Server Admin to display graphs.

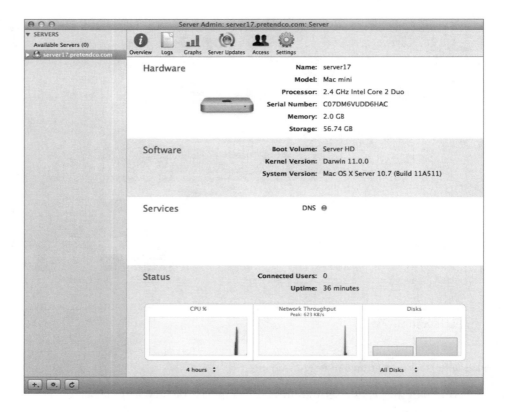

3 Click Logs to view the system log, kernel log, secure log, or software update log.

4 Click Graphs to view a graphical history of server CPU and network activity.

Once Graphs is selected, you can choose to view network traffic and CPU usage over varying lengths of time (past day; 1, 2, 4, 6, 12, and 24 hours; 2, 3, 5, and 7 days; and past week) by selecting either option from the pop-up menu at the bottom of the window.

5 Click Server Updates to use Software Update to remotely update the server's software.

6 Click Access to restrict who can access the server's various services and who can administer and monitor those services. You will use this to manage service access control lists (SACLs) in the next chapter.

7 Click Settings, and then click the General tab to enable or disable various protocols and services.

8 Click the Network tab to see the computer name, local host name, and network inter-face information. The computer name is what OS X computers will see in the Finder window sidebar if your server offers file- or screen-sharing services.

9 Click the Date & Time tab to control whether you use the Network Time Server, which is important if you are in a Kerberos environment. You can also set the time zone here.

10 Click the Alerts tab to configure the sending of an email message to a specified address when one of three criteria is met:

▶ A disk has less than x percent of free space, where x is determined by you.

▶ New software updates are available for the server.

▶ A certificate is expired or about to expire.

11 Select each of the checkboxes.

12 Click the Add (+) button, and enter an email address such as student17@pretendco.com, and click Save.

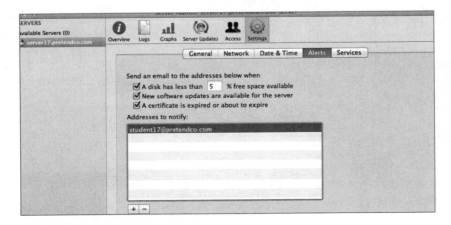

13 Click the Services tab to select various services you can manage with Server Admin.

Note that in the figure below, the checkbox for the DNS service is selected. This is because there was no DNS record available for your Lion Server's IPv4 address, so the Server Assistant automatically enabled the DNS service.

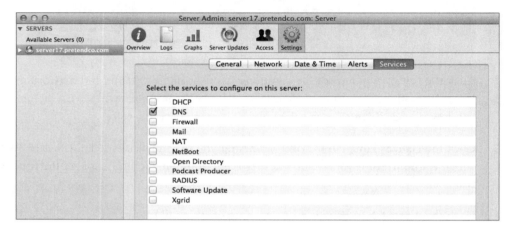

Working with Services

You use the Server app to configure most common services of Lion Server, but you can also use Server Admin to enable and configure various other services. To work with a particular service on a server, select the checkbox next to the service, and then click the Save button at the bottom of the window.

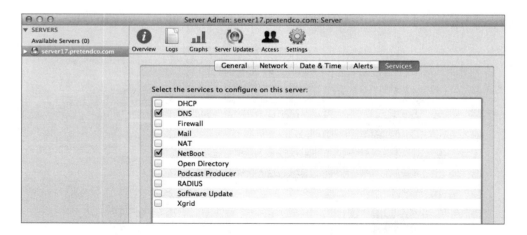

Next, click the disclosure triangle beside the server to reveal the list of services offered by the server, and then click the service. Use the buttons at the top of the window to manage the service's settings and to display status information, including logs for some services.

To start or stop a service, select the service (rather than the server entry) under your server, and then click Start *Service Name* or Stop *Service Name* at the bottom left of Server Admin. You can also use the Server menu and choose Start Service, Stop Service, or Soft Restart service, depending on the service.

You can allow Server Admin to have several windows open at once by choosing New Server Admin Window from the Server menu, and you can be connected to several servers simultaneously by clicking the Add (+) pop-up menu at the bottom of the window and choosing Add Server. Table 1.1 defines the Lion Server services available in Server Admin.

Table 1.1   Lion Server Services List

Service	Function
DHCP	Distributes IP address and associated information
DNS	Maps IP addresses to names
Firewall	Protects ports against attacks
Mail	Mail service
NAT	Network Address Translation
NetBoot	Network booting and installing service
Open Directory	Shared directory and authentication service
Podcast Producer	Automates and shares processing of podcast creation
RADIUS	Authentication for access to wireless network
Software Update	Offers Apple software updates stored locally
Xgrid	Manages processing jobs across a grid of Macs

When you select certain services, including Mail, Podcast Producer, RADIUS, and Xgrid, and then click Overview for that service, there is a Configure *Service Name* button available.

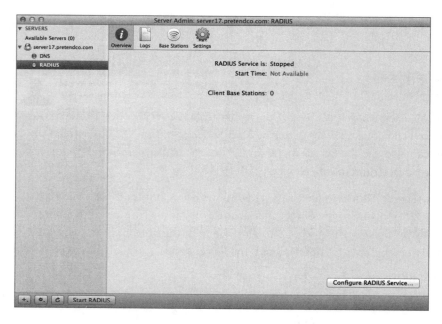

When you click that Configure *Service Name* button, a new window opens and presents a step-by-step assistant that helps you through the setup of that service.

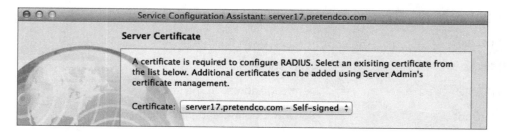

Exporting and Importing Settings

You can export (and subsequently import) both service settings and server settings by choosing Server > Export > Service Settings and/or Server > Export > Server Admin Preferences. When exporting your Server Admin preferences, you can save the single file anywhere you choose. When saving service settings, you are presented with a dialog showing all the currently running services that you can configure with Server Admin. You simply select the checkbox next to the services whose settings you want to save, and then click OK. Find a location suitable for saving those preferences, and save them.

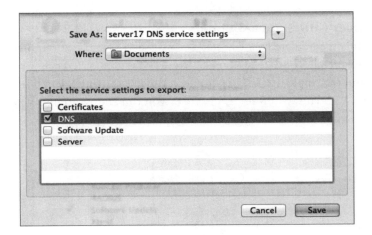

Conversely, when you are ready to import a service setting, choose Server > Import and locate the appropriate file.

Enabling Screen Sharing

Using Server Admin, you can control the screen of a remote Lion Server. You must first connect and authenticate to the server so you can see the Overview window and other various services windows. Select the remote server in the list of servers, and from the Server menu, choose Share Server's Screen. This opens the Screen Sharing application.

An authentication pane appears, asking you for that server's local administrator user name and password. Once you enter the information requested and click Connect, a new window appears, allowing you to share control of the keyboard and mouse of that remote server.

NOTE ▶ The Name field automatically contains the name of the user you are currently logged in as. However, you need to enter credentials for an administrative user on the computer you are attempting to control with the Screen Sharing application.

Updating your Lion Server with Software Update

After installation and setup are complete, you can update your server locally or remotely. Locally, you would use the Software Update preferences pane of System Preferences or select Software Update from the Apple menu. You should choose to show the details of the updates and select which updates you want to install, or you can choose to install all updates. Next, authenticate as a local administrator to begin the update process.

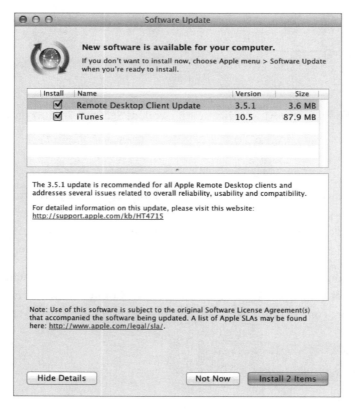

Alternatively, you can run Software Update remotely by using the Server app or Server Admin to update your computer running Lion Server. Software Update uses the server's connection to the Internet to check for the latest software updates for the server. The Server app will send you an email alert if there is a Software Update (if you entered an email address in the Alerts pane). You can also have Server Admin alert you to the presence of software updates by setting an email address and clicking the checkbox requesting notification of such updates. This is done under the Settings tab of Server Admin.

Plan for software updates. As updates to the server software become available from Apple, you will want to apply them to your servers. This should be done carefully. Your installation may contain third-party software or custom installations that have not been fully qualified with the updated software. Always preflight updates on nonproduction servers before rolling out the changes. Updates from Apple are important and will add value to your implementation. However, you should evaluate the updates according to your organizaton's needs and apply them when appropriate, not just because they are available.

It's possible to use the Lion Server Software Update service to provide Software Updates; your server downloads the updates from Apple, and computers on your local network can download the updates from your server's Software Update service.

To use the Server app to install an available Software Update:

1   Open the Server app, and connect to your Lion Server.

2   In the left column, click Status.

3 If there is an alert for an available software update, double-click that alert.

4 Review information about the software update, then click Install.

Using the Server Status Dashboard Widget

The Server Status Dashboard widget permits an administrator to monitor several aspects of your server. It is included with Lion Server.

The Server Status widget will monitor:

► Various services and their status

► CPU utilization

► Network load

► Disk usage

The Server Status Dashboard widget is installed when you configure a computer as a Lion Server. If you simply install or copy the Lion Server application, but do not configure a Mac as a Lion Server, the Server Status widget does not get installed.

> **NOTE** ► You can copy the Server Status widget to a Lion computer by copying Server Status from /Library/Widgets on your server to your Lion computer.

To use the Server Status Dashboard widget:

1   Activate Dashboard by clicking Launchpad in the Dock, then clicking **Dashboard** (or by pressing the Dashboard button on your keyboard).

2   Click the Plus (+) button in the lower-left corner.

3   Select the Server Status widget from the list at the bottom of the screen.

4   Once the Server Status widget appears, enter your server's IP address or DNS host name and local administrator's credentials, and then click Done.

Once you're connected, you will see three icons across the middle of the widget, and clicking each one will reveal (in order from left to right) CPU utilization, network activity, and free disk space. Clicking each icon will also update the graphic above the icons with the relevant information for your server. Moving your mouse over the graphic will show used and free totals for disk usage and will permit you to change the view of network activity and CPU usage over time (last hour, last day, last week).

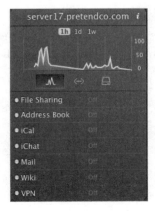

You can also open a second widget and connect to the same server should you want to monitor more than one item simultaneously, such as the percentage of disk space (used and free) and network activity.

Moving the Service Data to a Different Volume

Starting with Lion Server v10.7.2, you can configure your Lion Server to store data for various services on a volume other than the boot volume. The list of services includes Calendar and Contacts, Mail, Podcast, and Wiki, as well as the PostgreSQL databases.

If you use the Server app to choose a different service data volume, it automatically stops the appropriate services, creates a folder on the volume of your choice (/Volumes/*volume_name*/Library/Server), copies the existing service data to the new folder, configures services to use the new location, and starts the services again.

Using the Server app, you can choose a different volume for service data.

1   If necessary, on your administrator computer, open the Server app and connect to your server.

2   In the Server app sidebar, select your server and click Settings.

3   Next to the Service Data field, click Edit.

4   Inspect the current Service Data Size, as well as how much space is available on any listed volume. If you have another volume available on which to store the service data, you could select that volume and click Choose.

Because it is possible that you do not have any extra volumes in your test environment, the rest of the exercises for this book are written with the assumption that the service data is stored on the boot volume. So, for the purposes of these exercises, click Cancel to close the window.

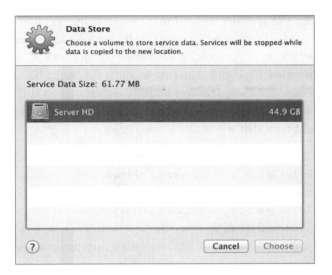

Configuring SSL Certificates

Here's a problem: You want the users who use your services to trust that you are who you say you are, and to be able to encrypt network traffic with your server. One solution is for you to take computers and devices that you can control, and configure them to trust your server's self-signed SSL certificate. When you ran the Server app on your remote administrator computer, you saw a message that the SSL certificate was untrusted, but it was simple to click Show Certificate and select the option to always trust that certificate. But what about computers that you have never seen before? One solution to the problem of proving your identity is for your server to use an SSL certificate that's "signed" by a Certificate Authority (CA) that most computers and devices are configured to trust.

Signing relies on public key infrastructure (PKI) – the use of public and private keys. Grossly simplified, a key is a cryptographic blob of data, and within PKI, public and private keys are created in a way that they are mathematically linked: Data encrypted, or signed, with one key can be decrypted only by using the other key, and if you can decrypt data with one key, it proves that the data was encrypted with the other key. The public key is made publicly available, and of course the private key should be kept private and optionally encrypted with a passphrase.

Public and private keys are related to certificates, which we use to prove identity; an identity is the combination of a private key, its corresponding public key, and a certificate.

A certificate identifies the keyholder and specifies the permitted usage of the certificate. A certificate must be either self-signed, or signed by another CA. It's possible to have a hierarchical chain of certificates, where one CA's certificate is signed by another CA ; a CA whose certificate is signed by another CA is called an intermediate CA, and a CA that signs its own certificate is called a root CA. How does one know if she can trust a CA? After all, since a root CA signed its own SSL certificate, the organization in control of a root CA simply says that you should trust that it is who it claims to be.

The answer is that trust has to start somewhere. In Lion and Lion Server, Apple includes a collection of root CAs that Apple has determined are worthy of trust, and your Mac computers and iOS devices configured to trust those root CAs. By extension, you also trust any certificate or intermediate CA whose signature chain ends with one of the root CAs that Apple has determined you should trust. You can use Keychain Access to view the list of trusted root CAs. Open Keychain Access (in the Utilities folder). In the upper-left Keychains column, click System Roots.

Your Lion Server has a default SSL certificate that's self-signed. That's a good start, but no other computers or devices will trust services that use that certificate. In order to get a CA to sign your certificate, you can use the Server app and optionally Keychain Access in the following steps. Specific steps to accomplish this objective are in the next section. They include:

▶ creating a new self-signed SSL certificate.

▶ using the new self-signed certificate to generate a Certificate Signing Request (CSR).

▶ submitting your CSR to a Certificate Authority (CA).

▶ replacing the self-signed certificate with the certificate signed by the CA.

▶ using Keychain Access to import the CA's certificate, in cases in which you use an intermediate CA that isn't signed by a trusted root CA, or a root CA that isn't trusted.

▶ configuring your Lion Server services to use your newly signed certificate.

Note that before the CA signs your SSL certificate, it:

▶ charges you money (yes, there are some free CAs, but most computers and devices are not configured to trust them).

▶ verifies your identity (otherwise, why trust the CA?).

▶ uses its private key to sign your certificate (from your CSR).

To finish the story, computers and devices can now use your server's services, without getting a warning that your SSL certificate is not trusted, and Lion Server and the users of services can use public and private keys to verify identity and encrypt messages.

Viewing Your Server's Default Certificate

You can use Keychain Access to display the default certificate. Because you need to inspect the Keychain that resides on your Lion Server, you have to log in directly on your Lion Server (or use a screen sharing method).

1 Log in on your server with the name ladmin and password ladminpw.

2 After you log in for the first time as a new user, you may need to complete the Mac OS X Setup Assistant. If necessary, scroll to the "Start Using Mac OS X Lion" button and click it.

3 If the iCloud preferences opens automatically, quit System Preferences.

4 Open Keychain Access (click Launchpad, click Utilities, and click Keychain Access).

5 In the Category column, click My Certificates to filter what Keychain Access displays.

6 In the Keychains column, click System to show items that are for the entire system, not for the user who is currently logged in.

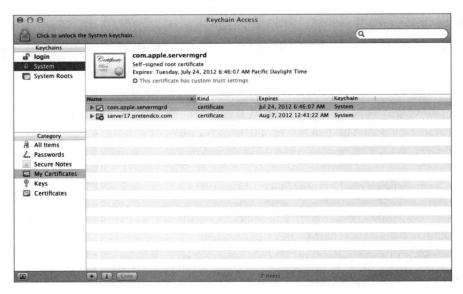

7 There should be two items: com.apple.servermgrd, which is used for remote administration with the Server app, and another item with the host name of your server.

Double-click the certificate with your host name.

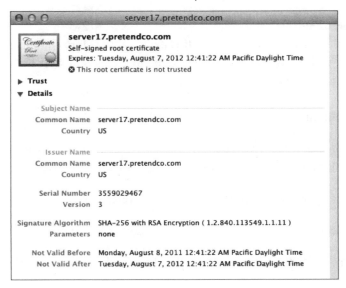

8   If necessary, click the Details disclosure triangle to view the details for the certificate.

The red text that states "This root certificate is not trusted" indicates that not even your server trusts this certificate. Even though you can configure computers to trust this certificate, you may decide to get a Certificate Authority (CA) to sign a certificate that you can use, so users are not warned that your SSL certificate is not trusted when they attempt to use services that use that SSL certificate.

Creating a Self-Signed Certificate

Use the Server app to create a new self-signed certificate, which is the first step towards getting a signed certificate.

For this task, you can switch back to your administrator computer.

1   If necessary, open the Server app, and connect to your Lion Server.

2   In the Next Steps section, click Review Certificates.

3   Server app displays explanatory text about certificates. Click the blue text link Server.

This produces the same results as selecting your server in the left column of the Server app, and then clicking the Settings tab.

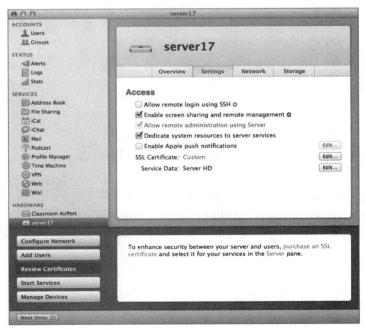

4 Next to the SSL Certificate field, click Edit.

5 Click the Action pop-up menu (looks like a gear), and choose Manage Certificates.

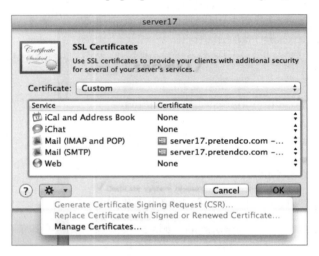

6 Select the certificate that was generated automatically when you first configured your Lion Server.

It should match the host name of your Lion Server. If you installed Lion Server on a computer that was already running Lion, you would likely see its Bonjour name instead of its host name.

7 Click the Details disclosure triangle.

Note that the Common Name and Country are filled in, but there is no other information about your organization.

Because the certificate does not have much information, no CA will sign a CSR generated from this automatically-created certificate. However, the Server app will not allow you to remove this default certificate until you create a new certificate identity.

8 Click the Add button, and choose Create a Certificate Identity.

9 In the Name field, your server's Host Name should be automatically populated. It is crucial that you select the checkbox to "Let me override defaults" so that you can specify additional information, such as your city and state.

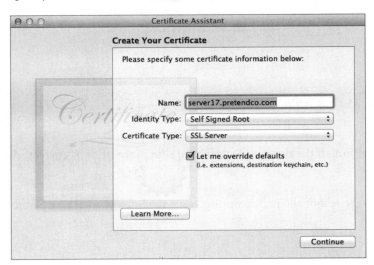

10 Click Continue to move on to the next step.

11 At the warning that you are creating a self-signed certificate, click Continue.

12 Accept the defaults for Serial number and Validity Period, and click Continue.

13 In the pane below, enter valid information for every single field. Consider specifying an email address for your organization that will remain active even if you leave the organization, rather than your personal email address.

In the Name (Common Name) field, enter your server's host name.

To be perfectly compliant with the standards, when you enter your State/Province, use its full name, instead of an abbreviation.

NOTE ▶ Because you are running the Server app on your administrator computer, the Certificate Assistant automatically populates the Name (Common Name) with information from your administrator computer, so you will need to change that information.

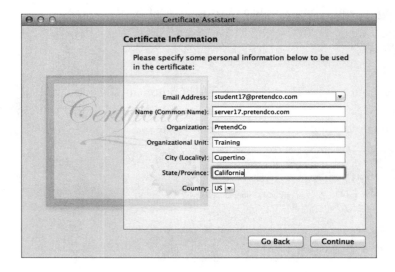

14 After you have filled out all the fields and confirmed the information is correct, click Continue.

15 Click Continue for the rest of the panes, until you see the Subject Alternate Name Extension pane.

The Certificate Assistant uses the IPv4 address of your administrator computer to populate the iPAddress field, so if necessary, update the iPAddress field to match the IPv4 address of your Lion Server, then click Continue.

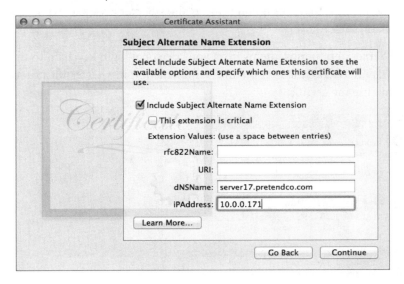

16 At the Conclusion pane, don't worry that you see "This root certificate is not trusted" in red letters, because you haven't asked a CA to sign it yet. Click Done to close the Certificate Assistant.

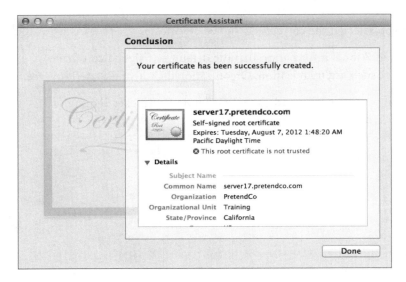

NOTE ▶ You may need to wait a few moments before the next step is available. You may need to click the Server app window to proceed with the next step.

17 When you see the window that asks if you want to allow Server access to export a key from your keychain, click Allow.

This allows the Server app to move items from your personal login keychain to the System keychain, and to store the new certificate information in /etc/certificates so other services can use the certificate.

Creating a Certificate Signing Request

Now create a Certificate Signing Request (CSR) that you can send to a Certificate Authority (CA).

1 Select the self-signed certificate you just created.

2 Confirm that you selected the correct self-signed certificate.

You should see additional information that the default self-signed certificate does not contain, such as Organization, Organizational Unit, and State/Province.

3 Click the Action pop-up menu, and choose Generate Certificate Signing Request (CSR).

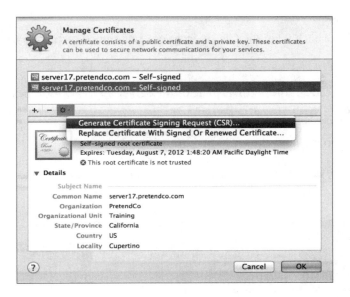

4   The following pane explains that you can use the plain text below to request a signed certificate from a CA.

Click Save to save the file (by default it saves it in your Documents folder).

You need to choose an appropriate CA for your organization's needs, send the CSR to the CA, and prove your identity to the CA. After some period of time, you will receive a signed certificate from the CA.

For this example, we used the test SSL certificate from a CA (in this case, Verisign). Because this is a test, there's no payment or verification of identity required.

Importing the Signed Certificate

After you receive the certificate back from the CA, replace your self-signed certificate with the signed certificate.

1   To import a signed certificate, in the Settings pane of the Server app, click Edit next to the SSL Certificate field.

2   Click the Action pop-up menu, and choose Manage Certificates.

3   Select the self-signed certificate that you generated. Use the Details to confirm that you chose the correct certificate.

4   Click the Action pop-up menu, and choose Replace Certificate With Signed Or Renewed Certificate.

5   Drag the certificate over the text "Drag a file containing the new certificate here."

Ignore the text about dragging the private key; when you created the self-signed certificate earlier, you automatically generated a public key and a private key, and your private key is in your keychain, so you do not need to provide it again.

6 Click Replace Certificate.

Configuring Lion Server Services to Use a Certificate

Now that you've installed the signed certificate, you should use the Server app to configure services to use that certificate. You can choose to have all services use the same certificate, or choose Custom and assign different services to use different certificates (or to not use SSL).

1 In the Server app, next to the SSL Certificate field, click Edit.

2 Click the Certificate pop-up menu, and choose your signed certificate.

3 Click OK.

This configures most of your Lion Server services to use this certificate. You would click Custom if you wanted to have at least one service use a different certificate, or to not use SSL.

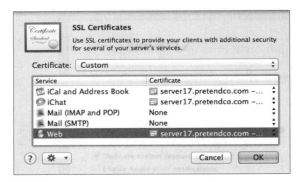

As you can see from the figure, the following Lion Server services can use SSL:

▶ iCal and Address Book

▶ iChat

▶ Mail (IMAP and POP)

▶ Mail (SMTP)

▶ Web (as you will see in the Web Services chapter, you can granularly specify an SSL certificate per web site you host)

Some other services that can use SSL, but are not shown in the Server app:

▶ com.apple.servermgrd (for remote administration with the Server app)

▶ RADIUS

▶ Open Directory services

▶ Xgrid

▶ VPN

Verifying That You Trust a CA

When choosing a CA to use, make sure that it's a root CA that most computers and devices are configured to trust. It's not very useful for you to have a CA sign your certificate, if not many computers or devices will trust that certificate.

You can use Keychain Access to determine whether your computer trusts the CA that issued a particular certificate.

You need to perform these tasks on your Lion Server, either logged in at your Lion Server or using remote screen sharing.

1   Open Keychain Access on your Lion Server.

2   As the Server app automatically adds certificates to your System keychain, click System in the Keychains column.

3   In the Category column, click My Certificates.

4   Select a certificate, in this case your new server17.pretendco.com. This certificate is the one that does not have a red x icon.

You can see that the "Issued by" field is "VeriSign Trial Secure Server CA - G2." Note the red x icon and the text, "This certificate was signed by an unknown authority." This is a root CA that is not trusted by computers and devices by default, so even if you used this signed certificate for Lion Server services, the people who access your services would experience trouble. In some cases the service might silently fail, and in the case of Safari, they would see an alert that Safari can't verify the identity (for the purposes of the example, the Web service has been started).

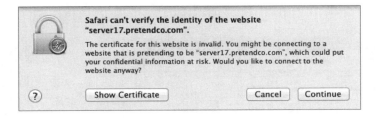

5   Click Show Certificate to reveal the certificate signature chain.

In this case, the certificate for server17.pretendco.com has a red x icon and the text "This certificate was signed by an untrusted issuer."

6   Click the CA, and see "This certificate was signed by an unknown authority."

7   Click the disclosure triangle for Details, and see that the issuer is "VeriSign Trial Secure Server CA Root - G2."

Because the root CA (that signed the intermediate CA, that in turn signed your certificate) is not in your computer's System Roots keychain, your computer doesn't trust the intermediate CA and doesn't trust the certificate either.

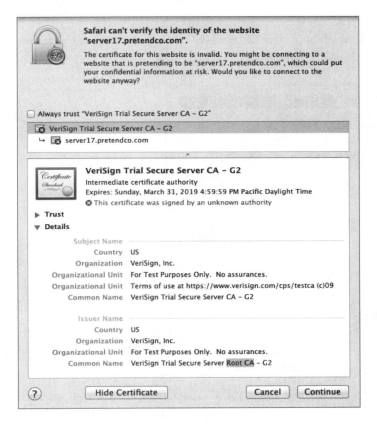

8   Click the disclosure triangle for Trust.

9   Click the Use System Defaults pop-up menu, choose Always Trust, and if necessary, provide local administrator credentials.

You just added the certificate to your personal keychain, so that you trust it, but this will not affect any other computers or devices, or any other users that log in to that computer.

Another option would be to download, install, and trust the certificate for the root CA that signed the intermediate CA. However, that step would need to be done for every computer or device that uses SSL-enabled services from your Lion Server, which is probably not a realistic option.

Here is a view of the certificate chain after the test root CA has been added to the System keychain, with a setting of Always Trust.

Troubleshooting

If you install Lion Server on a Mac running Lion, you need an active connection to the Internet to download additional components. Confirm that your network connection to the Internet is active, and is not blocked by a firewall.

One common problem found in server installations is incompatibility with third-party hardware and software configurations. Isolate the changes to your system when you run into problems, and keep the variables to a minimum.

Inspecting Logs

Lion and Lion Server log events to various log files. You can view logs in the Console application, Server Admin, and starting with version 10.7.2, you can select Logs in the sidebar of the Server app. In the figure below, the Server app displays the contents of the System Log (/var/log/system.log) and highlights all instances of the word that was entered in the search field in the lower-right corner.

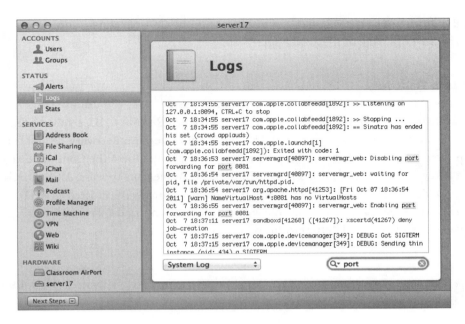

When you click the pop-up menu to choose a log, the list of logs displayed by the Server app varies depending on the services that you have configured. Here is an example of the choices available for a server that has had several services configured.

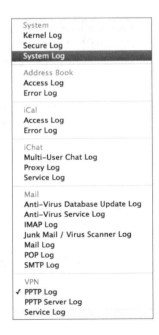

Throughout this book, you will view various logs with the Console application, Server Admin, or the Logs pane of the Server app.

Using Lion Recovery

If you suspect a disk error is causing problems during installation, you can use Disk Utility while booted into the Lion Recovery volume named Recovery HD, a volume that is hidden from view in tools such as Disk Utility. To boot into Lion Recovery, reboot (or turn on) your Mac, then after you hear the startup chime, hold down the Command key and the R key, and keep holding Command-R until the Apple icon appears. Alternatively, you could hold down the Option key after a reboot and manually select Recovery HD from the Startup Manager list of available volumes. Lion Recovery displays a Mac OS X menu bar and a Mac OS X Utilities window.

> **NOTE ▶** If you see a login window or your own desktop and icons, it is possible that either your Mac does not have a Recovery HD volume, or that you didn't hold Command-R early enough, so restart and try again.

Open the Disk Utility after you boot into Lion Recovery. You can use the Disk Utility's First Aid tab to run the Repair Disk and Repair Disk Permissions, or if you want to try a fresh installation of Lion and then install Lion Server, you can use the Erase tab to erase your entire disk or volume.

For more information about Lion Recovery, including Lion Internet Recovery, see the Apple Support Document HT4718, "OS X Lion: About Lion Recovery" at http://support.apple.com/kb/HT4718.

To monitor the Recovery HD logs, you can choose Window > Installer Log, then from the Detail Level pop-up menu, choose Show Errors Only, Show Errors and Progress, or Show All Logs.

What You've Learned

▶ Lion Server requires a Mac computer with a Core 2 Duo or better Intel processor, 2 GB of RAM, and at least 10 GB of available disk space.

▶ The Server app Assistant guides you through the initial configuration of your server.

▶ You can configure Lion Server remotely using the Server app.

▶ The computer name appears in the Finder window sidebar if screen sharing or file sharing services are enabled.

▶ The primary DNS name allows computers and devices to access Lion Server services by using a DNS name like server17.pretendco.com.

▶ The local hostname allows computers on the same subnet to access services using the Bonjour name, which ends in .local.

▶ You can administer a Lion Server from an administrator computer by installing the Server app and optionally the Server Admin Tools.

▶ Apple provides updates to Lion Server through the Software Update service. To ensure that your system is up to date, run Software Update on a regular basis.

▶ You use the Server app to configure, manage, and monitor Lion Server.

▶ You use Server Admin to configure and monitor some additional Lion Server services.

▶ You can use the Server Status widget to monitor the state of various services, disk usage, and CPU and network use over time.

▶ You can use the Server app to change the volume that your server uses to store the data for many of its services. The Server app stops the services before it copies the data to the selected volume, and then starts the services again.

▶ You can provide identity verification and traffic encryption by using an SSL certificate, which uses public key infrastructure (PKI) public keys and private keys.

▶ An SSL certificate is a digital file that contains identity and a public key, and is signed, self-signed, or signed by a certificate authority (CA).

▶ You can pay a CA to verify your identity and sign your SSL certificate, so that other computers and devices will trust that your server is who it claims to be when they access its SSL-enabled services.

▶ Lion and Lion Server have a number of root CAs that Apple specifies you should trust; any one of those root CAs can sign an SSL certificate for an intermediate CA, and via a chain of CAs, can eventually sign your SSL public key certificate.

▶ You can use the Console application, Server Admin, and the Server app to view various logs.

References

The following documents provide more information about installing Lion Server. Many other documents are available at http://www.apple.com/macosx/server/resources/documentation.html.

Lion Server Administration Guides

Lion Server: Advanced Administration
http://help.apple.com/advancedserveradmin/mac/10.7/

Lion Server: Upgrading and Migrating
http://images.apple.com/macosx/server/docs/Upgrading_and_Migrating_v10.7.pdf

Apple Knowledge Base Documents

You can check for new and updated Knowledge Base documents at http://www.apple.com/support/.

Document HT1349, "How to find the serial number of your Apple hardware product"

Document HT4827, "How to disable Lion Server"

Document DL1420, "Migration Assistant Update for Mac OS X Snow Leopard"

Document DL1402, "Mac OS X Server v10.6.8 Update Combo v1.1"

Document HT4886, "Mac mini Server (Mid 2011): How to install Lion Server on a software RAID volume"

Document HT4649, "OS X Lion: "Some features of Mac OS X Lion are not supported for the disk (volume name)" appears during installation"

Document HT4718, "About Lion Recovery"

Document HT4750, "Lion Server: Additional information about the "Dedicate system resources to server services" setting"

Document HT4766, "Lion Server: Installing Lion Server on a blank volume"

Document HT4770, "Lion Server: Installation requires Internet access"

Document HT4814, "How to administer Lion Server remotely using Server App"

Document TS3960, "Server App or Server Admin can't connect to a new Lion server"

Document TS3926, "OS X Lion: Installer reports "This disk cannot be used to start up your computer""

Document HT4771, "Mac OS X Server v10.6: Hosting Software Updates for OS X Lion or Lion Server"

Document HT1822, "Mac OS X Server: Admin tools compatibility information"

Document TS3887, "Unable to connect to the Internet after running NAT Gateway Setup Assistant"

Document SP630, "OS X Lion Server - Technical Specifications"

Document HT4746, "Lion Server: Mass deployment strategies"

Document HT1310, "Startup Manager: How to select a startup volume"

Documents

X.509
http://en.wikipedia.org/wiki/X.509

Internet X.509 Public Key Infrastructure Certificate and CRL Profile
http://www.ietf.org/rfc/rfc2459.txt

Chapter Review

1. What are the minimum hardware requirements for installing Lion Server?

2. What tool do you use to configure Lion Server if you have an unconfigured Lion Server?

3. If you are installing Lion Server on a Mac with Lion, what's one configuration step you should take before installing Lion Server?

4. What are three kinds of names associated with your Lion Server, and what are they used for?

5. How can you install the Server app on an administrator computer?

6. What are three ways to keep Lion Server up to date with the latest versions of software?

7. What three applications can you use to display graphs of various performance characteristics of your Lion Server?

8. What's the difference between a root certificate authority (CA) and an intermediate CA?

9. What's the problem with just using a self-signed SSL certificate?

Answers

1. The minimum requirements are:

   ▶ Mac computer with an Intel Core 2 Duo, Core i3, Core i5, Core i7, or Xeon processor

   ▶ 2 GB of RAM (more for high-demand servers running multiple services)

   ▶ 10 GB of available disk space

2. You use the Server app to configure an unconfigured Lion Server.

3. You should configure your Mac with Lion to use a manually-assigned IPv4 address.

4. You can use the Server app to configure these three names:

   ▶ Computer Name is what appears in the Finder sidebar if your server offers file sharing services.

   ▶ Bonjour name is appended with .local and is used for services discovery.

   ▶ DNS host name - Computers and devices can access services offered by your Lion Server by using your Lion Server's DNS host name, even if they are not on its local network, as long as the host name corresponds with an IPv4 address that is reachable and not blocked by firewalls.

5. You can use the Mac App Store to download the Server app to an administrator computer, or just copy the Server app to an administrator computer.

6. You can:

   ▶ Log in to your Lion Server, and from the Apple menu, choose Software Update;

   ▶ Use the Alerts section of the Server app to install available software updates; or,

   ▶ Click Server Updates in the toolbar of Server Admin, select the update(s) to install, and then click Install.

7. The Server app, Server Admin, and the Server Status widget all display graphs.

8. An intermediate CA's public key certificate is signed by another CA. A root CA's public key certificate is signed by itself. Note that there is a set of root CAs that Lion and Lion Server trust.

9. Computers and devices that access services that use a self-signed SSL certificate will see a message that the SSL certificate is not trusted. It is a security risk to teach users to just trust any SSL certificate that causes a warning.

2

Time

Goals

This chapter takes approximately three hours to complete.

Understand Authentication and Authorization

Create and Configure Local User Accounts

Create and Configure Local Group Accounts

Configure Limited Administrator Accounts for Monitoring and Administering

Configure Service Access Control Lists (SACLs)

Enable and Use Virtual Private Network (VPN) Service

Chapter 2

Authenticating and Authorizing Accounts

Authentication is the process by which a person identifies *which user account he or she wants to use on the system*. This is similar to, but slightly different from, saying that authentication is how a person proves his or her identity to a system. The distinction is useful because multiple people may share the same user name and password, or one person may have multiple user accounts on the same system. In each case, the person supplies user account *credentials* (which usually consist of a name and a password) to identify the user account the person wants to use, and if the supplied credentials are valid, the person successfully authenticates. While there are other methods of authenticating a user account, such as smart cards or voice print, the combination of name and password is the most common (and is assumed for this chapter).

Authorization is the process that determines what an authenticated user account is *allowed to do* on the system. A *service access control list* (SACL) controls whether or not a user account is authorized to use a given Lion Server service. In Chapter 6, "Providing File Services," you will learn more about how a user is authorized (or not) to access a particular file.

In this chapter you will use:

▶   the Server app and Workgroup Manager to configure local user and group accounts.

▶   the Server app and Server Admin to configure access to services.

▶   Workgroup Manager to export and import local user and group accounts.

▶   the Server app to import local accounts.

Managing Access to Services

When configuring any server for access by users, you'll need to determine what services the server will provide and what levels of user access to assign. For many of the services this book will cover, such as file sharing, you'll need to create specific user accounts on your server.

When considering the creation of user accounts, you'll want to determine how to best set up your users, how to organize them into groups that match the needs of your organization, and how to best maintain this information over time. As with any service or information technology task, the best approach is to thoroughly plan your requirements and approach before starting to implement a solution.

Using Authentication and Authorization

Authentication occurs in many different contexts in Lion and Lion Server, but it most commonly involves using a login window. For example, when you start up a Lion computer, you may have to enter a user name and password in an initial login window before being allowed to use the system at all.

Authentication also occurs when you attempt to connect to a network file service, whether via AFP or SMB.

A user must authenticate before accessing these services, even if logging in just as a guest user. Depending on what he or she is trying to access, the user may or may not get feedback on whether *he or she entered the wrong password* (authentication) or *is not allowed access to the service* (authorization). For instance, if you enter a wrong password at the login window, the login window will simply shake and return you to the login window; this is the behavior for many authentication dialogs in Lion and Lion Server.

If you do not have *authorization* to log in at a computer, even if the user name and password are correct, the login window will again shake and return to the login window. The user experience is the same, despite the different reasons for the user not being able to access a service.

Below is a window that indicates that either authentication or authorization failed. In fact, for this example, the wrong password was provided, so the user was not authenticated, and without authentication, there is no authorization to use the Podcast service.

And here is a window that indicates that even though the *authentication* may have succeeded, the *authorization* failed:

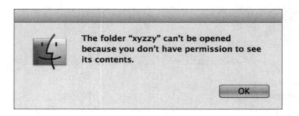

Creating and Administering User and Administrator Server Accounts

A number of tools are available to create and administer user and group accounts. The Users & Groups system preference on Lion Server is just like the Users & Groups system preference for Lion—you use it to define local users and perform very basic administration of local groups. However, System Preferences does not have a remote mode; you have to use tools such as Screen Sharing or Apple Remote Desktop to remotely administer System Preferences on a Lion Server.

This chapter focuses on using the Server app, Server Admin, and Workgroup Manager to remotely manage local user and group accounts, and to remotely manage access to the services Lion Server provides.

Like Lion, Lion Server stores local user and group accounts in the local directory domain (also known as local directory node). You will learn about managing *network* accounts in Chapter 3, "Using Open Directory."

To administer a server with the Server app, Server Admin, or Workgroup Manager, you must authenticate as an administrator (or, for Server Admin, a user that has limited administrative privileges) using those applications. This is required whether you use those applications at the server locally or remotely from another computer.

> **NOTE ▶** When you select the checkbox labeled "Remember this password in my keychain," you store your credentials in your keychain. This means that the next time you attempt to access this service, if your keychain is unlocked, you will not be prompted to authenticate, or your user name and password may be entered automatically, depending on the tool and service. See *Apple Pro Training Series: OS X Lion Support Essentials*, Chapter 2, "User Accounts," for information about the keychain.

Using the Server App for Configuring User Accounts

To grant a person specific permissions on Lion Server, you must set up a user account for that person. The Server app is the primary tool you will use in this chapter for creating and configuring user accounts on Lion Server. You'll use the Server app to create *network* user accounts in the next chapter.

NOTE ▶ It is common to drop the word *account* from the term *user account*.

Standard *local* user accounts on Lion enable a person to access files and applications local to that computer. Similarly, local user accounts on Lion Server permit users who log in locally (at the server) to access files or services (such as mail and file sharing services) that are located on the server, but they also give remote users access to server-shared folders and associated files. When you use another computer, you can use a server's local user account to remotely access various services offered by that server, but you cannot use it at another computer's login window to log in to that computer (unless that other computer also has that local user account defined in its local directory domain—this is a complication you should avoid by using a centralized directory, which is covered in the next chapter).

When you use the Server app to create a user, you can specify the following settings:

▶ Full Name
▶ Account Name
▶ Email Address
▶ Password
▶ Whether or not the user can administer the server

A user account's *Full Name* is also known as a *long name* or *name*; it is common practice to use a person's full name, with the first letter of each name capitalized, and a space between each word in the name. The name can contain no more than 255 bytes, so character sets that occupy multiple bytes per character have a lower maximum number of characters.

The *Account Name*, also known as *short name*, is an abbreviated name, usually consisting of all lowercase characters. A user can authenticate using the Full Name or Account Name. Lion and Lion Server use a user's first account name when creating a home folder for that user. Carefully consider the first account name before assigning it, because it is not a trivial task to change a user's account name. You are not permitted to use the space character in a user's initial account name; it must contain at least one letter, and can contain only the following characters:

▶   a through z

▶   A through Z

▶   0 through 9

▶   _ (underscore)

▶   - (hyphen)

▶   . (period)

For a little more information about the user, select the user, Control-click (or right-click) a user, and choose Advanced Options.

In the advanced settings pane, you can view and modify several more attributes of a user account.

The full list of attributes listed in the advanced settings pane is:

► User ID

► Group

► Account Name

► Aliases

► Login Shell

► Home Directory

You should not modify these attributes without completely understanding the ramifications of the change.

NOTE ► Invalid settings can prevent the user from logging in or accessing resources.

A full explanation of all of these attributes is outside the scope of this book, but some are important enough that they are explained in the following sections.

The *User ID* (UID) is a numerical value that the system uses to differentiate one user from another. Though users gain access to the system with a name or short name, each name is associated with a UID, and the UID is used in making authorization decisions. In the unlikely event that two users are logged in with different names and passwords, but with the same UID, when they access documents and folders, the system will consider them to be the same owner. Because of this, the system will provide both users with the same access to documents and folders, a situation you should avoid.

NOTE ▶ The Server app allows you to configure multiple users with the same UID, but this is not recommended.

The *Group* is the primary group that the user is associated with, even though the user may be associated with multiple groups.

It is recommended that you not change the *Account Name* in the advanced settings pane, because this could prevent the user from accessing resources.

You can assign one or more *Aliases* for a user account. An alias allows a user to authenticate with a shorter or otherwise more convenient string of text.

Configuring Administrator Accounts

An administrator account is a special type of user account on Lion Server that enables the user to administer the server. A user with an administrator account can create, edit, and delete user accounts, as well as modify the settings of various running services on the Lion Server where the administrator account exists. The administrator uses the Server app to perform basic account and service management, Server Admin to configure advanced service settings, and Workgroup Manager as another tool to edit users and groups, and to import and export accounts.

To give a user the ability to administer the server, designate that user as an administrator: when creating a new user with the Server app, select the "Allow user to administer this server" checkbox, as shown in the figure below.

When you make a user account an administrator, the operating system makes that user account a member of the local group that has the Full Name of Administrators. Any member of the administrators group can use the Server app, Workgroup Manager, and Server Admin, and can unlock all the preferences in System Preferences. Any member of the administrators group can also change file ownership and can run commands as the root user in the command line environment, so consider carefully before enabling a user account to be a member of the administrators group.

In the section "Limiting Administration Capabilities," you will learn how to use Server Admin to delegate to nonadministrative users the ability to administer or monitor services with Server Admin, without making them members of the administrators group.

Configuring Local User Accounts

Lion Server maintains a list of local user accounts for managing access to resources. In this section, you will use the Server app to:

▶ create local users that can access services and files on your Lion Server.

▶ give a local user the ability to administer your Lion Server.

▶ create local groups.

▶ assign local users to a local group.

▶ assign local groups to a local user.

▶ assign local groups to a local group.

> **NOTE** ▶ During this entire chapter, you will be using your administrator computer to configure your Lion Server. This demonstrates that you can perform server configuration from any computer with Lion that has network access to your server computer.

Creating Local Users that can Access Services and Files on your Lion Server

1   On your administrator computer, use the Server app to connect to your Lion server.

2   In the Next Steps section, click Add Users, and view the text that states your server can provide local user accounts. You should also consider configuring it to manage network accounts–this process will be explained in the next chapter, "Using Open Directory." For now, you will create local accounts only.

3 Click Next Steps to close the Next Steps section.

4 In the Server app sidebar, click Users.

5 In the Users pane of the Server app, click the Add (+) button.

6 Enter the following information into the following fields:

Full Name: Localuser 1

Account Name: localuser1

Leave email address field empty.

Password: local

Verify: local

7 Click Done to create the user.

8 Create another user with the following attributes:

Full Name: Localuser 2

Account Name: localuser2

Leave email address field empty.

Password: local

Verify: local

You now have three local users: your Local Admin, and the two users you just created. You are not yet offering any services on your server, but if you started the File Sharing service, for example, you could provide credentials for any of these users to access that service.

Giving a Local User the Ability to Administer your Lion Server

It is simple to make a local user an administrator. Just select the checkbox for "Allow user to administer this server." You can enable this when you create the user, or at any time afterwards. You'll create a user and make it an administrator.

NOTE ▶ When you select this checkbox for a user, you add him or her to the local group named admin. You can use the credentials for any user in the admin group to access secure system preferences like the Users & Groups and Security panes, among other privileges. Be careful about which users you assign as part of the local group admin.

1 Double-click the user Localuser 2.

2   Select the checkbox "Allow user to administer this server."

3   Click Done to modify the user.

Note that in the list of users, there is no indication that any user is an administrator user.

Confirming that the User is an Administrator

Test the new administrator access as the user you just promoted to an administrator.

1   Choose Manage > Close.

2 Choose Manage > Connect to Server.

3 Select your server and click Continue.

4 Deselect the "Remember this password in my keychain" checkbox.

5 Connect to your server. Rather than using the credentials for the user Local Admin, use the credentials for the user Localuser 2 (Administrator Name: localuser2; Administrator Password: local).

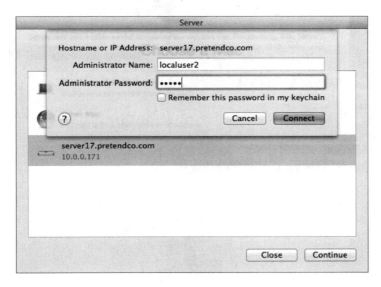

6 Still authenticated as Localuser 2, create another local user account:

▶ Name: Localuser 3

▶ Short Names: localuser3

▶ Password: local

▶ Verify: local

Removing a User's Administrative Status

Make Localuser 2 a nonadministrative user.

1 Choose Manage > Close.

2 Choose Manage > Connect to Server.

3   Select your server and click Continue.

4   Instead of Localuser 2, authenticate as Local Admin (Administrator Name: ladmin; Administrator Password: ladminpw).

5   Double-click Localuser 2.

6   Deselect the checkbox labeled "Allow user to administer this server," and then click Save.

Creating local groups

Groups allow you to assign privileges to groups of users, so you don't have to modify each user individually.

1   In the Server app sidebar, click Groups.

2   In the Groups pane of the Server app, click the Add (+) button.

3   Enter the following information into the following fields:

Full Name: Contractors

Account Name: contractors

4   Click Done to create the group.

5 Create three more groups:

Full Name: Employees

Account Name: employees

Full Name: Engineering

Account Name: engineering

Full Name: All Staff

Account Name: allstaff

You should now have four local groups.

Assigning Local Users to a Local Group

The most common approach for populating groups with users is to select a group and add one or more users to it. On your server, you will select a group, and then add users to the group. When you use the Server app to add a user to a group, you can't just enter the name; you have to actually choose a user from a list that appears when you start typing. You could also choose Browse, then select users and groups from the new window that appears, and drag them into the list of members.

1 From the list of groups, double-click Contractors.

2 Click the Add (+) button to start adding users to this group.

3   Start typing the word local. You should see a list of accounts appear.

4   Choose the user Localuser 1.

5   Click Add again to add another user.

6   Start typing local again. Note that this time the list doesn't include the account that is already in the group.

7   Choose the user Localuser 2.

Now there are two members of the group Contractors.

8 Click Done.

Assigning Local Groups to a Local User

Just as you can assign a user to a group, you can edit a user to add groups to that user. The effect is the same: you add a user as a member of a group. Add a group to a user, then confirm by looking at that group's list of members.

1 In the Server app sidebar, click Users.

2 Double-click the user Local User 3.

3 Click the Add (+) button to start adding groups to this user.

4 Start typing the word Contractors. You should see a list of groups appear.

5 Choose Contractors.

6 Click Done.

7 Click Groups in the Server app sidebar.

8 Double-click Contractors.

9   Confirm that Local User 3 is also listed as a member of the group.

Assigning Local Groups to a Local Group

You can make a group a member of another group. This way, when you want to allow a group of groups to access the same resource, you can configure the parent group, instead of separately configuring each group. You will make two groups a member of a third group.

1   In the Server app sidebar, click Groups to see a list of your groups.

2   Double-click All Staff.

3   Click Add, and start typing Contractors.

4   Choose Contractors.

5   Click Add, and start typing Employees.

6   Choose Employees.

7   Click Done.

In this example you added only groups, but you can add both users and groups as members of a group.

Using Workgroup Manager to Export and Import Users and Groups

Workgroup Manager is another great tool for creating and managing accounts. Workgroup Manager works closely with a specific directory domain. So far, you have seen the local directory domain, and in the next chapter you will learn about using a network domain.

There are some things that the Server app does, like automatically adding users to the appropriate service access control lists (SACLs), that Workgroup Manager does not do.

Likewise, Workgroup Manager has some functionality that the Server app does not have, such as the ability to:

▶ import users from a character-delimited text file that does not have a valid header line that defines how the data in the file is structured.

▶ export users to a character-delimited file for use with another OS X Server.

▶ create computer accounts and computer group accounts.

▶ manage preferences for user, group, computer, and computer group accounts.

▶ configure password policy for specific users.

▶ update extra information associated with a user account such as address, phone, and homepage.

▶ display and edit information from one directory node only.

> **NOTE** ▶ You can use the Server app to import user accounts from a text file that does have a valid header line by choosing Manage > Import Accounts from File.

You can create user accounts individually, or you can import them from a properly formatted file. The file could be created on your own, created with a third-party tool, restored from another server, or imported from an export of the current server. To export and import user and group accounts from a Lion Server computer, use the Export and Import commands in Workgroup Manager.

To export user and group accounts defined in Workgroup Manager, first select the accounts you want to export, choose the Export command from the Server menu, and then specify a name and location for the resulting file.

User passwords are *never* exported, so anytime you export and then later import users from a file, you will need to set their passwords after you import the users.

> **NOTE** ▶ You must export each category of accounts separately; you must export users, and then export user groups, if you want to export all your accounts. The Export function saves only the accounts selected in the current Workgroup Manager view.

To import accounts using Workgroup manager, use the Import command from the Server menu. In the Import dialog, choose "Ignore new record" from the Duplicate Handling pop-up menu. This setting will skip any records if a user with that UID already exists on your server. This prevents you from damaging or overwriting any existing accounts.

You do not want to export your Local Admin account. Because the Local Admin user ID is 501, and the other users have user IDs starting with 1025, you will sort the list of users by their user IDs to make it easier to separate the Local Administrator account from the rest of the user accounts. By default, Workgroup Manager displays the list of users by User Name in alphabetical order.

Use the following steps to create two new user accounts, export your user accounts, delete them, and then import them. Because user passwords are not exported, you will also assign passwords again.

Creating New Users with Workgroup Manager

1   On your server computer, open Launchpad, click the Server folder, and click Workgroup Manager.

2   In the Workgroup Manager Connect window, enter the host name and local administrator credentials, then click Connect.

Because the local node can be used for authentication only to resources hosted on the server, you will be notified that your directory node is not visible to the network. You will learn about directory services in Chapter 3, "Using Open Directory."

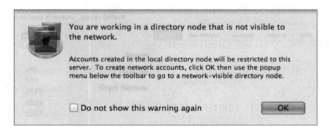

3 Click OK to dismiss the directory node notification.

4 If necessary, click Accounts in the toolbar.

Note that there is text under the toolbar to remind you which credentials you used to authenticate to Workgroup Manager.

5 If necessary, click the Users button above the accounts list.

6 Click New User in the toolbar.

7 Click OK when you get the message that "New users may not have access to services." This is a warning that service access control lists (SACLs) may be in effect, and you may have to specifically grant access to services for this new user.

When you create users with the Server app, the Server app automatically adds that new user to appropriate SACLs; Workgroup Manager does not do this. You will learn how to configure SACLs later in this chapter, in the section, "Controlling Access With Server Access Control Lists (SACLs)".

8 In the Basic pane, enter the following information for the first new user. Note that Workgroup Manager automatically generates the first short name based on the Name field, and you must double-click that automatically generated short name in order to change it, although once you click Save, you cannot change the new user's first short name.

▶ Name: Localuser 4

▶ Short Names: localuser4

▶ Password: local

▶ Verify: local

Of course, do not use such an insecure password in a non-lab environment.

9   Leave the other settings at their default values; be sure you don't select "User can administer this server."

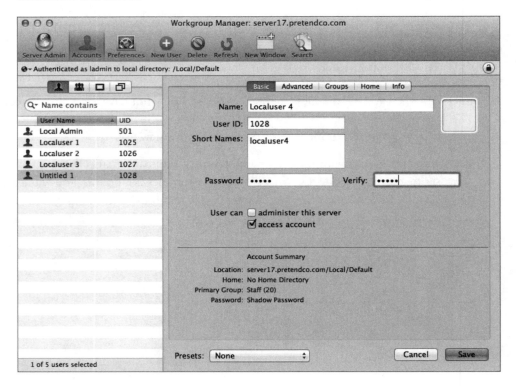

Note that Workgroup Manager and the Server app use different names for the same information. Workgroup Manager uses Name, and the Server app uses Full Name.

10   Click Save.

11 Create another user the same way you just did, with the following attributes:

▶ Name: Localuser 5

▶ Short Names: localuser5

▶ Password: local

▶ Verify: local

NOTE ▶ You will see the "New users may not have access to services" warning. That is expected, and a good reminder. Unless you will never create users with the Server app, do not select the checkbox "Do not show this warning again."

Exporting Users with Workgroup Manager

1 In Workgroup Manager, click the word *UID* in the UID column to sort the user list from low UID to high UID.

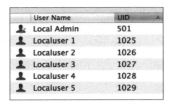

2 Select the user accounts Localuser 4 and Localuser 5. Do not select the Local Admin account for this export.

You can select and deselect multiple users by using the Command or Shift key while making your selection.

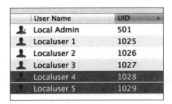

3 Choose Server > Export.

4 In the Save As window, specify the filename Chapter2Users, press Command-D to navigate to your desktop, and then click Export.

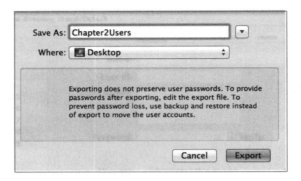

5 In Workgroup Manager, with Localuser 4 and Localuser 5 still selected, click Delete in the toolbar.

6 When you are asked "Delete selected users?" confirm by clicking Delete.

7 Confirm that Workgroup no longer lists Localuser 4 or Localuser 5.

Importing a Formatted List of Users with Workgroup Manager

Workgroup Manager can import a list of users that has been exported from a Lion Server. The first line is a header line that defines how the text is formatted, and what data is included in the file. The user data follows the header line, and is formatted in a combination of character-delimited text and eXtensible Markup Language (XML), which makes the data easily readable to computers.

You'll simulate importing user records from another server by importing the user records you just exported in the previous section.

1 In the Finder, double-click the file Chapter2Users. The file opens in TextEdit.

2 View the contents of the file. It is formatted to be convenient for computers to process, and the information is not necessarily easy for a human to quickly scan without careful inspection.

3 Quit TextEdit.

4   In Workgroup Manager, choose Server > Import.

5   In the Import Users pane, navigate to select the file you just exported, Chapter2Users. Leave all the settings at their default values.

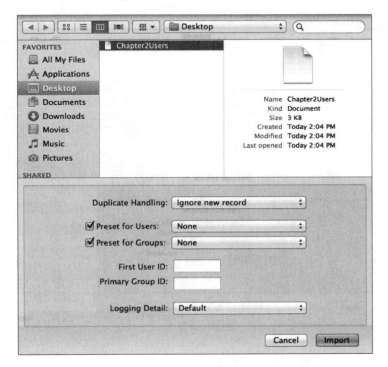

6   Click Import.

The users you previously exported and deleted are imported.

When you inspect an imported user's Basic pane, you will see dots in the Password and Verify fields, which may lead you to believe passwords have been imported. However, there are no passwords included in this import file, so you need to set a password for each user account.

7   In the list of users, select Localuser 4 and Localuser 5.

8   Click the Basic button to display the Basic pane for these two users. Note that both checkboxes have a dash to indicate that there are multiple records selected, and the value of the checkbox may vary between records.

9 Enter the password local in the Password and Verify fields, and then click Save.

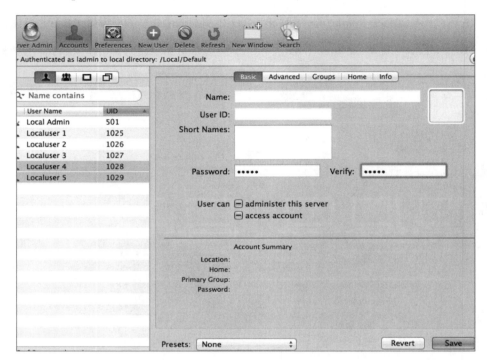

Of course, you should always use secure passwords in a production environment.

Importing a Text List of Users with Workgroup Manager

If you have a text file that contains a list of users from a source other than another OS X Server, you can import this list of users, but you need to specify what kind of data the text file contains at the time you import the file.

NOTE ▶ As of the current writing, the import file must be at least three entries long. Otherwise, the import will silently fail.

First, configure TextEdit to create plain text files, then create a sample list of users:

1 Click Launchpad, then open TextEdit.

2 Choose Format > Make Plain Text.

3 Choose TextEdit > Preferences.

4 Select Plain text.

5 Deselect the checkbox "Check spelling as you type."

6 Close the Preferences window.

7 Since the current Untitled document was created before you set the preference for new documents to be plain text, choose Format > Make Plain Text.

Define three new users with the following attributes separated by the colon character (:):

Last name

First name

Real name

Short name

Password

1 Enter the following text:

1:Textuser:Textuser 1:textuser1:text

2:Textuser:Textuser 2:textuser2:text

3:Textuser:Textuser 3:textuser3:text

NOTE ▸ Be sure to press Return at the end of the last line. In the next few steps, you will specify that the Newline character will signify the end of a record.

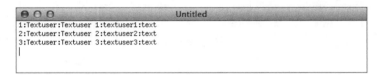

2 Choose File > Save.

3 Press Command-D to open your Desktop folder.

4 Name the file Chapter2TextImport.txt.

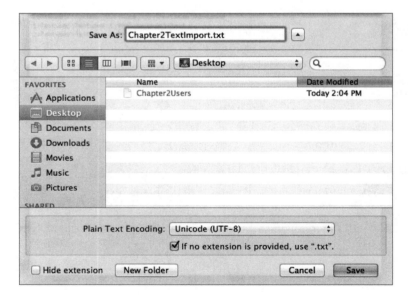

5 Click Save.

6 Quit Textedit.

Now you can use Workgroup Manager to import this text file.

1   In Workgroup Manager, choose Server > Import.

2   In the Import Users pane, press Command-D to open your Desktop folder and select the file Chapter2TextImport.txt.

Leave all the settings at their default values.

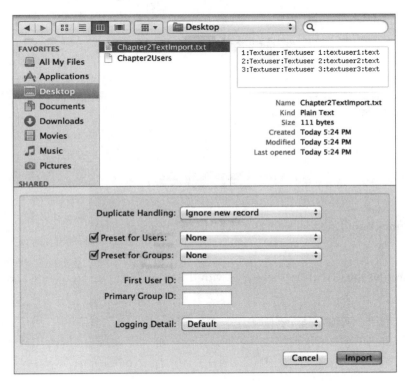

3   Click Import.

4   Ensure the Record type pop-up menu is set to Users.

5   In the Field Mappings pane, click the Attribute pop-up menu for the first value, which is the last name of the user.

6   Since LastName is not listed in the list of default attributes, choose Other to show a larger list.

7   Press L to jump to the first entry that starts with the letter L, choose LastName and click OK.

8   Set the following Values to use the following Attributes:

1: LastName

Textuser: FirstName

Textuser 1: Real Name

textuser1: Short Names

text: Password

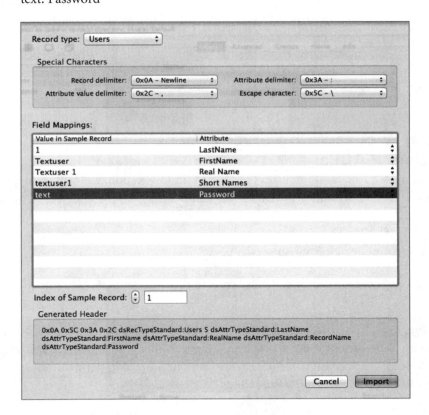

Workgroup Manager automatically generates and displays a header (under the text Generated Header near the bottom of the Import pane) that is similar to the header of the text file you generated when you exported users with Workgroup Manager.

NOTE ▶ If you periodically import users from a delimited text file, you can avoid the hassle of specifying which values get assigned to which attributes. Select the header text at the bottom of the import pane, copy the text, paste the text into a new text file, and use the header in future import files.

9   Click Import.

You do not need to change the user passwords, because they were imported in the text file. Remember that you cannot export passwords with Workgroup Manager, but you can import user passwords when you import user accounts.

Now that you have successfully imported users, you can drag the import files (Chapter2Users and Chapter2TextImport.txt) to the Trash.

Controlling Access With Server Access Control Lists (SACLs)

Authorization is used throughout Lion and Lion Server. In this section, you will learn how Lion Server allows and denies authorization for the ability to:

▶   access Lion Server services.

▶   administer and monitor Lion Server services.

You will learn about how Lion Server controls access to files in Chapter 6, "Providing File Services."

When connecting to a server with one of the Lion Server administration tools, including the Server app, Server Admin, and Workgroup Manager, after you authenticate, Lion Server checks to see if the account you connected with is authorized to perform administrative and monitoring functions using those tools.

When you connect to a Lion Server service, such as the Address Book service, Lion Server checks to see if the account with which you connected is authorized to access the service. Lion Server uses service access control lists (SACLs) to make authorization decisions. If a service does not have a SACL, then any user account that successfully authenticates can access the service. However, if a Lion Server service does have a SACL, then once a user account successfully authenticates, Lion Server checks that user account against the SACL to determine whether that user account is allowed to use the service.

You could use SACLs to allow all users to access file sharing services, but restrict Secure Shell (SSH) connections to administrators.

SACLs are stored simply through membership in a specially named group. For example, the SSH SACL is controlled by membership in the group named Remote Login Group (with the short name com.apple.access_ssh). Once you configure SACLs, it's possible that you may see similarly named groups on your system. In most circumstances, it is best to not directly modify those group files; instead, use the Server app and Server Admin to configure SACLs. To modify SACLs, you need to have administrative rights on the server.

Configuring Service ACLs

You can configure SACLs for individual users, groups, or a mix of both. You may find that long-term administration will be easier if you assign SACLs based on organizational roles assigned to groups rather than to individual people. This will make it much easier when there are changes within your organization, because you'll need to change only group membership rather than individual file and service permissions for each person. However, the examples in the book involve users instead of groups, so you do not have to remember which user is a member of which group.

When you enable File Sharing with the Server app, it automatically enables the AFP service for Apple file sharing and the SMB service for Windows clients (you will learn more about these in Chapter 6, "Providing File Services"). So, in this example, you will configure a SACL for AFP and for SMB. Perform these steps on your remote administrator computer:

1   On your administrator computer, make sure you do not have any AFP volumes mounted. If your server's entry in the Finder window's sidebar displays an Eject button, click that button.

2   If necessary, open Server Admin and connect to your server as ladmin.

3   Select your server in the sidebar.

4   Click Access in the toolbar.

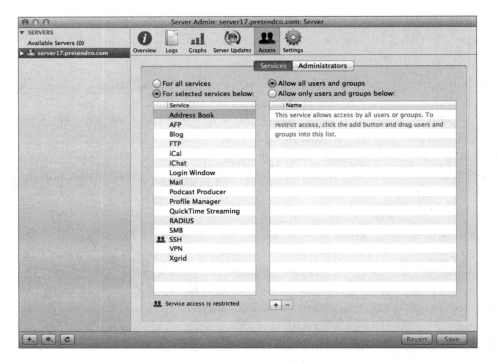

Note that there is an icon next to the SSH service. The Server Assistant automatically created a SACL for SSH to allow only administrator users access to the secure shell (SSH) service (the SACL for SSH is not displayed in the figure above).

Setting up the SACL for AFP

5   Select "For selected services below," and select AFP.

6   Select "Allow only users and groups below."

7   Click the Add (+) button near the bottom to open the Users & Groups window.

8   Select the user Localuser 2, drag it into the list of allowed users and groups, and click Save.

    NOTE ▶ You can enter local in the Users & Groups window search field to limit the users displayed.

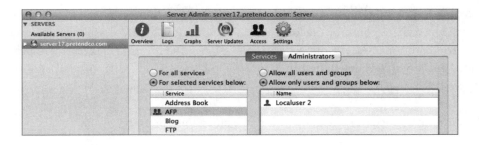

Turning On File Sharing

9   If necessary, open the Server app and connect to your server as ladmin.

10   Click File Sharing in the Server app sidebar.

11   Click the On/Off switch to turn on the service.

Testing the SACL for AFP

12   On your administrator computer, click the Finder in your Dock to switch to the Finder.

13   Choose Go > Connect to Server.

14   Enter afp://server17.pretendco.com and press Return.

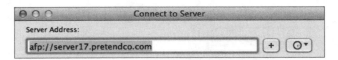

15   Enter the credentials for a user that's not in the SACL for AFP (name: localuser1 and password: local) and click Connect.

NOTE ▶ Your authentication window may look different. If you installed Lion Server over Lion, a share point for the local administrator with Guest access is enabled, so you will additionally see "Connect as Guest" as an authentication choice. If you provided an AppleID when configuring Lion or Lion Server, you will also see "Using an Apple ID" as an authentication choice.

16 You cannot connect. The window will shake and allow you to try again.

If there is no response, you can cancel the connection attempt by clicking the x in the Connecting to Server window.

17 If you do not see the authentication window, Choose Go > Connect to Server again, enter afp://server17.pretendco.com, and press Return.

Enter the credentials for a user that is in the SACL for AFP (Name: localuser2 and Password: local) and click Connect.

18 You should immediately see the default list of shared folders from your AFP server.

19 Choose Users and click OK.

20 Confirm that the Finder opens to a window with the Users folder from the AFP server. It contains the home folder for the ladmin user on the server.

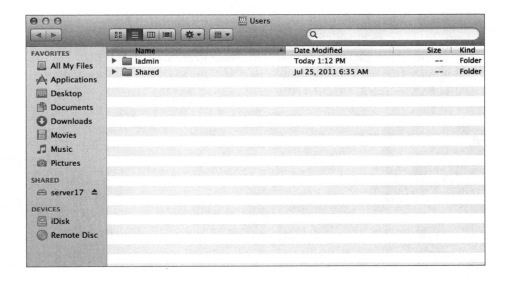

21 Click Eject next to your server name in the Finder window sidebar.

Inspecting the SACLs in the Server App

22 In the Users pane of the Server app, Control-click Localuser 1 and choose Edit Access to Services.

Note that the checkbox for File Sharing is not selected, and it is not deselected either. There is a dash, which indicates that the information that the checkbox represents is more complex than simply selected or deselected. In this case, Localuser 1 cannot use AFP, but because there is no SACL for SMB, any user, including Localuser 1, can use SMB.

23   Click Cancel to close the list of services that Localuser 1 can access.

24   In the Users pane of the Server app, Control-click Localuser 2 and choose Edit Access to Services.

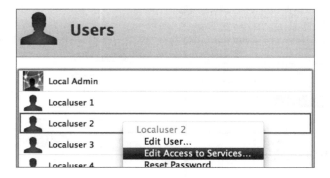

Note that the checkbox for File Sharing is selected but not available for you to edit. Localuser 2 can use AFP because it is listed in the SACL for AFP, but as there is no SACL for SMB, any user, including Localuser 2, can use SMB.

25 Click Cancel to close the list of services that Localuser 2 can access.

Creating a SACL for SMB

26 In Server Admin, select SMB in the "For selected services below" column.

27 Select "Allow only users and groups below."

28 If necessary, click the Add (+) button near the bottom to open the Users & Groups window.

29 Select Localuser 2 and drag it into the list of allowed users and groups.

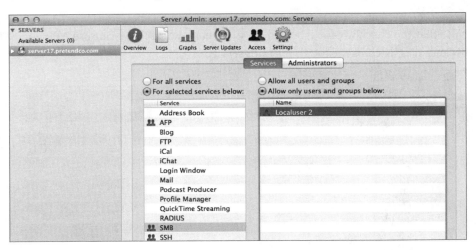

30 Click Save.

Inspecting the SACLs again in the Server App

31 In the Users pane of the Server app, Control-click Localuser 1 and choose Edit Access to Services.

Note that the checkbox for File Sharing is now simply deselected. In this case, because there are SACLs for AFP and for SMB, and Localuser 1 is not listed in either SACL, Localuser 1 cannot use AFP and cannot use SMB.

32 Click Cancel to close the list of services that Localuser 1 can access.

33 In the Users pane of the Server app, Control-click Localuser 2 and choose Edit Access to Services.

Note that the checkbox for File Sharing is selected. Localuser 2 can use AFP and SMB because it is listed in the SACL for both services.

34 Click Cancel to close the list of services that Localuser 2 can access.

Modifying the SACLs with the Server App

35 In the Users pane of the Server app, Control-click Localuser 1 and choose Edit Access to Services.

36 Select the checkbox for File Sharing.

37 Click OK to save the change.

Inspecting the SACLs in Server Admin

38 Click Refresh in the lower-left corner of the Server Admin window.

39 Click AFP in the list of services.

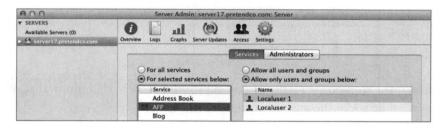

40 Click SMB in the list of services.

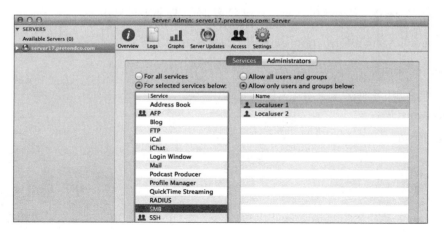

Note that the Server app added Localuser 1 to the SACL for both AFP and for SMB.

Creating New Users with the Server App and with Workgroup Manager

41 In the Server app, create a new user with the following attributes:

▶ Full Name: sacl1

▶ Account Name: sacl1

▶ Password: sacl

▶ Verify: sacl

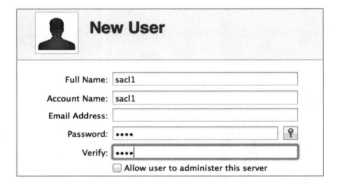

42 If necessary, open Workgroup Manager, connect to your server as ladmin, and click OK at the warning about the local domain.

43 In Workgroup Manager, click New User in the toolbar.

44 At the "New users may not have access to services" window, click OK.

45 Enter the following information, and then click Save:

▶ Name: sacl2

▶ Short Names: sacl2

▶ Password: sacl

▶ Verify: sacl

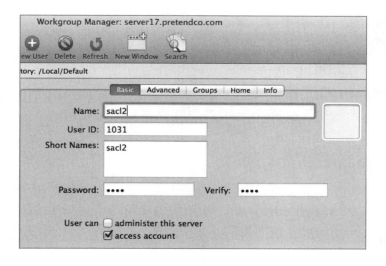

Inspecting the SACLs in Server Admin

46 Click Refresh in the lower-left corner of Server Admin.

47 Click AFP in the list of services.

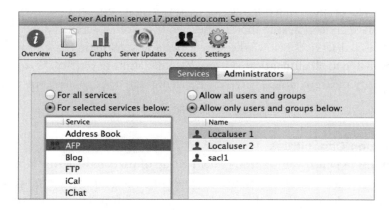

48 Click SMB in the list of services.

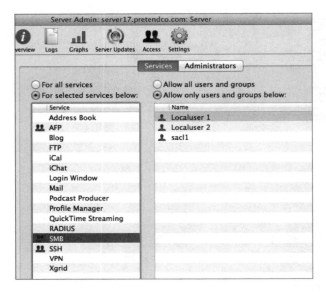

Note that the Server app added the user sacl1 to the SACL for both AFP and SMB, but Workgroup Manager did not add the user sacl2 to and SACL. This is why Workgroup Manager displays the warning when you click New User.

You'll notice that when you're specifying different access for specific services that services with controlled access have an icon next to their names, while the other services don't have an icon. If "For selected services below" is selected, and a service doesn't display an icon, that service is available to all authenticated users. You may want to restrict those other services as a security measure, unless you truly do want them open to everyone who successfully authenticates.

Limiting Administration Capabilities

There are often situations in which you want to grant a group of users only partial administration abilities. These are cases in which the roles of your organization might require a group of users to be able to do something that requires administrator privileges, but you don't feel comfortable granting full administrator rights to those users. An example of this situation may be in a school environment. You may have a group of interns responsible for monitoring your services. Another group may be responsible for managing the images available with the NetBoot service. Using the limited administrator features, you can configure access as described in the following steps while not granting access to the entire server. In the examples, you will use users instead of groups, so you do not have to remember which users are members of which groups.

Adding Limited Administration Capabilities for Local Users

1   If necessary, open Server Admin and connect to your server as ladmin.

2   Select your server in the sidebar.

3   Click Access in the toolbar.

4   Click Administrators.

5   In the left column of the access pane, confirm that "For all services" is selected.

6   If necessary, click Add to open the Users & Groups window.

7   Enter local in the Users & Groups search field to narrow the list of names displayed.

8   Drag Localuser 1 and Localuser 2 into the "Allow to administer or monitor" list.

9   Confirm that Localuser 1's permission is set to Monitor.

10   In the Permission pop-up menu next to Localuser 2, change Monitor to Administer.

11 Click Save.

12 In order for users to monitor or administer services, add some services to the list of services that appear in the Server Admin sidebar.

Click Settings in the toolbar, then click Services.

13 Select the checkbox for every available service, and then click Save.

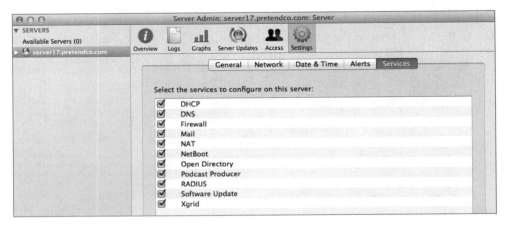

Confirming Limited Administrator Ability to Monitor Services

14 Confirm that your server is selected in the Server Admin sidebar.

15 Choose Server > Disconnect.

16 Choose Server > Connect.

17 Authenticate as the user with the limited administrative ability to monitor services: localuser1 (password: local).

18 Now that you're authenticated as Localuser 1, click Graphs in the toolbar, and confirm that you can view the CPU Usage and Network Traffic graphs.

19 If necessary, click the disclosure triangle to display a list of services.

20 Select a service in the Server Admin sidebar, like NetBoot, and confirm that you can view, but cannot make any changes.

Confirming Limited Administrator Ability to Administer Services

21 Choose Server > Disconnect.

22 Choose Server > Connect.

23 Authenticate as a user with the limited administrative ability to administer services: localuser2 (password: local).

24 In the Server Admin sidebar, click NetBoot as a sample service, and then click Settings in the toolbar.

Confirm that you could make changes if you wanted: There are checkboxes that are available for you to edit.

Do not make any changes at this time.

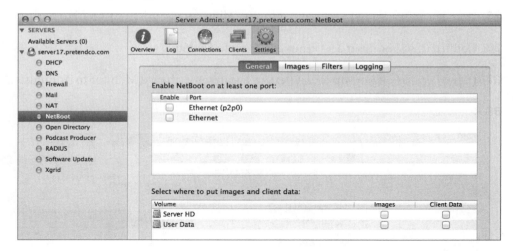

25 Click the various buttons in the toolbar and confirm that you cannot make any changes under Access or Settings. The Localuser 2 account is not a full administrator account; it can only administer the services you made available with Server Admin.

Configuring a Limited Administration for a Specific Service Only
In many cases, you will find that even limited administrator access is too broad, and you may want to restrict access to only certain services for those groups.

26 Choose Server > Disconnect.

27 Choose Server > Connect.

28 Authenticate as ladmin (password: ladminpw).

29 Click your server in the Server Admin window sidebar.

30 Click Access in the toolbar, then click Administrators.

31 Select "For selected services below."

32 Select NetBoot.

33 If necessary, click Add to open the Users & Groups window.

34 Enter local in the Users & Groups search field.

35 Drag Localuser 1 and Localuser 2 into the "Allow to administer or monitor" list.

36 Confirm that Localuser 1's Permission is set to Monitor.

37 In the Permission pop-up menu next to Localuser 2, change Monitor to Administer.

38 Click Save.

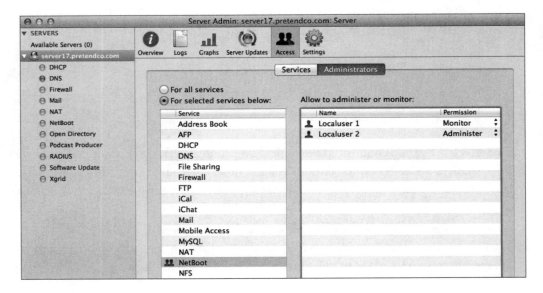

This configuration will grant Locauser 1 extra access to monitor the NetBoot service (such as logs), and will grant only Localuser 2 access to make changes to the NetBoot configuration. Any other service will require the user to be an administrator.

39   Select another service in the Server Admin sidebar, such as Address Book.

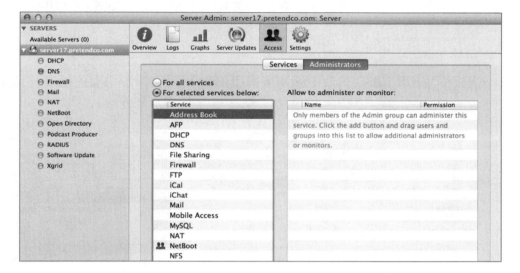

Note that only users that are in the administrator group can administer the Address Book service.

Cleaning Up Authorization on Your Server

For the next chapter, you want the server returned to a state where all the users can connect and only administrators have administrative access. Follow these steps to open your server access back up to everyone:

1   If necessary, open Server Admin, connect to your server as an administrator, and select your server in the Server Admin sidebar.

2   Click Access.

3 Click Services.

4 Select "For all services."

5 Select "Allow all users and groups."

6 Ensure that the list of allowed users and groups is empty. If there are any entries, select them and click the Remove (–) button.

7 Click Save.

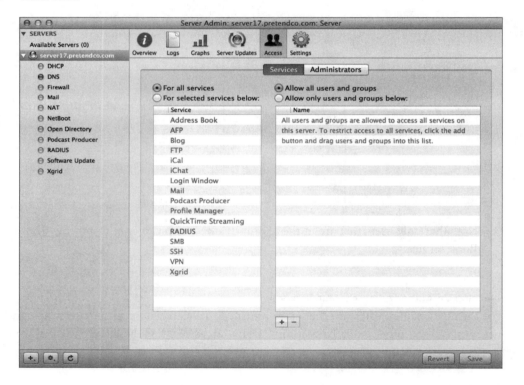

8 Click Administrators.

9 Select "For all services."

10 Ensure that the list of users and groups is empty. If there are any entries, select them and click the Remove (–) button.

11 Click Save.

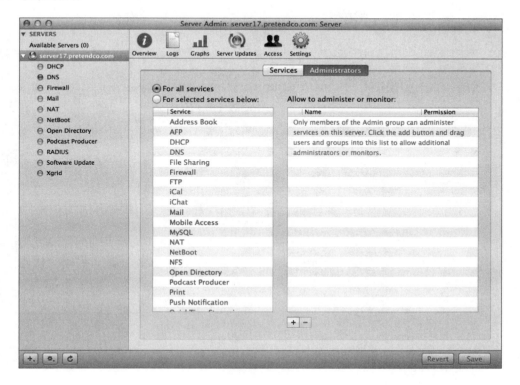

Restore the original SSH SACL.

12 Click Services.

13 Click "For selected services" below.

14 Select SSH.

15 If necessary, click Add to show the Users & Groups window.

16 Click Groups in the Users & Groups window.

17 If necessary, click the x icon in the search field to remove any text filter.

18 Drag Administrators to the list of allowed users and groups.

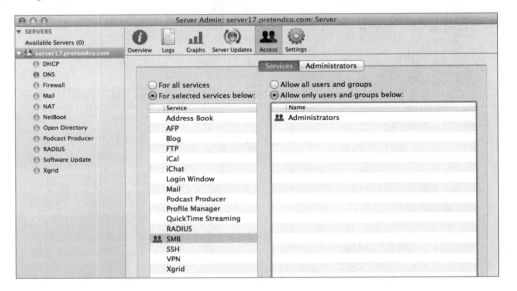

19 Click Save.

Removing the Currently Unused Services from the Server Admin Sidebar

To prevent confusion, remove the services that you are not using.

1 Click Settings.

2 Deselect the checkbox for each of the services and click Save.

If your server did not find appropriate DNS records when you configured Lion Server for the first time, the DNS service will be running, and Server Admin will automatically re-select the checkbox for DNS.

Note that Server Admin now displays no services or only the DNS service in the sidebar, depending on the availability of DNS records at the time you first configured your Lion Server.

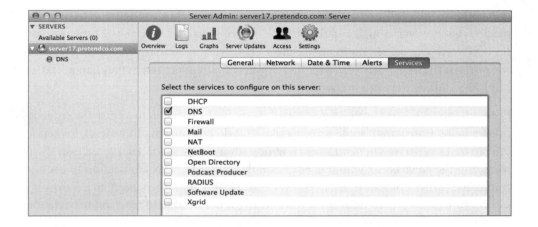

Turning off File Sharing with the Server App

To prevent confusion in future chapters, turn off the File Sharing service with the Server app.

1 If necessary, open the Server app and connect to your Lion Server as an administrator.

2 Click File Sharing in the Server app sidebar.

3 If File Sharing is still running, click the On/Off switch to turn off the service.

Configuring Virtual Private Network (VPN) Service

Now that you have some users defined for your server, one of the services you can provide for them right away is Virtual Private Network (VPN). Lion Server provides VPN service using the Layer 2 Tunneling Protocol (L2TP) protocol.

You can configure your users' computers and devices to use VPN so that when they are outside of your organization's internal network, they have a secure connection to your internal network. Having a VPN connection is like having an impossibly long Ethernet cable from a user's computer or device somewhere else in the world to your internal network; your users can use VPN to encrypt all traffic between their computer or device and computers inside your organization's internal network.

Don't confuse a firewall and VPN; a firewall can block network traffic based on several different possible criteria, such as the port number and source or destination address, and there is no authentication involved, but a user must authenticate in order to use the VPN service. If you provide VPN service for your users, you can use a firewall to allow services that you provide to all users, like the web and wiki service, but configure your firewall to block outside access to mail and file services. When your users are on the other side of the firewall from your server, they can use the VPN service to establish a connection as if they were on your internal network, and the firewall will not affect them; they can access all the services as if they were not remote.

Even though your server can offer many of its services using SSL to secure the content of data being transferred, some services, like AFP, do not use SSL. In general, for services offered by Lion Server, *authentication* is almost always secure and encrypted over the network, but the *payloads* may not be. For example, without a VPN connection to encrypt traffic, the content of files transferred over AFP are not encrypted. So if an eavesdropper can capture unencrypted network traffic, he might not be able to reassemble credentials, but he can reassemble information to which you probably don't want him to have access.

To ensure confidentiality, authentication, and communications integrity, both the VPN service and the VPN clients must use the same shared secret, which is like a passphrase. In order to establish a VPN connection, a user must still authenticate with his or her username and password.

You'll configure your server to offer VPN service, and then save the settings into a configuration profile that you can install on any Mac running Lion. Having a configuration profile for a client computer makes it easy to set up a VPN connection; you don't need to enter the information that you would otherwise need to manually enter, such as the service type, VPN server address, and shared secret. You'll install the configuration profile on your administrator computer, which quickly configures the VPN client service.

The most difficult part of establishing a VPN connection falls outside the scope of this book; you need to be sure that the router passes the appropriate traffic from outside your network to your server so that VPN clients can establish and maintain a VPN connection. See the Apple Knowledge Base article TS169 (http://support.apple.com/kb/TS1629), " Well known TCP and UDP ports used by Apple software products" for more information.

Configuring VPN with the Server App

1   On your administrator computer, if you are not already connected to your server, open the Server app, connect to your server, and authenticate as ladmin with the password ladminpw.

2   Select VPN in the Server app sidebar.

3   Select the checkbox for "Show shared secret."

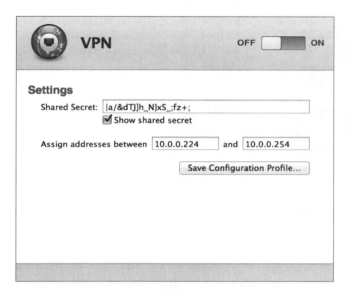

This shared secret is a random string of characters that your VPN clients need to provide, in addition to their user credentials, when they attempt to access the VPN service. You can change the string to something else, but it's best if this is a random string. You can include this shared secret in the configuration profile that you distribute to users. If the shared secret changes, you need to save the configuration profile again, distribute it to your users, and have them install the configuration profile.

4   Change the Assign addresses fields to a range that does not conflict with any existing DHCP service. For the purposes of this exercise, enter 10.0.0.175 and 10.0.0.176, which allows two IPv4 addresses for VPN clients.

5   Click the On/Off switch to turn on the service

6   Click Save Configuration Profile.

7 Press Command-D to change the destination folder to your Desktop.

8 Confirm that the VPN Host is your server's host name.

9 Click Save.

10 Quit the Server app.

Installing the VPN Profile on Your Administrator Computer

On your administrator computer, open and install the VPN configuration profile, and then open a connection.

1 From the Desktop, open the file VPN.mobileconfig.

2 Click Show Profile.

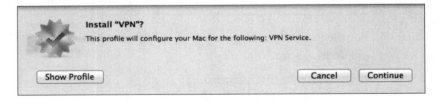

3 Scroll through the Profile and inspect its settings.

4 Click Continue.

5 Click Continue at the confirmation question.

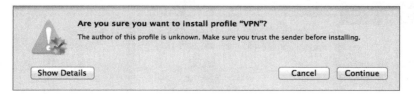

6 In the Enter settings for "VPN" pane, leave the username blank, so that each user of this computer will be required to enter his or her own username, and click Install.

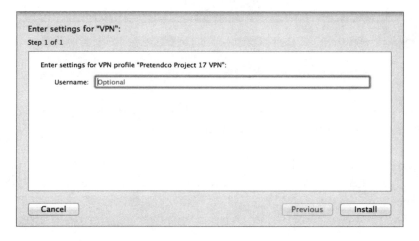

7 If asked, provide administrator credentials and click OK.

The profile appears in the Profiles preferences list of profiles.

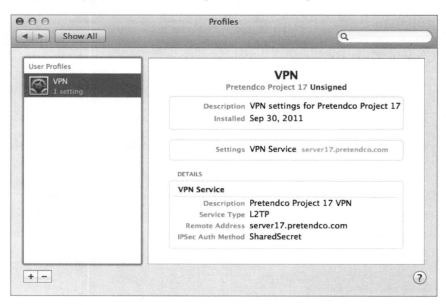

Configure the VPN icon to appear in the menu bar so that the currently logged-in user can start a VPN connection without opening System Preferences.

NOTE ▶ The configuration profile for the VPN service is available to all users of this computer, but the checkbox to display the VPN status in the menu bar affects only the currently logged in user.

8 Click Show All to return to the list of all preferences.

9 Click Network.

10 Select the newly installed VPN entry in the list of interfaces.

11 Select the checkbox "Show VPN status in menu bar."

12 Click Connect.

13 At the VPN Connection pane, use the credentials for Localuser 2 (name: localuser2; password: local) and click OK.

If you successfully authenticate and make a VPN connection, the Status field changes to "Connected," and you see connection information in the network preference (Connect Time, IP Address, and Sent and Received traffic meters).

You also see the connected time in the menu bar.

14 Click Disconnect.

Cleaning Up

Remove the VPN Profile to prepare for the other exercises.

1 In the Network preferences, deselect the checkbox "Show VPN status in menu bar."

2 Click Show All.

3 Open Profiles.

4 Select the VPN profile.

5 Click Remove (–).

6   Click Remove to remove the profile.

7   If asked, provide your credentials (Name: Local Admin; Password: ladminpw) and click OK.

8   Note that when there are no profiles, Profiles is not displayed in the available preferences.

9   Quit System Preferences.

10   In the Server app, click the On/Off switch for the VPN service to turn it off.

11   In the Finder, drag the VPN.mobileconfig to the Trash.

Troubleshooting

It can be confusing to know which tool to use if you aren't familiar with its capabilities. When you create a user with the Server app, if there are SACLs configured for a select list of services, the Server app automatically adds that new user to the SACLs. This can be confusing if you carefully construct a SACL to restrict access to the AFP service, and then wonder why the user you created with the Server app is not restricted from using the AFP service.

For service ACLs, it can be somewhat confusing if users are trying to connect to a service for which they don't have permission. Despite the fact that they have entered their password correctly, they may believe that they haven't, because they see the authentication window shake or see an error message. It may be useful to have users try to authenticate to a service that they do have access to, so you can confirm that their password isn't the problem.

Troubleshooting Importing Users

When you use the Server app or Workgroup Manager to import users or groups, a log file is automatically created in a folder named ImportExport in your Library/Logs folder of your home folder. Since you imported users in earlier exercises, you can use the Console application to inspect the import log.

On your administrator computer, open the Console application.

1   If the Console application is not already running, open LaunchPad, open Utilities, and open Console.

2   If there is no sidebar displayed for the Console window, click Show Log List in the toolbar.

    The Console application displays logs from several locations on your computer. The tilde character (~) is a symbol for your home folder, so ~/Library/Logs is a folder in your home folder, and is for logs specifically related to your user account. The /var/log and /Library/Logs folders are for system logs. You will look for a log file in the ImportExport folder in your ~/Library/Logs folder.

3   Click the disclosure triangle for ~/Library/Logs to display the contents of that folder, then click the disclosure triangle for ImportExport to display the contents of that folder.

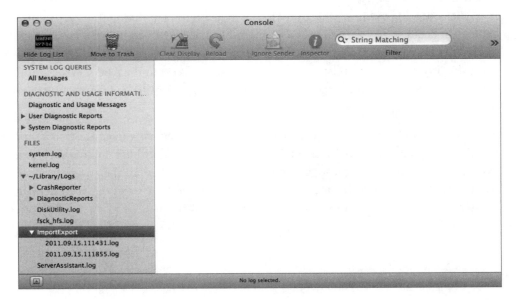

4 Select a log file under ImportExport.

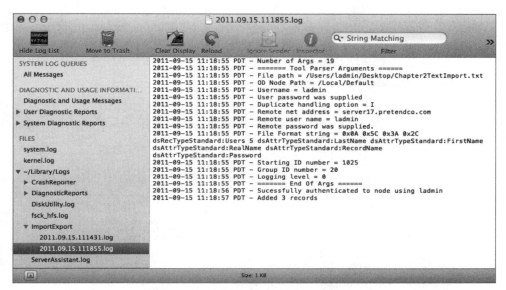

Note that this log file shows that you imported a number of users without error. Some problems associated with importing accounts, if they occur, will appear in these log files.

Using Logs to Troubleshoot VPN service

The VPN service writes log messages to /var/log/ppp/vpnd.log, but when you use the Server app to view the logs, you don't need to know the log locations. Use the Server app to inspect information related to the VPN service. You might not understand all the information, but you might compare information about a trouble-free connection with information related to someone experiencing problems. You'll examine the information for Localuser 2, who made a successful connection. In general, it is a good idea to keep examples of "known good" logs, so that you can use them as a reference when you are using logs to troubleshoot problems.

1 On your administrator computer, if you are not already connected to your server, open the Server app, connect to your server, and authenticate as ladmin with the password ladminpw.

2 Select Logs in the Server app sidebar.

3   Click the logs pop-up menu, and choose Service Log under the VPN section.

When you enter text in the search field, the Server app highlights entries that contain the text you entered.

4   In the search field, enter localuser2.

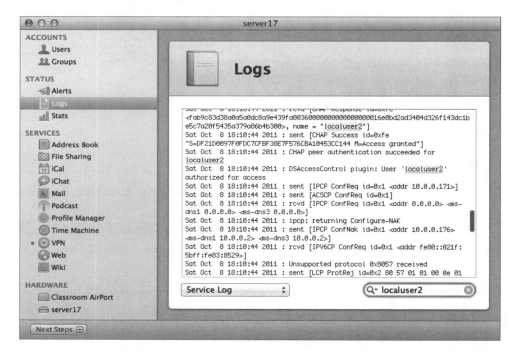

Note that the text you enter is highlighted as you type it.

What You've Learned

▶   Authentication gets a user into the server. Authorization determines what the user can do after getting in.

▶   You can create local user accounts and group accounts in Lion Server with the Users & Groups preference, the Server app, and Workgroup Manager.

▶   You can use the logs in your ~/Library/Logs/ImportExport folder to view information related to importing users.

▶ An administrator account is the same as a user account, except it has the authority to administer the server.

▶ It is more convenient to configure permissions for a group than it is to individually configure multiple users.

▶ A group can have users and groups as members; groups can be members of other groups.

▶ Group accounts enable administrators to quickly assign a set of permissions to multiple users. You create and manage group accounts with the Server app and with Workgroup Manager. You can add users to groups and group membership to user accounts.

▶ Lion Server includes support for service acess control lists (SACLs), which limit access for certain services to specified users or groups.

▶ Lion Server allows you to assign specific administrative permissions for services (administer or monitor in Server Admin) to users and groups, without adding them to the admin group.

▶ You can provide Virtual Private Network (VPN) service for your users to help them protect their network traffic from being captured and analyzed by eavesdroppers.

▶ Using the Server app, you can create a configuration profile that contains the VPN service settings, including the shared secret, to make it easy for Macs running Lion to use your server's VPN service.

References

The following documents provide more information about topics in this chapter. Additional resources are available at http://www.apple.com/macosx/server/resources.

Lion Server Administration Guides

Lion Server: Advanced Server Administration
http://help.apple.com/advancedserveradmin/mac/10.7/

Apple Knowledge Base Documents

You can check for new and updated Knowledge Base documents at http://www.apple.com/support/.

Document TS1629, "Well known TCP and UDP ports used by Apple software products"

Chapter Review

1. Describe the difference between authentication and authorization, and give an example of each.
2. What is the difference between user and administrator accounts on Lion Server?
3. Which applications can you use to configure Lion Server local user and group settings?
4. What tool can you use to import and export user accounts?
5. Which two formats of files can you use to import users with Workgroup Manager?
6. Can you export user passwords with Workgroup Manager?
7. What tool can you use to authorize a non-administrator user to administer or monitor specific services on Lion Server?
8. What is the difference between service ACLs and limited administrator settings?
9. What is an easy way to help your users running Lion to quickly configure their computers to use your server's VPN service?

Answers

1. Authentication is the process by which the system requires you to provide information before it allows you to access a specific account. An example is entering a name and password while connecting to a Lion Server's Apple Filing Protocol service. Authorization refers to the process by which permissions are used to regulate a user's access to specific resources, such as files and shared folders, once the user has been successfully authenticated.

2. User accounts provide basic access to a computer or server, whereas administrator accounts allow a person to administer the computer. On Lion Server, an administrator account is typically used for changing settings on the server computer itself, usually through the Server app, Server Admin, or Workgroup Manager.

3. You can use the Users & Groups preferences, the Server app, and Workgroup Manager to create and configure local users and groups.

4. You can use Workgroup Manager to import and export user accounts. Additionally, as you will see in the next chapter, you can use the Server app to import network users after you authenticate as a directory administrator.

5. You can use Workgroup Manager to import a character-delimited text file with user information, but you need to use Workgroup Manager to define the characteristics of the information contained in the file. You can also import a text file that has a header line at the beginning of the file that defines the contents of the file, such as a file exported from another OS X Server.

6. No. You can only import user passwords; you cannot export user passwords when you export users with Workgroup Manager.

7. You can use Server Admin to give a non-administrative user the ability to use Server Admin to administer or monitor specific services.

8. Service ACLs determine which users are allowed to utilize a given service, whereas limited administrator settings control which nonadministrative users can monitor or change a service with Server Admin.

9. Select VPN in the Server app sidebar, click Save Configuration Profile, and distribute the resulting .mobileconfig file to your users. When a user of a computer running Lion opens the .mobileconfig file, the Profiles preferences automatically opens and prompts the user to install the configuration profile.

3

Time

Goals

This chapter takes approximately four hours to complete.

Understand the four Open Directory server roles you can configure on OS X Lion Server

Configure OS X Lion Server as an Open Directory server with the Server app and with Server Admin

Use the Users & Groups preferences to bind to an Open Directory server

Configure global and per-user password policy

Locate and identify Open Directory–related log files

Examine the contents of an Open Directory archive and restore those contents

Describe authentication types

Understand basic Kerberos infrastructure

Chapter 3

Using Open Directory

This chapter describes how using a directory service can help you manage users and resources on your network. You will learn about the features of Apple's Open Directory services and how these services can be integrated with other directory services in a mixed environment. You will also learn how to set up and manage directories and user accounts with the Server app, Server Admin, and Workgroup Manager. Finally, you'll become familiar with common Open Directory services issues and learn how to resolve them.

Open Directory is extremely versatile when dealing with a variety of other directory services, such as Active Directory, eDirectory, and Network Information Service (NIS), but mixed platform directory service scenarios are outside the scope of this document.

If you have two extra Lion Server computers, you can follow the exercises to use one as an Open Directory replica and the other as a server connected to the Open Directory replica. If you do not have extra servers, simply read through those exercises.

Introducing Directory Services Concepts

Giving a user multiple user accounts on different computers can cause problems. For instance, if each computer in a network has its own authentication database, a user might have to remember a different password for each computer. Even if you assign the user the same password on every computer, the information can become inconsistent over time, because the user may change a password in one location but forget to do so in another. You can solve this problem by using a single source of identification and authentication information.

Directory services provide this central repository for information about the computers, applications, and users in an organization. With directory services, you can maintain consistent information about all the users—such as their names, passwords, and preferences—as well as about printers and other network resources. You can maintain this information in a single location rather than on individual computers. The result is that you can use directory services to:

▶ provide a common user experience.

▶ provide easier access to networked resources such as printers and servers.

▶ allow users to log in on multiple computers using a single account.

For example, once you *bind* Lion computers to an Open Directory service (to bind is to configure one computer to use the directory services offered by another), users can freely log in to any bound Lion computer and have their session managed based on who they are, what group they belong to, what computer they logged in at, and what computer group the computer belongs to. Using a shared directory service also permits a user's home folder to be located on another server and to be mounted automatically on whatever computer the user logs in to, as long as that computer is bound to the shared directory.

What Is Open Directory?

Open Directory is the extensible directory-services architecture that is built into OS X Lion and OS X Lion Server. Open Directory acts as an intermediary between directories (which store information about users and resources) and the applications and system software processes that want to use the information.

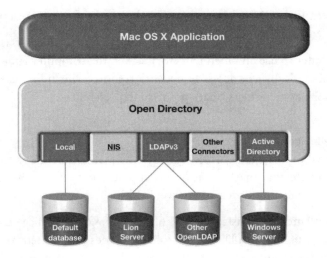

The Open Directory service is actually a set of services on Lion Server that provide identification, authentication, and client management.

Many services on OS X require information from the Open Directory service to function. The Open Directory service can securely store and validate the passwords of users who want to log in to client computers on your network or use other network resources that require authentication. You can also use the Open Directory service to enforce policies, such as password expiration and minimum length, and to manage user preferences.

You can use the Open Directory service to provide authentication to Windows users for file and print services, as well as other services that Lion Server provides.

Overview of Open Directory Service Components

Open Directory provides a centralized source for identification and authentication. For identification, Open Directory uses OpenLDAP, an open source implementation of the Lightweight Directory Access Protocol (LDAP), a standard protocol used for accessing directory service data. Open Directory uses LDAPv3 to provide read-and-write access to the directory data.

The Open Directory service leverages other open source technologies, such as Kerberos, and combines them with powerful server-administration tools to deliver robust directory and authentication services that are easy to set up and manage. Because there are no per-seat or per-user license fees, Open Directory can scale to the needs of an organization without adding high costs to an IT budget.

After you bind an OS X computer to use an Open Directory server, the computer running OS X or Lion Server automatically gets access to network resources, including user authentication services, network home folders, share points, and preferences.

Understanding Open Directory Masters

A Lion Server that is configured to manage network accounts and provide directory services is referred to as an Open Directory master. The Server app does not refer to the term Open Directory master, but you will see this term in Server Admin.

In addition to the role of Open Directory master, the role of Open Directory replica exists; both provide directory services, but an Open Directory replica provides a replicated version of directory information, which is synchronized with the Open Directory master periodically. For clarity in terminology, we refer to a Lion Server that is an Open Directory server as either a master or a replica (even though technically, each replica is also a master).

As you plan directory services for your network, consider the need to share user and resource information among multiple Lion computers. If the need is low, little directory planning is necessary; everything can be accessed from a local server directory. However, if you want to share information among computers, you need to set up at least one Open Directory server (an Open Directory master). And, if you want to provide high availability of directory services, you should set up at least one additional Lion Server to be an Open Directory replica.

Understanding Open Directory Replicas

If you already have an Open Directory master server set up, you can configure at least one more Lion server as a directory replica to provide the same directory information and authentication information as the master. The replica server hosts a copy of the master's LDAP directory, its Password Server authentication database, and its Kerberos KDC. When authentication data is transferred from the master to any replica, that data is encrypted as it is copied over.

You can use replicas to scale your directory infrastructure and improve search-and-retrieval time on distributed networks, and to provide high availability of Open Directory services. Replication also protects against network outages, because client systems can use any replica in your organization.

You can create nested replicas—that is, replicas of replicas. One master can have up to 32 replicas, and those replicas can have 32 replicas each; one master plus 32 replicas plus 32 × 32 replicas of those replicas totals 1057 Open Directory servers for a single Open Directory domain. Nesting replicas is accomplished by joining one replica to your Open Directory master, and then joining other replicas to that first replica.

The following figure has one Open Directory master and one replica that is also a *relay*, a replica that in turn has at least one replica. There are also three replicas that are simply replicas in the figure.

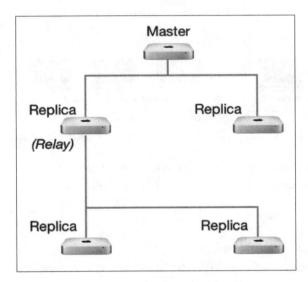

Understanding Open Directory Locales

Open Directory locales is a new feature with Lion Server that makes it easy for you to distribute the load among appropriate Open Directory servers. An Open Directory locale is a group of Open Directory servers that service a specified subnet; you use Server Admin to define a locale, then associate one or more Open Directory servers and one or more subnets with that locale. When a client computer is bound to any of your Open Directory servers, if that client computer is in a subnet associated with a locale, that client computer will prefer the Open Directory server(s) associated with that locale. This is an improvement over the situation with previous versions of OS X and OS X Server, which required manual intervention, DNS records that vary by location, or deployment workflow modifications, in order to get client computers to use an appropriate Open Directory server in an organization with multiple locations or networks.

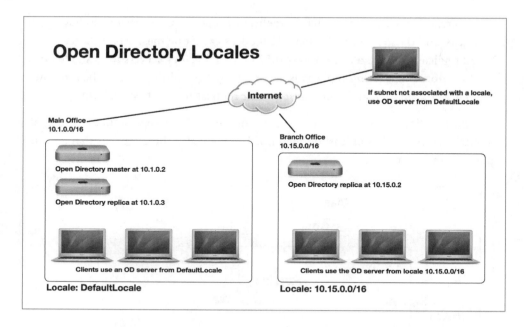

Please note that configuring Open Directory locales is outside the scope of this book; see help.apple.com/advancedserveradmin for more information on configuring Open Directory locales.

Understanding Using Another Open Directory Server

If you intend to set up multiple servers, it would be extremely inefficient to populate each server with the same user accounts. Instead, you can bind your Lion Server to another directory system. In this role, the server gets authentication, user information, and other directory information from some other server's directory service. This way, users can authenticate to your Lion Server with an account defined in your server's local directory, or with an account defined in any directory node that your server is bound to. The other directory node could be an Open Directory or an Active Directory system.

There are a number of ways to bind your Lion Server to another directory service. One way is to use the Server app. When you use the Server app to bind Lion Server to another directory service, you may note that it first walks you through the steps of becoming an Open Directory master. This is particularly useful for groups within a larger organization. If you are the administrator for a group of users within a larger organization, you can use your Lion Server to provide additional services or to create additional groups of people, without bothering the people who administer resources for the larger organization, regardless of what directory service your larger organization uses.

Some services, like the Profile Manager, require that your server be configured to manage network accounts, also known as being an Open Directory master. That's fine, because it is possible for your server to both be an Open Directory master and be bound to another Open Directory service.

You can configure your Lion Server to use another server's directory services, and you should be aware that your configuration choices affect whether all users from another directory service have access to your Lion Server's services, or if only users you "import" are authorized to use services offered by your Lion Server (see the section Using the Server App to Import Users).

Preparing to Configure Open Directory Services

There are several methods available to configure your Lion Server to provide directory services, use another directory service, or both. You will learn which tool is appropriate for your needs.

In order to provide the full range of Open Directory services, your Lion Server must have forward and reverse DNS records available before you configure it as an Open Directory master.

In the next two sections you will learn which tools are appropriate to use, and how to confirm your DNS records.

Choosing Tools to Configure Directory Services

There are a number of ways to configure Lion Server to offer Open Directory services. How do you choose which method to use? It depends on your needs. You should understand the ramifications of using each tool.

Choosing Tools to Configure as an Open Directory Master

In order to configure your Lion Server as a directory server, also known as an Open Directory master, you can choose between using these two tools:

▶ The Server app
▶ Server Admin

Both tools perform a series of tasks, including:

▶ configuring OpenLDAP, Kerberos (if the server is not already part of a Kerberos realm), and Password Server databases.

▶ adding the new directory service to the authentication search path so your .

▶ creating a network group named Workgroup.

▶ adding the local group "Local Accounts" to the network group Workgroup.

▶ creating an SSL certificate, signed by a new intermediate certificate authority (CA), which is in turn signed by a new root CA.

▶ adding the root CA and intermediate CA to the System keychain of your Lion Server.

▶ creating an Access Control Entry (ACE) to the Public share point to allow Read & Write access for the network group Workgroup.

The Server app performs the following tasks that Server Admin does not perform:

▶ Configuring the Lion Server to trust the CA and Intermediate CA

▶ Creating service access control lists (SACLs) for a set of services

▶ Adding all existing local users to those SACLs, so that the existing local users are authorized to access each service if that service is running

The services for which SACLs are created appear in the Server app when you select a user and choose Edit access to services:

▶ Address Book

▶ File Sharing (This is actually a SACL for AFP and a SACL for SMB.)

▶ iCal Server

▶ iChat Server

▶ Mail Server

▶ Podcast

▶ Profile Manager

▶ Time Machine

▶ VPN

While the Server app automatically configures a Kerberos realm based on the host name of your Lion Server, when you use Server Admin instead of the Server app to configure your Lion Server as an Open Directory master, you can specify a different Kerberos realm name, such as a realm name that reflects your organization name rather than the name of the server. Additionally, Server Admin offers easy access to view logs and inspect SACLs for services.

Understanding Choices for Directory Services with Server Admin

If you require more options than the Server app offers, you can use Server Admin to configure Lion Server to provide Open Directory services. You can configure Lion Server's Open Directory services in a number of ways using Server Admin:

▶ As a standalone server—Remove the existing directory configuration so that the server does not provide directory information to other computers or get directory information from an existing system. The local directory can't be shared.

▶ As a server connected to a directory system—You can set up the server to provide services that require user accounts and authentication, such as file and mail services, but use accounts that are set up on another server.

▶ As an Open Directory replica—A server hosts a replicated version of a directory. The replica is synchronized with the master periodically.

▶ As an Open Directory master—A server can provide directory information and authentication information to other systems.

If your Lion Server has not yet been configured with any directory service role, you'll see these choices:

▶ Set up an Open Directory master
▶ Connect to another directory
▶ Set up an Open Directory replica

If your Lion Server is configured as an Open Directory master, you'll see these choices:

▶ Set up a standalone directory
▶ Connect to another directory
▶ Set up an Open Directory replica

If your Lion server is configured as an Open Directory replica, you'll see these choices:

▶ Promote replica to an Open Directory master
▶ Decommission replica and connect to another directory
▶ Decommission replica and set up a standalone directory

If your Lion Server is configured to use another directory service, you'll see these choices:

▸ Remain connected and set up an Open Directory master

▸ Remain connected and set up an Open Directory replica

▸ Disconnect and set up a standalone directory

As illustrated by the list above, Server Admin has a flexible and dynamic set of configuration choices based on the current directory services configuration.

Choosing Tools to Configure as an Open Directory Replica

You cannot use the Server app to configure your server as a replica of another Open Directory master. You can use Server Admin (or use command-line tools, which are outside the scope of this book).

Choosing Tools to Configure to Connect to Another Directory Service

If you want your Lion Server to simply take advantage of a centralized directory service, and not offer directory services itself, you can bind your Lion Server to another directory service, so users can use credentials hosted by the centralized directory service to access services on your Lion Server.

The preferred procedure to bind your Lion Server to another directory service is to first use the Users & Groups pane in System Preferences to bind, then use Server Admin to prepare services to use the Kerberos realm of the other directory service.

You can also use Directory Utility to configure binding to another directory service, but you don't need the advanced options that Directory Utility offers if you are binding to another Open Directory service.

To bind to another directory service, you can choose Manage > Connect to Directory in the Server app. However, if your Lion Server is not already an Open Directory master, then the Server app automatically opens the "Configure Network Users and Groups" assistant. If you cancel that assistant, you cannot continue with binding to another directory service. In this case, this means that in order to use the Server app to bind to another directory service, you have to first configure your server as an Open Directory master, which creates SACLs for a list of services. So, in order for users from another directory service to use services on your newly-bound Lion Server, you need to "import" those users with the Server app, which adds them to SACLs, otherwise users from the other directory service can use only the Wiki service from your Lion Server.

NOTE ▶ This is not an issue if you first use Server Admin to configure your server to be an Open Directory master, because that does not establish SACLs. You can then use the Server app to choose Manage > Connect to Directory.

Confirming DNS Records for Lion Server

You can use the Server app to make changes to your server's host name or IP address, or to confirm that your server's host name and primary IP address match the available DNS records.

Before configuring a server as an Open Directory master or replica, you should use the Network Utility to confirm that your server's host name and primary IP address have appropriate DNS records available.

If you installed or configured Lion Server in an environment with a DNS record available for the IP address you assigned to your server during setup, Server Assistant does not set up or start the DNS service. However, if you installed or configured Lion Server in an environment without a DNS record available for the IP address you assigned to your server during setup, the Server app creates the appropriate DNS zones and records for its host name and IP address, and then starts the DNS service.

The exercises in this book assume that your Lion administrator computer has access to the DNS records of your Lion servers, and the exercise steps instruct you to use the host name, or fully qualified domain names (FQDNs) of your servers (like server17.pretendco. com). You can use your servers' Bonjour names (for example, server-17.local), but it is a good idea to always use the host name with the server tools; if there are problems with the availability of DNS records, you are more likely to notice them while using the tools and to take the time to address and resolve the DNS issues before continuing.

MORE INFO ▶ See "Troubleshooting Network Configuration" in Chapter 6, "Network Configuration," in the book *Apple Pro Training Series: OS X Lion Support Essentials* for information on using Network Utility to confirm DNS records.

Use Network Utility to confirm that your server has appropriate DNS records available for your Lion Server:

1   On your administrator computer, open the Server app.

2   From the Tools menu, choose Screen Sharing.

3   Enter the host name of your server (server17.pretendco.com).

4   Authenticate as ladmin to share the screen of your server (password: ladminpw).

5 In the login window of your server, if you are not already logged in, log in as ladmin (password: ladminpw).

6 Open Launchpad, open Utilities, and then open Network Utility.

7 Click the Lookup tab.

8 Enter your server's host name in the text field (server17.pretendco.com).

9 Click Lookup.

10 Confirm that the Answer section contains your server's IP address.

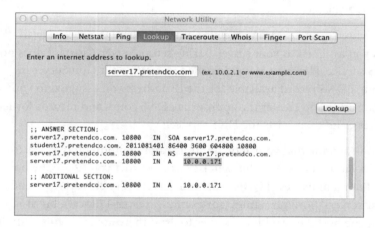

11 In the text field, enter your server's IP address, and then click Lookup.

12 Confirm that the Answer section contains your server's host name.

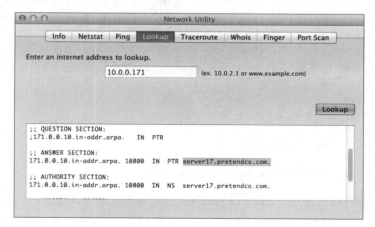

13 Quit Network Utility.

14 On your Lion Server, log out.

15 On your administrator computer, quit Screen Sharing.

You will perform this basic procedure of using Network Utility to confirm forward DNS records and reverse DNS records, whenever you configure a Lion Server to be an Open Directory master, an Open Directory replica, or just a member server.

Configuring Open Directory Services

Now that you understand which tools are appropriate, and you have confirmed your DNS records, you can configure your Lion Server to provide and use directory services.

Configuring Lion Server as an Open Directory Master

If your Lion Server is not already configured as an Open Directory master or connected to another directory service, you can configure directory services using one of the following options in the Manage menu of the Server app:

▶ Manage Network Accounts

▶ Connect to Directory

These two options in the Server app are the most likely to be used by a Lion Server administrator; other options are available with Server Admin. When you choose Manage Network Accounts, the Server app walks you through configuring your server as an Open Directory master. When you choose Connect to Directory, the Server app walks you through configuring your server to use another directory service, but it first prompts you to configure your server as an Open Directory master.

Using the Server App to Choose "Manage Network Accounts"

Using the Server app is the recommended way of configuring your Lion Server to manage network accounts, or in other words, to become an Open Directory master.

This exercise is valid only for a server that is not already an Open Directory master or replica, and is not bound to another directory service. You will use the Next Steps section to configure your Lion Server as an Open Directory master.

NOTE ▶ The default account name for a directory administrator account is ""dirad-min." However, when binding two Lion Server directory servers, ensure that each server's directory administrator account has a unique account name. See help.apple.com/advancedserveradmin for more information.

1 On your administrator computer, open the Server app and connect to your server as a local administrator (Administrator Name: ladmin; Administrator Password: ladminpw).

2 If necessary, click Next Steps to reveal the Next Steps section, and click Add Users.

3 In the Next Sections text on the right, click "manage network accounts" (you could also choose Manage > Manage Network Accounts with the same result).

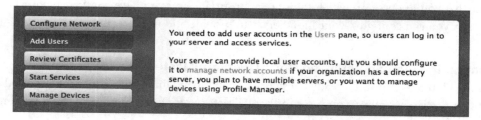

4 In the Configure Network Users and Groups pane, click Next.

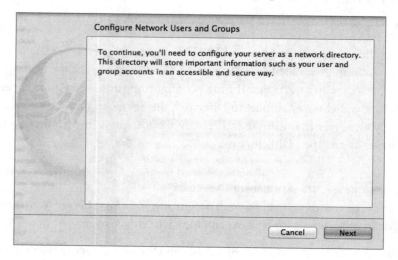

5 In the Directory Administrator pane, enter a password for the diradmin account.

For the purposes of this example, specify the password diradminpw. Of course, in a production environment, you would use a secure password. You might also consider using non-standard names for this account, instead of Directory Administrator and diradmin.

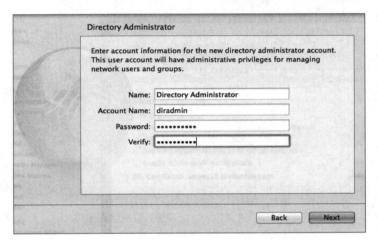

6   Click Next.

7   In the Organization Information pane, you should see information automatically inserted from when you initially configured your Lion Server.

If you installed Lion Server from Lion, these fields might be blank.

You can change the information here, but for the purposes of the example, leave the fields as they are, and click Next.

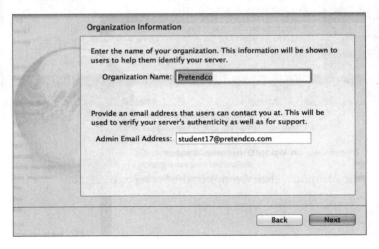

8 In the Confirm Settings pane, click Set Up.

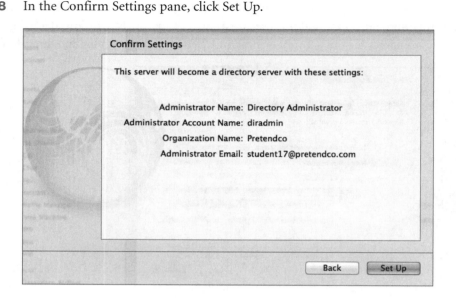

9 Wait a few moments while the Server app sets up your Lion Server as a network directory server, also known as an Open Directory master.

When the Server app has completed, you will be returned to the Server app.

Note that the Server app updated the text in the Next Steps section.

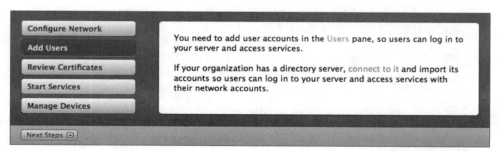

Inspecting the Effects of Becoming an Open Directory Master

1 On your administrator computer, click Groups in the Server app sidebar.

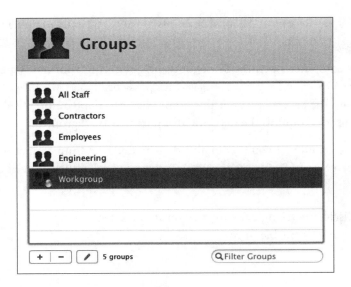

Note that in addition to any local groups you may already have, there is a new network group named Workgroup, with a blue globe as part of its icon.

2   Double-click the network group Workgroup.

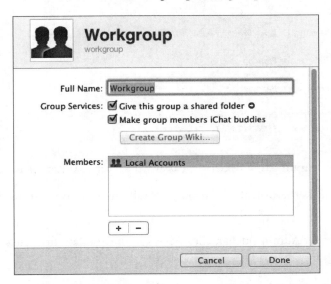

At this time, the only member of this group is the local group named "Local Accounts." The Server app displays only the Local Accounts group in the list of groups if you choose View > Show System Accounts. All local accounts are automatically members of the local group "Local Accounts."

On your administrator computer, open the Server app and connect to your new Open Directory master (server17.pretendco.com, as ladmin with password ladminpw). When you create new users with the Server app after this point, the Server app automatically adds the new network user account to the network group named Workgroup.

3   On your administrator computer, if you do not already have Server Admin connected to your Lion Server, open Server Admin, connect to your server, and authenticate as a local administrator.

4   If necessary, click the disclosure triangle for your server in the sidebar of Server Admin to display the services available to configure.

5   Select Open Directory.

6   Click Overview.

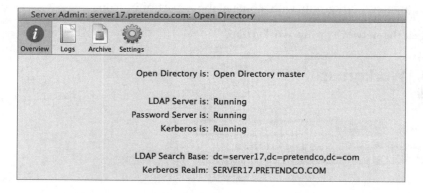

Note that three services are running: LDAP Server, Password Server, and Kerberos.

The LDAP Search Base, and Kerberos realm, which by default are based on your host name, are displayed.

7   Click your server in the Server Admin sidebar, click Access in the Toolbar, then click Services.

Note that various services have icons next to them, indicating that they have SACLs.

8   Select Address Book, one of the services that has a SACL enabled.

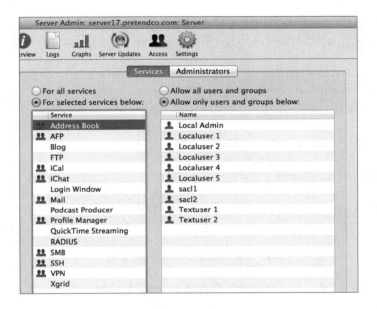

Note that the Server app automatically added all your local users to the SACL for Address Book, so they can access that service. When you create a new user with the Server app, it will automatically add the new network user to the appropriate SACLs.

9   Select the SSH service.

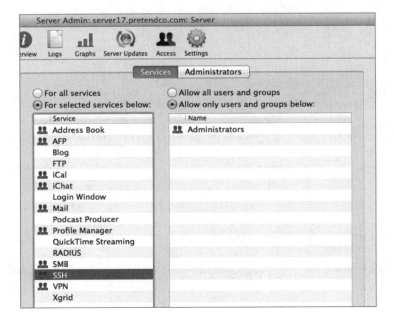

The SSH SACL still allows only members of the local group Administrators to access the SSH service; it is not included in the list of services that automatically get updated.

Next, inspect the System keychain on your Lion Server. You'll need to log in on your server in order to inspect the keychain.

10 Select your server in the Server Admin sidebar.

11 Choose View > Share Server's Screen.

12 Provide local administrator credentials (ladmin with password ladminpw) and click Connect.

13 If necessary, log in on your Lion Server as your local administrator.

14 On your Lion Server, use Launchpad to open Keychain in the Utilities folder.

15 Under Keychains, click System.

16 Under Category, click My Certificates.

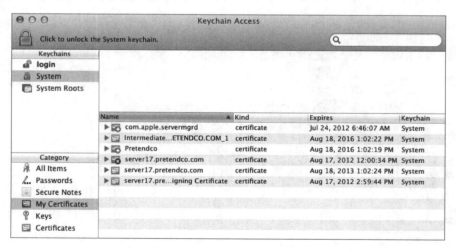

17 Double-click the root CA for your organization, in this example, Pretendco.

18 Click the disclosure triangle for Trust, and confirm that "When using this certificate" is set to Always Trust.

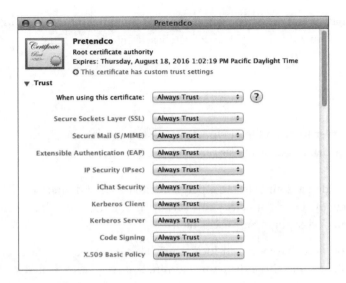

19 Click the disclosure triangle for Trust again to minimize the information displayed about Trust.

Under Details, confirm that your organization name (Pretendco) is used as the value for Common Name and Organization, the Organizational Unit is MACOSX OpenDirectory Root CA, and the Email Address is that which you specified earlier.

Confirm that the information in the Issuer section contains the same information as contained in the Subject Name; this root CA is definitely self-signed.

20 Quit Keychain Access.

21 Quit Screen Sharing.

Once you have set up your server to be an Open Directory master, you can configure other computers on your network to access the server's directory services.

> **NOTE ▶** Once you have added accounts to the Open Directory shared domain on your server, do not change the Open Directory role setting. If you do, you will lose all your account information and orphan your users' data.

To recap, you began with a local database for your local users. That database still exists. The administrator of that database has the short name ladmin. You have now created a secondary, shared LDAP database. The administrator of that database has the short name diradmin. Each database is separate, and managing either one requires different credentials. You have also created a Password Server database to store user passwords, as well as a Kerberos Key Distribution Center (KDC). You will learn about those later in this chapter.

Configuring Lion Server as an Open Directory Replica

In this section you will step through the process of hosting a replica of your Lion Server Open Directory master. If you have only one Lion Server and one Lion client, you can read through this exercise, but not perform the steps. This exercise assumes that you have another Lion Server at 10.1.18.1 that you want to configure as a replica of 10.1.17.1, and that your administrator computer and both server computers can access forward and reverse DNS records for both servers.

> **NOTE ▶** You can set up a second server to use as an Open Directory replica by following the same setup instructions as in Chapter 1, "Installing and Configuring OS X Lion Server," except you should use 10.1.18.1 as the IP address and server18 as the computer name.

> See the section "Configuring DNS to Support Multiple Open Directory Servers" at the end of this chapter to set up your server17 to host DNS records for the host name server18.pretendco.com and the IP address 10.1.18.1.

Use the following steps to confirm the DNS records for the server that you will promote to an Open Directory replica:

1 On your administrator computer, open the Server app.

2 From the Tools menu, choose Screen Sharing.

3 Enter the host name of the server that you will configure as an Open Directory replica.

4 Authenticate as ladmin to share the screen of your server.

5 At the login window of your server, if you are not already logged in, log in as ladmin (password: ladminpw).

6 Open Launchpad, click Utilities, and then click Network Utility.

7 Click the Lookup tab.

8 Enter your server's host name in the text field.

9 Click Lookup.

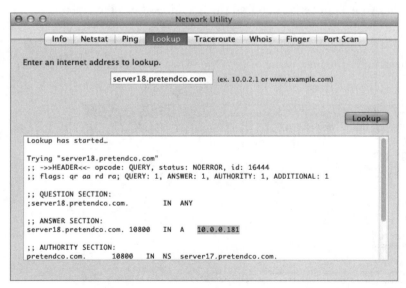

10 Confirm that the Answer section contains your server's host name and IP address.

11 In the text field, enter your server's IP address and then click Lookup.

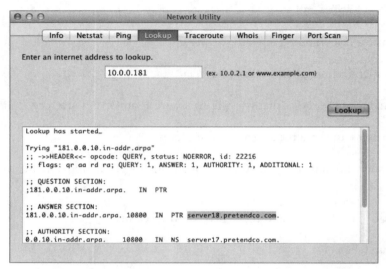

12 Confirm that the Answer section contains your server's host name.

Finally, confirm that your Lion Server can find the IP address from the Open Directory master's host name.

13 In the text field, enter the host name of the Open Directory master and then click Lookup.

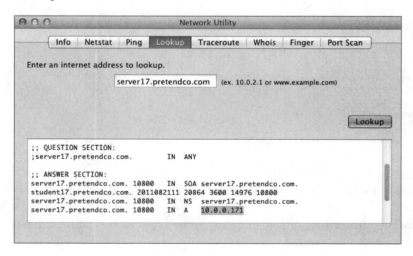

Confirm that the Answer section contains the IP address of your Open Directory master. Explaining the other information in the Answer section is outside the scope of this book.

14 On your Lion Server, quit Network Utility.

15 On your Lion Server, log out.

16 On your administrator computer, quit screen sharing.

Use the following steps to promote your Lion Server to an Open Directory replica:

1 On your administrator computer, open Server Admin and connect to server18. pretendco.com

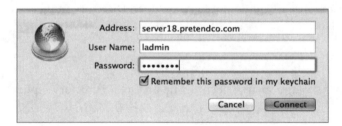

2 If you get the following message, "This server does not have any services marked as configured." click Continue.

3 If you're not automatically brought to Services, with server18.pretendco.com selected in the Server Admin sidebar, click Settings in the toolbar, and then click Services.

4 Enable the checkbox to add Open Directory to the list of services, and click Save.

5 If necessary, click the disclosure triangle to show the services for server18.pretendco. com in the Server Admin sidebar.

6 Click Open Directory under server18.pretendco.com.

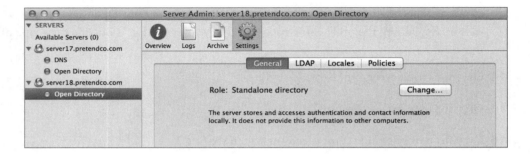

Confirm that server18's role is Standalone Directory.

7 Click Settings in the toolbar, click General, and click the Change button to open Open Directory Assistant, just as you did when you created an Open Directory master.

NOTE ▶ You can't create a replica if you do not have an Open Directory master.

If this server is already an Open Directory master, the current LDAP database will be emptied of all its contents.

8 Once the Open Directory Assistant opens, select "Set up an Open Directory replica" and click Continue.

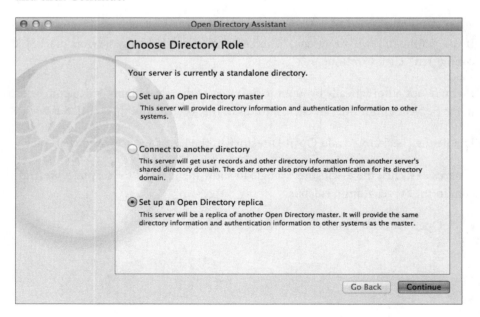

9 Configure the replica with the following parameters (be sure to use the DNS name of the Open Directory master, as opposed to the IP address or Bonjour name):

▶ IP address or DNS name of master: server17.pretendco.com

▶ Domain administrator's short name: diradmin

▶ Domain administrator's password: diradminpw

▶ CA administrator's email: student17@pretendco.com

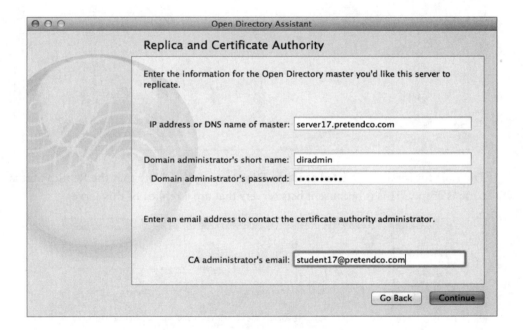

10 Click Continue.

11 Click Continue in the Confirm Settings window.

12 Click Done in the Summary window.

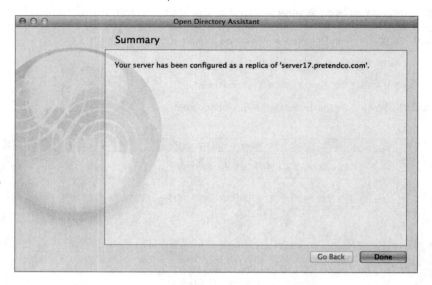

The Role for server18 is listed as Open Directory replica. Note that the Replica Status pane is empty. This is because it lists servers that are a replica of this server.

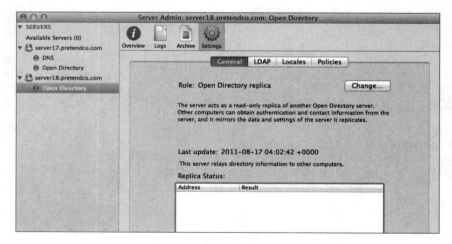

13 Click Overview in the toolbar.

Note that server18 is now an Open Directory replica and offers all three services: LDAP Server, Password Server, and Kerberos. The Kerberos realm is based on the host name of the Open Directory master.

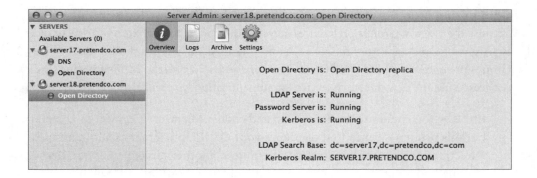

14 In the Server Admin sidebar, select Open Directory under server17.pretendco.com, click Settings, and then click General.

Note that server17's Role is Open Directory master, and server18.pretendco.com is listed as a replica.

Once you have set up your server to be an Open Directory replica, other computers can connect to it as needed. The Open Directory master will update replicas automatically whenever there is a change in directory information.

Once a single replica has been established, other Lion Servers can be set up as replicas of replicas. This increases the redundancy and potentially improves the performance of the entire Open Directory structure.

> **TIP** Because replication and Kerberos use timestamps, it's best to use NTP to synchronize the clocks on all Open Directory masters, replicas, and servers using existing masters. You can use Server Admin to enable NTP services, as well as to specify an NTP server to use.

Configuring Lion Server to use another Open Directory Server

Because the Users & Groups preferences automatically offers to configure your client or server to trust your Open Directory master's CA and Intermediate CA, you should use the Users & Groups preferences to bind to an Open Directory server. In order to configure your server's services to use the new directory service for authentication, you will also use Server Admin.

> **NOTE** ▸ You could use the Server app and choose Manage > Connect to Directory, but this prompts you to first configure your OS X Lion Server as another Open Directory master, then it allows you to bind to another directory service. Because that method automatically creates SACLs, only users you "import" will be able to use services (other than the Wiki service) that your Lion Server offers.

This exercise assumes:

▸ you have a replica configured at 10.1.18.1 from the previous exercise.

▸ you have a third server that you set up with the same instructions that you used in Chapter 1, "Installing and Configuring OS X Lion Server," except you used 10.1.19.1 as the IP address and server19 as the computer name.

▸ you will configure a standalone Lion Server at 10.1.19.1 to bind to the replica at 10.1.18.1.

▸ you have forward and reverse DNS records available for these servers.

If these requirements are not met, you can read through this exercise but not complete it.

1 On your administrator computer, open the Server App, choose Manage > Connect to Server, choose the server you want to bind (server19.pretendco.com), and authenticate as ladmin (password: ladminpw).

2 If you see the "Server can't verify the identity" dialog, click Show Certificate, enable the "Always trust" checkbox, click Continue, authenticate to make changes to your Certificate Trust Settings, and click Continue.

3   From the Tools menu, choose Screen Sharing.

4   In the Connect to Shared Computer window, type your server's host name (server19.pretendco.com), and click Connect.

5   If necessary, in the Screen Sharing authentication window, enter credentials for server19 (Name: ladmin and password: ladminpw).

6   If you are not already logged in to server19, log in (name: ladmin and password: ladminpw).

7   Use Network Utility to confirm forward and reverse DNS records for server19.pretendco. com (see the section Confirming DNS Records for Lion Server for exact steps), and confirm forward DNS records for the Open Directory replica and the Open Directory master (server18.pretendco.com and server17.pretendco.com, respectively).

8   Open System Preferences from the Apple menu.

9   Select Users & Groups.

10 Select Login Options.

11 If necessary, click the lock in the lower-left corner and provide local administrator credentials.

12 Click Join.

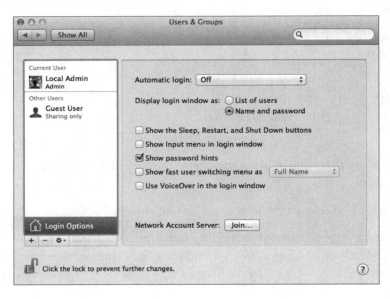

13 Enter the host name of your Open Directory replica, server18.pretendco.com (if you have only an Open Directory master, use this instead: server17.pretendco.com), and then click OK.

14 In the "This server provides SSL certificates" dialog, click Trust.

15 In the "This server does not provide a secure (SSL) connection" window, click Continue.

By default, an Open Directory master does not provide LDAP services over SSL; for many organizations this is not a concern because the information stored in the LDAP directory is not considered sensitive.

16 In the Client Computer ID window, leave the Client Computer ID, which is generated from your host name, as it is.

You have the option to bind anonymously or set up authenticated binding.

Anonymous binding is appropriate when binding with Lion clients, but you should use authenticated binding, which mutually authenticates the client and the Open

Directory service, when binding a Lion Server to an Open Directory master. An authenticated bind creates a computer record in the Open Directory service; this computer record is used to mutually authenticate the bind.

Provide directory administrator credentials for the authenticated bind: use the Directory Administrator credentials, since you already know those credentials. Enter diradmin for the User Name, diradminpw for the Password, and click OK.

17 At the Users & Groups preferences, note that the server now is listed as the Network Account Server.

Quit System Preferences.

18   Log out as ladmin on server19.

19   On your administrator computer, quit screen sharing.

Next, you will use Server Admin to prepare your member server's services to offer services to network users.

20   On your administrator computer, open Server Admin.

21   If server19 is not already listed in the sidebar of Server Admin, click the Add (+) pop-up menu in the lower-left corner of Server Admin, choose Add Server, enter server19.pretendco.com, enter your local administrator credentials, and click Connect.

22   Choose server19.pretendco.com in the Server Admin sidebar, click Settings, and then click Services.

23   Select the checkbox for Open Directory and click Save.

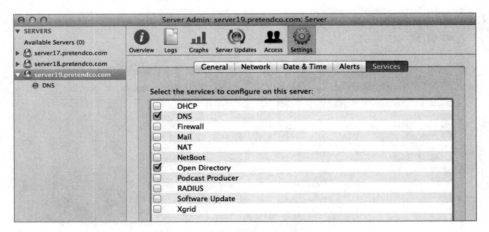

24   If necessary, click the disclosure triangle for server19.pretendco.com to reveal the available services.

25   Select Open Directory for server19.pretendco.com in the Server Admin sidebar.

26 If necessary, click Settings, and then click General.

27 Note that the Role is listed as: Connected to another directory.

Click Kerberize Services.

28 Provide diradmin credentials and click OK.

server19 is now configured to accept Kerberos credentials to authenticate any user in the Open Directory service to whom server19 is bound.

NOTE ▶ Don't worry if the Kerberize Services button still appears; you don't need to click it again.

29 Inspect the SACLs for services offered by server19.

Select server19.pretendco.com in the Server Admin sidebar, then click Access.

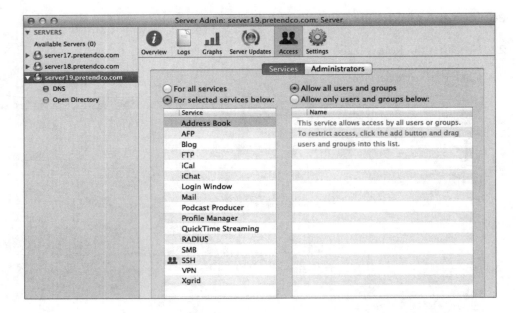

Note that server19 doesn't have any SACLs, except for the SSH service. If you had used the Server App (instead of the Users & Groups preferences) to bind, SACLs would exist for various services.

Using Directory Utility Remotely

You can still use Directory Utility instead of System Preferences; in fact, the Users & Groups preferences offer a shortcut to Directory Utility, which is located in /System/Library/CoreServices. Directory Utility offers a little more control than the Join button of the Users & Groups preferences, and it allows you to control a remote computer from Lion or Lion Server, so you don't need to rely on screen sharing being available.

Use the following exercise to use Open Directory on Lion to connect to Lion Server to confirm the settings for directory use.

This exercise assumes that you have a replica at 10.1.18.1, that you configured a stand-alone Lion Server at 10.1.19.1 to bind to the replica at 10.1.18.1, and that you have forward and reverse DNS records available for these servers.

1   On your administrator computer, if necessary, open the Server app.

2   From the Tools menu, choose Directory Utility.

3   You need to use Directory Utility to connect to your server and inspect the directory services that your server uses.

Choose File > Connect.

4   Enter the following information to authenticate to the remote server:

Address: server19.pretendco.com

User Name: ladmin

Password: ladminpw

Click Connect to connect.

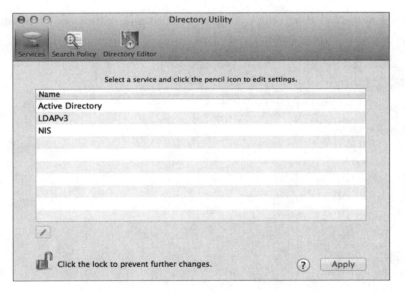

5   If necessary, click Services in the toolbar.

6 Double-click LDAPv3.

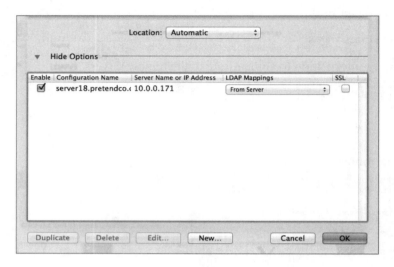

Note that the Configuration Name is based on the server's DNS name, but the Server Name is the IP address of the Open Directory master.

7 Select the server18.pretendco.com configuration and click Edit.

This opens the Connection pane, which contains detailed information about the connection to the Open Directory server.

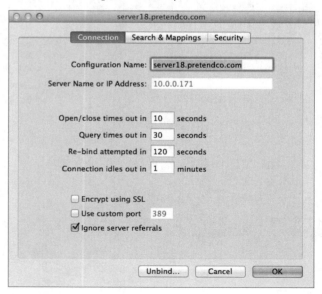

8   Click the Security tab.

This shows that server19 uses the computer record named server19$. Don't be alarmed that the checkbox "Disable clear text passwords" is disabled, because that applies when connecting to other LDAP services, not Open Directory servers.

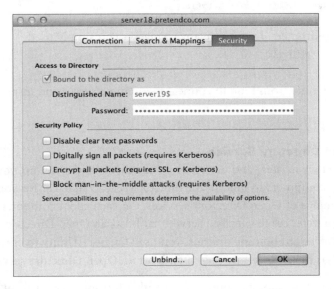

9   Click OK to dismiss the LDAP server listing.

10   Click Search Policy in the toolbar.

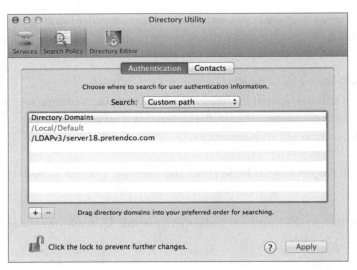

Confirm that the Open Directory server is listed. It will be listed starting with /LDAPv3/, followed by its IP address or DNS name.

11 Click Cancel to close the window.

12 Click Cancel again to close the list of LDAP servers.

13 Quit Directory Utility. If prompted, do not save any changes—you simply used Directory Utility to inspect settings.

You have now used Directory Utility from Lion to connect to a remote server and inspect settings remotely.

Binding Lion to Your Open Directory Service

Once you have an Open Directory master (and perhaps one or more replicas) set up, you must also configure the client computers to bind to the directory service in order for your client computers to take advantage of Open Directory services. On each client computer, you use the Users & Groups preferences to specify a server that hosts an Open Directory service, or if you need more-advanced binding options, you use Directory Utility to create an LDAP configuration that has the address and search path for an Open Directory server.

You will now configure your administrator computer to use authentication services from your Lion Server. You already configured a shared directory, and your Lion computers must be able to see the shared directory in order to authenticate against it. Any client bound to the Open Directory service can authenticate users using the data in the shared directory.

In an environment with many Open Directory replicas, you may consider binding Lion to a replica, which leaves the Open Directory master free to communicate with the replicas.

Using the Users & Groups Preferences to Bind

In the following steps, you will use System Preferences to bind your Lion computer to your Open Directory master. The steps are similar to binding a server to an Open Directory server, from the section immediately above.

1 On your Lion computer, open System Preferences and open the Users & Groups preferences.

2 If necessary, click the lock in the lower-left corner and provide local administrator credentials.

3 Click Join.

4 Enter the host name of your Open Directory replica, server18.pretendco.com (if you have only an Open Directory master, use this instead: server17.pretendco.com), and then click OK.

5 In the "This server provides SSL certificates" dialog, click Trust.

6 In the "This server does not provide a secure (SSL) connection" window, click Continue.

You will be returned to the Login Options pane, and the Network Account Server value is updated.

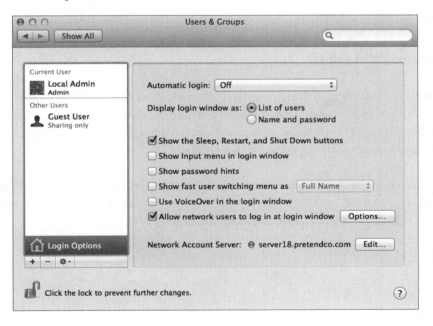

7 Quit System Preferences.

Managing Network User Accounts

Once you have created shared LDAP directories, you need to populate them with information. User account information is probably the most important type of information you can store in a directory. User accounts that are stored in a shared directory are accessible to all the computers that search that directory; those accounts are referred to as network user accounts or simply network users.

There are two main tools for managing network user accounts: the Server app and Workgroup Manager. The Server app offers basic management of users and services, and is the preferred tool unless you need more advanced options. Workgroup Manager offers more-advanced editing, but the Server app automatically adds users to service access control lists (SACLs) and adds users to the built-in group called Workgroup.

Using the Server App to Manage Network User Accounts

The Server app gives you the basic options for account management, including the account details, email address, services that a user is authorized to use, groups to which a user belongs, and global password policy.

When you create a user with the Server app, the user is automatically added to the network group named Workgroup.

> **NOTE ▶** When you create network user accounts outside of the Server app, such as with Workgroup Manager, those users are not automatically added to the group named Workgroup. Therefore, be careful when you use both the Server app and Workgroup Manager to create network user accounts.

1   If necessary, open the Server app on your administrator computer and connect to an Open Directory server. In this exercise you will use your Open Directory master, but you could also connect to an Open Directory replica.

2   Click Users in the sidebar.

3   Click Add (+).

4   Enter the following values:

   ▶ Full Name: Networkuser 1

   ▶ Account Name: networkuser1

   ▶ Password: network

Of course, you should use a secure password in a production environment.

5 Click Done.

6 Inspect the group membership for the newly created network user.

Double-click networkuser1.

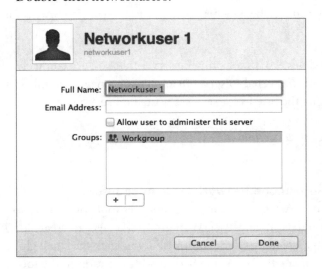

Note that the Server app automatically added Networkuser 1 to the network group Workgroup.

7 Click Done.

8   Inspect how SACLs are modified for the new user.

Control-click networkuser1, and choose Edit Access to Services.

The Server app automatically added the new network user to the existing SACLs for services offered by server17.

NOTE ▸ The Server app modifies SACLs for only the server that you are connected to with the Server app. If you are connected to server18 and create a new user, the Server app will not attempt to update the SACLs for services hosted on server17.

9   Click OK to close the Service Access window.

Using Workgroup Manager to Manage Network User Accounts

As an alternative to the Server app, Workgroup Manager is another tool you can use to create network user accounts. You have already used Workgroup Manager to create local accounts, but you can also use it to create network accounts. If you click the small globe icon in the upper left of the Accounts pane below the Server Admin button in the toolbar, you can choose a directory from a pop-up menu. This enables you to create user accounts in different directories. Use the Basic pane to create an account, and then use the other panes to set the account's attributes, such as login shell.

NOTE ▶ If you are creating user accounts that other computers will use, make sure you have chosen a shared directory from the directory pop-up menu before you create the account. Workgroup Manager will display a warning whenever you start to add accounts to the local directory; this will help prevent you from accidentally creating an account in the local directory instead of in a shared one.

NOTE ▶ You can also add users and/or groups from one directory to groups from another directory. This increases the flexibility of your system and servers and makes it easy to create an overly complex model across directory servers. Always be sure you know which directory you are editing before making changes.

Use the following steps to verify the configuration and to verify that Workgroup Manager can see both databases:

1 On your administrator computer, open Workgroup Manager, and if necessary, connect to your server computer using the following settings:

▶ Address: server17.pretendco.com

▶ User Name: ladmin

▶ Password: ladminpw

NOTE ▶ If you previously stored the password in the keychain, the password field gets automatically populated, and, for security reasons, shows eight characters regardless of how many characters are actually in the password.

2 If you get the message "You are working in a directory node that is not visible to the network," click OK.

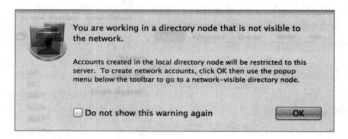

3 Click the globe icon to display the Directory Node pop-up menu, and choose Other.

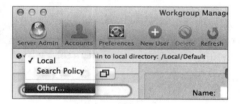

4 In the "Select a directory" pane that opens, select LDAPv3, select 127.0.0.1, and click OK.

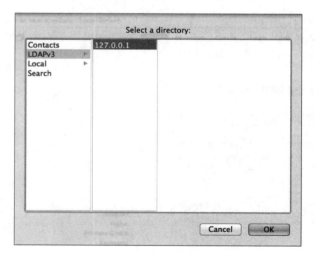

5 Because you authenticated as a local administrator, not as a directory administrator, you cannot edit the shared directory. You must authenticate with the Directory Administrator credentials.

Click the lock icon on the right under the toolbar.

6 Authenticate as diradmin (password: diradminpw). For now, leave the option to remember the password in the keychain deselected, and click Authenticate.

7 In the left pane of the Workgroup Manager window, click the Users button, and then click New User in the toolbar.

8 At the message "New users may not have access to services," click OK.

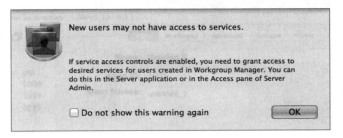

9 Enter the following values:

▶ Name: Networkuser 2

▶ Short Names: networkuser2

▶ Password: network

▶ Leave the other settings at their defaults.

Of course, you should use a secure password in a production environment.

10 Click Save.

You have just created a user account in your shared directory domain.

11 Create one more network user with the following values:

▶ Name: Networkuser 3

▶ Short Names: networkuser3

▶ Password: network

12 Click Save.

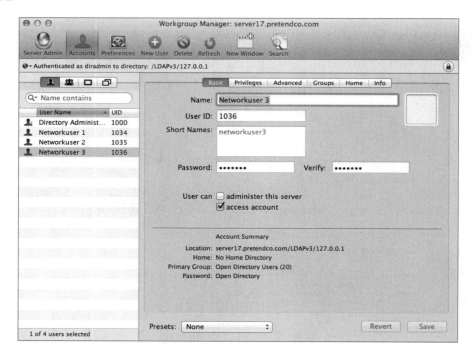

Now use the Server app to inspect the user that you just created with Workgroup Manager.

13 If necessary, on your administrator computer, close any connections you have open with the Server app.

14 On your administrator computer, open the Server app and connect to server17, and authenticate as your local administrator.

15 Inspect the group membership for the newly created network user.

Double-click Networkuser 2.

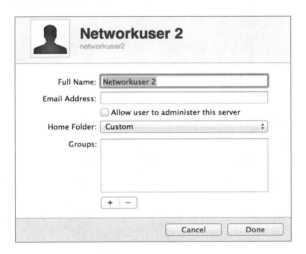

Note that this user, which you created with Workgroup Manager, is not a member of the network group Workgroup.

Additionally, this user has a Home Folder value visible, and it is set to Custom. This field is not visible when you use the Server app to inspect Networkuser 1.

Click Done to close the window.

16 Inspect how SACLs are modified for the new user.

Control-click Networkuser 2, and choose Edit Access to Services.

Because server17 has SACLs enabled for a default set of services, and Workgroup Manager did not modify the SACLs when you created Networkuser 2, this user is not authorized to access any of these services.

17 Click OK to close the Service Access window for user Networkuser 2.

You have just created one user with the Server app, and another user with Workgroup Manager. Carefully select the tool you and administrators in your organization will use to create new users, because as you've seen, the tools have different consequences.

Using the Server App to Import Users

If you configure your server to be an Open Directory master by using the Server app to choose Manage > Manage Network Accounts, after you bind to another directory service, users from the directory service you bind to will not be authorized to use services on your Lion Server unless you import them. You can import users, and you can import groups. In this exercise you will import a user.

The following exercise assumes there is a Lion Server configured as server20.pretendco. com at 10.0.0.201, and you will configure it as an Open Directory master.

1 On your administrator computer, use Screen Sharing to confirm that server20 uses the DNS service from your Open Directory master (10.0.0.171).

2 Use Network Utility to confirm forward and reverse DNS records for server20. pretendco.com (see the section Confirming DNS Records for Lion Server for exact steps), and confirm forward DNS records for the Open Directory replica and the Open Directory replica (server18.pretendco.com and server17.pretendco.com).

3 On your administrator computer, open the Server app and connect to server20.
pretendco.com as a local administrator.

4 From the Manage menu, choose Connect to Directory.

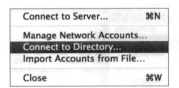

This opens an assistant that walks you through setting up server20 as an Open
Directory master.

5 In the Configure Network Users and Groups pane, click Next.

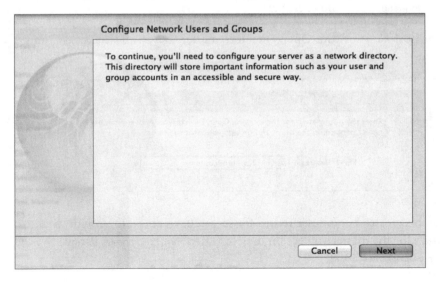

6   Because you should not have two directory administrator accounts with the same short name within the same directory realm, specify the following information and click Next:

▶   Name: Directory Administrator 20

▶   Account Name: diradmin20

▶   Password: diradmin20pw

▶   Verify: diradmin20pw

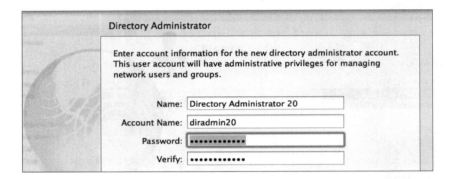

7   For the Organization Name and Admin Email Address, enter server20 and student20@pretendco.com and click Next.

8   Enter the host name of your Open Directory master (server17.pretendco.com) and click Next.

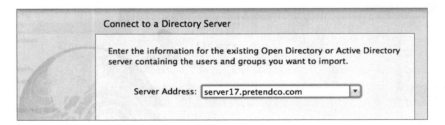

9   Because this creates a computer record for server20, you need to provide diradmin credentials for the master you are binding to (User Name: diradmin, Password diradminpw) and click Next.

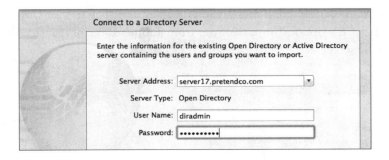

10 Click Set Up in the Confirm Settings pane.

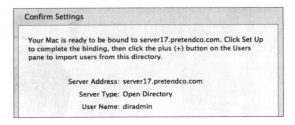

You now have server20 configured as an Open Directory master, and server20 is also bound to the Open Directory replica at server18. You can now import a user from the Open Directory master to enable that user to access services hosted on server20.

11 In the Users pane of the Server app, click Add (+).

12 Click the pop-up menu for Type, and choose Imported user from server18. pretendco.com.

NOTE ▶ If your server is connected to more than one other directory service, the pop-up menu includes the option "Imported user from another directory" instead of referring to a specific server.

13 In the search field, type networkuser1.

14 Select Networkuser 1, click Import, and then click Done.

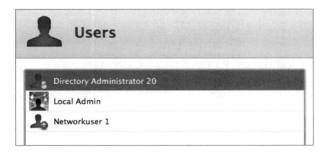

Note that the user Networkuser 1 has a blue icon with an arrow to indicate that it is an imported user. Additionally, the directory administrator account, Directory Administrator 20, appears in the list of users. As of the current writing, the Server app does not normally display a user if its short name is "diradmin."

15 Click Add (+) to create a new user.

16 Click the Type pop-up menu and choose New user.

Create this new user in server20's domain with the following information:

▶ Full Name: Server20networkuser 1

▶ Account Name: server20networkuser1

▶ Password: network

▶ Leave the other settings at their defaults.

17 Click Done to create the user.

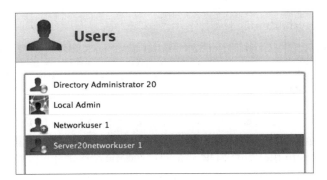

You see server20's directory administrator account, a local account, the imported account with the blue circle with an arrow, and the network account hosted by server20's domain, with a blue circle.

18 If necessary, open Server Admin, and connect to server20.pretendco.com as a local administrator.

19 Select server20.pretendco.com in the Server Admin sidebar, then click Access in the toolbar.

20 Select one of the services, like Address Book.

Confirm that Server20networkuser 1 is listed in the service's SACL.

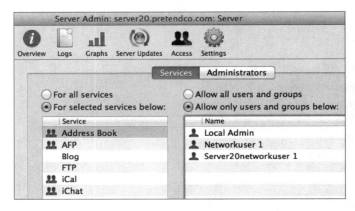

21 Close the windows in the Server app and in Server Admin.

Only the following users are authorized to use the default set of services offered by server20:

▶ Users local to server20, like Local Admin

▶ Network users defined in server20's Open Directory master databases, like Server20networkuser 1

▶ Imported users, like Networkuser 1

Remember that because you used the Users & Groups preferences to bind server19 to another Open Directory server, there were no SACLs created. But, because on server20 you used the Server app to bind to another Open Directory server, the Server app first helped you establish server20 as its own Open Directory master, then it bound to the other Open Directory server, the Server app created SACLs for services offered on server20.

The next step would be to use Server Admin to click the Kerberize Services button, but that is not shown here.

Configuring Authentication Methods on Lion Server

For authenticating users whose accounts are stored in directories on Lion Server, Open Directory offers a variety of options, including Kerberos and the many authentication methods that network services require. Open Directory can authenticate users by using:

▶ Single sign-on with the Kerberos KDC built in to Lion Server

▶ A password stored securely in the Open Directory Password Server database

▶ A password stored as several hashes—including NTLMv1 and NTLMv2 (NT LAN Manager); and Microsoft Challenge Handshake Authentication Protocol (MS-CHAPv2), used for VPN—in a location that only the root user can access

▶ An older crypt password stored directly in the user's account (on the local filesystem or in the user's record stored in a third-party LDAP directory), for backward compatibility with legacy systems

▶ Local-only accounts, in which a shadow password is used, stored in a location accessible only by root

In addition, Open Directory lets you set up a password policy that affects all users (except administrators), as well as specific password policies for each user, such as automatic password expiration and minimum password length. Open Directory password policies do not apply to shadow and crypt passwords. Even though Lion Server supports all these different authentication methods, you should not use all the methods. Crypt password support, for example, is provided for backward compatibility with older computers, but using crypt passwords is not as secure as using Kerberos or the Open Directory Password Server.

Configuring User Authentication

To authenticate a user, Open Directory first must determine which authentication option to use: Kerberos, Open Directory Password Server, shadow password, or crypt password. The user's account contains information that specifies which authentication option to select. This information is called the authentication authority attribute. The attribute is not limited to specifying a single authentication option. For instance, an authentication authority attribute could specify that a user can be authenticated both by Kerberos and Open Directory Password Server.

You can change a user's authentication authority attribute by changing the user password type in the Advanced pane of Workgroup Manager. By default, the password type is Open Directory, which means that Lion Server uses either Kerberos or Open Directory Password Server. Open Directory passwords are stored securely in a separate database, not in the user account. Shadow hash passwords are stored securely as part of the user record, a crypt password is generally stored as part of the user record, in a way that is readable by users other than the root user—a situation you should avoid.

A user's account might not contain an authentication authority attribute. If a user's account contains no authentication authority attribute, Lion Server assumes that a crypt password is stored in the user's account.

> **NOTE** ▶ Crypt passwords are inherently less secure because they are stored in the directory database and are subject to dictionary attacks.

Disabling a User Account

If you want to prevent a user from logging in, you can temporarily disable that user by using Workgroup Manager to remove access to his or her account. Doing so does not delete the user, nor does it change his or her User ID or any other information. It also doesn't delete any of the user's settings, preferences, or files. It simply prevents that user from authenticating and gaining access to the server via any method.

1 On server17, open Workgroup Manager and select the directory where the account that you want to disable resides. Generally, you will disable network user accounts, but you can also disable local user accounts.

2 Click the Accounts button, select the account, click the Basic tab, and deselect the "access account" checkbox.

3 Save the changes.

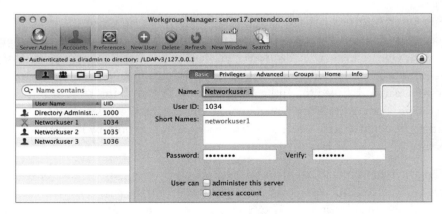

> **NOTE** ▶ When a user account is disabled, you'll see a red X through the user's icon in the list of users.

Setting Account Password Policies

Once you create new users, it's useful to establish password policies for their network accounts. (There is more on setting these policies later in this chapter.) Should the users change their passwords next time they log in? Should there be a minimum password length? You can use the Server app, Workgroup Manager, and Server Admin to establish these and other policies for your users. Policies can apply to just one user or to all users.

Password policies applied with Workgroup Manager are called user account settings and are set for each user by clicking the Advanced button, and then clicking the Options button.

> **TIP** ▶ Per-user policies can be set for more than one user by selecting more users prior to clicking the Advanced tab and subsequent Options button.

There are also some password policies that you can apply with the Server app and with Server Admin that are called global policies. In Lion Server, user account settings may override global policies. Administrators are exempt from both types of policies. You'll learn how to set global policies later in this chapter.

Setting User Account Settings (Per-User Password Policies)

You will now set policies on a per-user basis, as opposed to for multiple users.

1 Open Workgroup Manager and make sure you are in the LDAP directory (/LDAPv3/127.0.0.1). Select all three network user accounts you created earlier in this chapter, and click the Advanced tab.

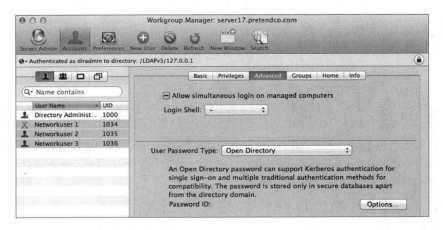

> **NOTE** ▶ If you accidentally include Directory Administrator in your selected list, you cannot click Options, because you cannot modify password policy for the user that you are authenticated as. Additionally, Administrators are exempt from password policy.

2   Click the Options button.

3   Use the text fields and checkboxes to configure the following settings:

▶   Allow the user to log in

▶   Disable login on specific date (a year from today's date)

▶   Disable login after inactive for 90 days

▶   Disable login after user makes 10 failed attempts

▶   Allow the user to change the password

▶   Password must contain at least 3 characters

▶   Password must be reset every 90 days

▶   Password must be changed at next login

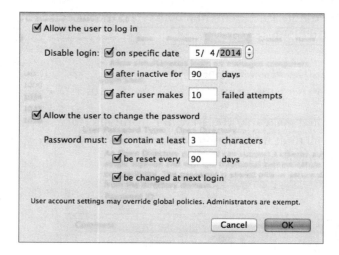

"Allow the user to log in" and "Allow the user to change the password" will already be selected.

The next time any of the highlighted users logs in, he or she will need to change his or her password; the new password will need to be at least 3 characters long; and the account will be disabled on the date you chose.

NOTE ▶ If you choose more than one user, dashes appear in all checkboxes to indicate the individual values may vary. Clicking a dash changes it to a checkbox, indicating that the selection is now selected or deselected for all highlighted users.

4 Click OK, and then click Save.

Note that because you enabled the checkbox "Allow the user to log in," the previously-disabled network account is no longer disabled.

Setting Single User Account Settings

Now you may want to have only one of those users not be able to change his or her password, as in the case of a novice user.

1 Select one of your users (networkuser1), click the Advanced tab if it's not already selected, and click the Options button.

2 Edit the checkboxes to disallow all options under the criteria for password, and deselect the checkbox allowing the user to change his or her password.

3   Click OK, and then click Save.

Now this user can't change his or her password, and it is still set to expire on a given date.

> **TIP** ▸ If you disable the checkbox for "Allow the user to log in" in the Advanced pane, then click the Basic pane, the checkbox for "User can access account" is still enabled. Click Refresh and the checkbox will be updated to be deselected as expected.

Testing User Account Policies

You will now use your Lion computer to test these policies.

1   On your Lion computer, use Server Admin to ensure that on server17.pretendco.com, AFP service is running and there are no SACLs that restrict access to the AFP service.

2   On your Lion computer, switch to the Finder and ensure that you do not have any network volumes mounted.

If the Eject button is displayed next to your server in the sidebar of the Finder, click Eject.

3   Choose Go > Connect to Server.

4   Enter afp://server17.pretendco.com.

5   Attempt to authenticate as networkuser1 (password: network).

6   You are prompted to enter a new password because you selected the checkbox "Password must be changed at next login" for this network user account.

7 Enter network in the Old Password field, and enter zz in the New Password and Verify fields, and then click Change Password.

8 Click OK at the message that your password does not meet the policy enforced by the server.

9 Enter networkuser1 in the New Password and Verify fields, and then click Change Password.

This should be a valid new password.

10 Since you entered a valid new password, you should see a list of share points.

Click Cancel. You do not need to mount any share points.

If you already mounted a share point, simply click Eject next to the icon for server17 in the Finder window sidebar.

Setting Global Password Policies

Open Directory enforces per-user and global password policies. For example, a user's password policy can specify a password expiration interval. If the user is logging in and Open Directory discovers that the user's password has expired, the user must replace the expired password. Open Directory can then authenticate the user.

Password policies can disable a user account on a certain date, after a number of days, after a period of inactivity, or after a number of failed login attempts. Password policies can also require passwords to be a minimum length, contain at least one letter, contain at least one numeral, be mixed case, contain a character that is neither a number nor a letter, differ from the account name, differ from recent passwords, or be changed periodically.

Open Directory applies the same password policy rules to Password Server and Kerberos. Password policies do not affect administrator accounts. Administrators are exempt from password policies because they can change the policies at will; therefore, administrator accounts are not vulnerable to a troublemaker exploiting the "disable login after user makes N failed attempts" policy by performing repeated failed authentication attempts for an administrator account. However, this makes administrator accounts potentially more vulnerable to brute force attacks that attempt to guess the administrator password with repeated guesses of different passwords, so it is crucial that you choose a strong password for each account in the Administrators group.

Kerberos and Open Directory Password Server maintain password policies separately. Lion Server synchronizes the Kerberos password policy rules with Open Directory Password Server password policy rules.

After global password policies are put into effect, they are enforced only for users who change their password, or users you create or import. For instance, the user Networkuser 1 with the password "networkuser1" will not be required to change his password, even though you may have set global password policy to require the password to be different from the short name. This is because the account and password existed prior to the establishment of the global policy. In this case, it is best to require the user to change his password at the next login, thus forcing him to make his password conform to the recently set global password policies.

1   Open the Server app if it's not already open, and connect to your Open Directory master as a local administrator.

2   Click Users in the Server app sidebar.

3   Click the action menu (looks like a gear with an arrow), and choose Edit Global Password Policy.

4   Choose your own criteria for when to disable the login, choose what parameters every user's password must meet, and click Save. Your settings may be different from what is shown in the figure below.

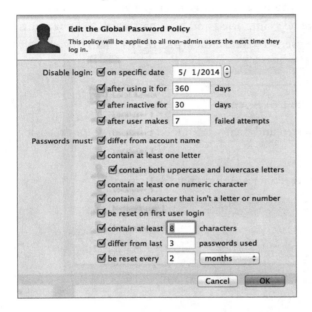

5   Use the steps from the previous exercise "Set Single User Account Settings" to require Networkuser 1 to change the password at the next login.

6   Use the steps from the previous exercise "Test User Account Policies" to attempt to connect to the AFP service as networkuser1, in order to be prompted to change Networkuser 1's password (which you should have set to networkuser1).

Attempt to specify a new password that does not match the global options you set in step 3, and confirm your global password policy settings.

If you successfully changed Networkuser 1's password, do not mount a network volume, in order to keep the rest of the exercises simple.

7   In the Server app, deselect all the checkboxes you just selected so that these options will not interfere with the rest of the exercises, and then click Save.

8   Use the Basic tab in Workgroup Manager to change Networkuser 1's password to the same password your other network users have: network.

9   Quit the Server app and Workgroup Manager.

> **TIP** It is important to obtain your organization's password policies if known prior to setting these options. If you miss certain criteria that are required by your organization and all users have been imported and have passwords set, changing these parameters may require users to change their passwords again to conform to the newer standards.

Examining Global Password Policy with Server Admin

1   Select your Open Directory master, and then select Open Directory from the list of services on the left.

2   Click Settings in the toolbar, click Policies, and then click Passwords.

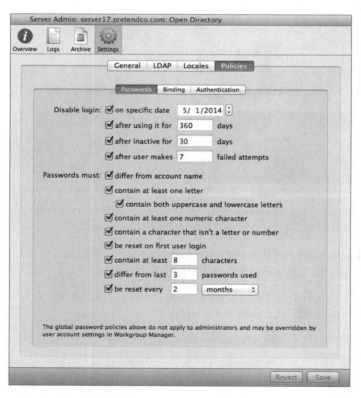

You can use either the Server app or Server Admin to set global password policy; they have the same options and the same effects. Remember that global password policy is only applied when a user changes their passwords, not when they authenticate.

Using Single Sign-On and Kerberos

Frequently, a user who is logged in on one computer needs to use resources located on another computer on the network. Users typically browse the network in the Finder and click to connect to the other computer. It would be a nuisance for users to have to enter a password for each connection. If you've deployed Open Directory, you've saved them that trouble. Open Directory provides a feature known as single sign-on, which relies on Kerberos. Single sign-on essentially means that when users log in, they automatically have access to other services they may need that day, such as email, file servers, chat servers, and VPN connectivity, without again entering their user credentials; in this way, Kerberos provides both identification and authentication services.

Defining Kerberos Terms

There are three main players in a complete Kerberos transaction:

▶ The user

▶ The service that the user is interested in accessing

▶ The KDC (Key Distribution Center), which is responsible for mediating between the user and the service, creating and routing secure tickets, and generally supplying the authentication mechanism

Within Kerberos there are different realms (specific databases or authentication domains). Each realm contains the authentication information for users and services, called Kerberos principals. For example, if you have a user with a long name of John Significant and a short name of johnsig on a KDC with the realm of SERVER17.PRETENDCO.COM, the user principal would be johnsig@SERVER17.PRETENDCO.COM. By convention, realms use all uppercase characters.

For a service to take advantage of Kerberos, it must be Kerberized (modified to work with Kerberos), which means that it can defer authentication of its users to a KDC. Not only can Lion Server provide a KDC when configured to host a shared LDAP directory, but it can also provide several Kerberized services. An example of a service principal would be afpserver/server17.pretendco.com@SERVER17.PRETENDCO.COM.

Finally, Kerberos enables you to keep a list of users in a single database called the KDC, which is configured on Lion Server once an Open Directory master has been created. When a network user logs in on a Mac OS X v10.4 or later client computer, that computer negotiates with the KDC. If the user provides the correct user name and password, the KDC provides an initial ticket called a Ticket Granting Ticket (TGT), which enables the user to subsequently ask for service tickets so he or she may connect to other servers and services on the network for the duration of the login session. During that time, the user can access any network service that has been Kerberized, without seeing a password dialog.

Kerberos is one of the components of Open Directory. The reason a user's password is stored in both the Password Server database and the Kerberos principal database is to allow users to authenticate to services that are not Kerberized. However, users must enter a password every time they access those s non-Kerberized services. Open Directory uses Password Server to provide support for those authentication protocols.

Because Kerberos is an open standard, Open Directory on Lion Server can be easily integrated into an existing Kerberos network. You can set up your Lion computers to use an existing KDC for authentication.

One security aspect to using Kerberos is that the tickets are time sensitive. Kerberos requires that the computers on your network be synchronized to within five minutes by default. Configure your Lion computers and your servers to use NTP, and synchronize to the same time server so this doesn't become an issue that prevents you from getting Kerberos tickets.

Examining Kerberos Tickets

Even though you do not have a home folder at this point, you can examine your Kerberos ticket.

1   Log in to your Lion computer as ladmin, if you are not already logged in as ladmin.

2   In the Finder, choose Go > Go to Folder.

3   Enter /System/Library/CoreServices and click Go.

4   Open Ticket Viewer.

5   Click Add Identity to obtain a new Kerberos ticket.

6 Enter the short name and password that you entered earlier in Workgroup Manager (networkuser1, network), and click Continue.

7 You should now see an entry for a valid Kerberos ticket, including its expiration date and time.

8 Click Remove Identity so your ticket will not interfere with any other exercises.

9 Quit Ticket Viewer.

Notice that even though you logged in at the login window as ladmin, you were able to get a Kerberos ticket as another user. This is because, although you authenticated locally to your administrator computer as ladmin, you authenticated against the Open Directory service for your network user account with Ticket Viewer.

Archiving and Restoring Open Directory Data

Once your Open Directory master (and any replicas) has been established, it is advisable to archive all your Open Directory data. This enables you to quickly recover all LDAP user information, passwords, and computer configuration information. It also permits you to transfer the Open Directory service from one computer to another by restoring the Open Directory information, provided that the IP address and host name of the new computer are the same as on the old one.

Understanding the Archival Structure

When you archive the Open Directory data, Server Admin creates an encrypted sparse disk image and stores it wherever you choose. The items archived include all three major components of Open Directory masters—the LDAP database, the Password Server database, and the Kerberos Key Distribution Center—along with the local database and passwords, the local KDC, and the host name and directory service files.

NOTE ▶ It is wise to store or copy this critical information to another device for safekeeping in case the server disks suffer catastrophic failure.

Archiving the Open Directory Master

You will now archive all the critical information related to your Open Directory master.

1   Open Server Admin if it is not already open. Select your Open Directory master, and select Open Directory in the service list on the left.

2   Click Archive in the toolbar.

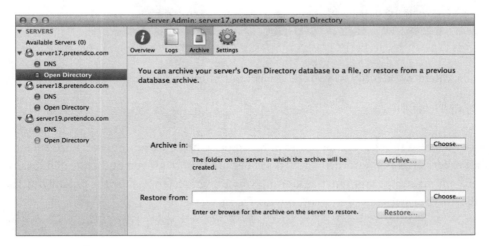

3   Click the Choose button next to the "Archive in" field. Navigate to the location where you want to save the archive disk image. For this exercise, navigate to /your Lion Server boot volume/Users/ladmin/Desktop.

The location you choose will be relative to the server you are connected to with Server Admin, not the Lion computer that you use to open Server Admin.

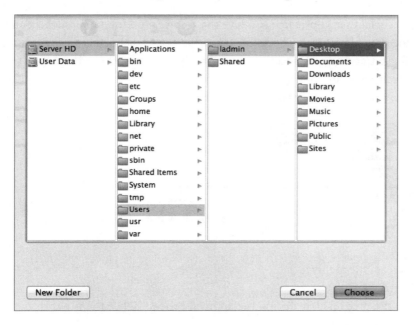

4   Click Choose to choose the location.

5   Click Archive to actually create the archive.

6   Enter the archive name ODArchive.

7   Enter a password. For this exercise, use the same password as your diradmin account: diradminpw.

> **NOTE ►** It is crucial that in practice you give the archive a useful name, such as one containing the date of archival. Check to ensure that the Caps Lock key is intentionally either enabled or disabled, and then record the password you used somewhere safe, like a Keychain Secure Note. For the purposes of this exercise, use the same password as the diradmin account password.

Please enter the name and password for this archive:

Archive Name:	ODArchive
Password:	••••••••••
Verify:	••••••••••

Cancel   OK

8   Click OK to create the archive.

You can now view the progress bar during the archival process. Once the progress bar disappears, the process is complete.

Inspecting the Contents of the Archive

The archive of your server's Open Directory databases won't do you much good if you just leave it on your server's hard drive and that hard drive becomes unavailable. However, for now, leave it there so you can use it to restore the Open Directory databases in an upcoming exercise. Use the following steps to copy the archive to your Lion computer in order to inspect it:

1   From the Server menu, choose Share Server's Screen.

2   Enter the password (ladminpw) and click Connect.

3   Using Screen Sharing, on your Lion Server, log in as your local administrator.

4   On your Lion Server, double-click the ODArchive.sparseimage to open it.

5   Enter the password you used to create the archive (diradminpw) and then click OK.

6   Note that in Lion, the Finder does not automatically display External disks on the
    Desktop by default, so it may not appear that anything has happened.

    Scroll down to the bottom of your Finder's sidebar, and click the ldap_bk disk image.

7   Confirm that the ldap_bk volume is populated with files. These files constitute the
    archive of your Open Directory master; you do not need to understand the con-
    tents of all files at this time, but take a quick look that the files that make an Open
    Directory backup possible: configuration information, certificates, and LDAP,
    Kerberos, and Password Server databases.

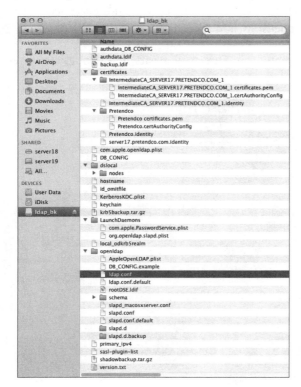

8　Eject the ldap_bk volume.

9　Log out of your Lion Server.

10　On your administrator computer, quit Screen Sharing.

Restoring Directory Data to the Open Directory Master

Once Open Directory data has been archived, it can be restored just as easily. In this exercise you will change your Lion Server from an Open Directory master to a standalone server—you'll destroy the Open Directory databases, simulating a catastrophic loss of your Lion Server. If you ever need to start from scratch for any reason, simply install Lion Server with the same IP address and DNS name as your old Open Directory master, configure a fresh new Open Directory master, and then restore from your archive. This exercise gives you a taste of how the process works.

1　Quit Workgroup Manager and the Server app if it is open on your administrator computer or any server, and open Server Admin on your administrator computer.

2　Select your Open Directory master (server17.pretendco.com), and then select Open Directory in the service list. Click Settings, and then click General.

3　Change the role of the server from an Open Directory master to a standalone server using the Change button, which opens Open Directory Assistant.

4　Select "Set up a standalone directory" and click Continue.

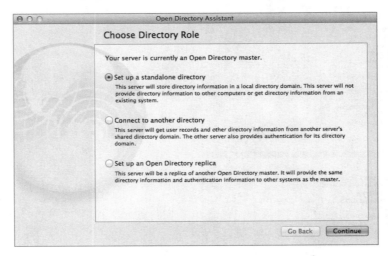

5   In the "Are you sure you want to destroy the current master" window, click Continue.

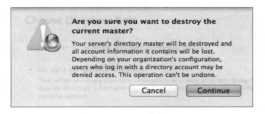

6   In the Confirm Settings pane, click Continue.

7   In the Summary pane, click Done to close the Open Directory Assistant.

You just removed the LDAP database, Password Server database, and Kerberos KDC—all of which constitute the Open Directory master.

You cannot restore from an Open Directory master archive until you first configure your server as an Open Directory master, which you will do in the next section.

Configuring an Open Directory Master with Server Admin

As an alternative to the Server app, you can use Server Admin to configure your server to host a shared LDAP directory, Password Server, and Kerberos Key Distribution Center (KDC), providing directory information and authentication services to other systems. You already configured an Open Directory master with the Server app, and now that you have destroyed your Open Directory master configuration, here is your chance to configure your Lion Server as an Open Directory master with the Server Admin.

In order for Server Admin to consistently display your DNS name rather than your IP address throughout the process of setting up an Open Directory master, use the DNS name rather than the IP address when using Server Admin.

> **NOTE ▶** The Server app is the preferred tool to use to configure your Lion Server as an Open Directory master, but these directions are included if you still prefer to use Server Admin.

1   On your Lion computer, if necessary, open Server Admin, and connect to your server (server17.pretendco.com) as ladmin (password: ladminpw).

2   In the sidebar of Server Admin, select the Open Directory service, click Settings, and then click General.

3 Click Change to open the Open Directory Assistant.

4 Select "Set up an Open Directory master," and click Continue.

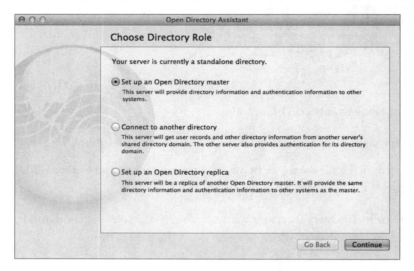

5 When setting up the new Directory Administrator account, you have the ability to change the name, short name, and user ID. For this exercise, leave the defaults.

For this exercise, use the password diradminpw and click Continue.

Of course, you should use a secure password in a production environment.

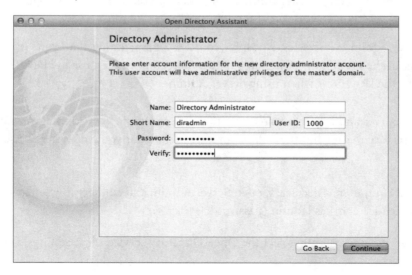

6 Verify that the automatically generated values for the Kerberos Realm and the LDAP Search Base fields match those in the following figure.

These values are somewhat arbitrary, but they are based on your server's host name, and you should leave them at the suggested defaults unless you have a compelling reason to do otherwise. Do not change these values for this exercise.

If either field references "local," close the Open Directory Assistant and recheck your DNS records.

Open Directory Assistant generates a Kerberos realm and an LDAP search base from your server's DNS name. You are allowed to change these values, but it keeps things predictable if you leave them at their defaults.

7 For Organization Name, type Pretendco.

8 For CA Administrator Email, type student17@pretendco.com.

Click Continue to accept these values.

9 Review the settings, and then click Continue in the Confirm Settings window.

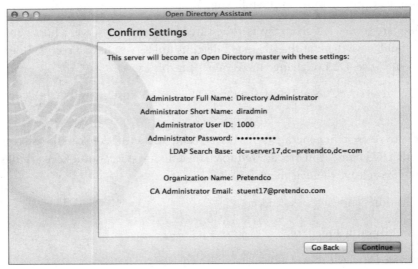

10 In the Summary window, click Done to quit the Open Directory Assistant.

11 Click Overview in the toolbar. You should see that the three services—LDAP Server, Password Server, and Kerberos—are running.

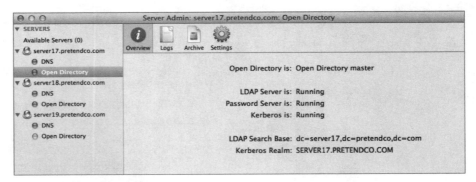

12 Click the Archive button in the toolbar.

13 Next to the Restore from field, click Choose, and navigate to the archive you created earlier. For this exercise, choose */your Lion Server boot volume*/Users/ladmin/Desktop/ODArchive.sparseimage.

The location you choose is relative to the server you are connected to with Server Admin, not the Lion computer that you use to open Server Admin.

Once you have your archive sparse image selected, click Choose.

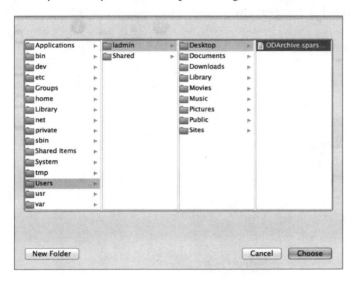

14 Click Restore.

15 Enter the password for the encrypted sparse disk image (diradminpw), and then click OK.

Server Admin displays information as it performs tasks related to the restore.

NOTE ▶ If you mount the disk image on your server, make sure you eject the ldap_bk disk image before you attempt the restore; one step in the restore process is to mount the disk image, and if the disk image is already mounted, the restore fails.

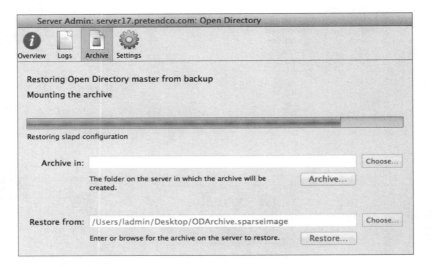

16 After the restore has completed, click Overview in the toolbar.

17 Open Workgroup Manager, connect to your Open Directory master, and confirm that the network users you created are restored.

You have now successfully restored Open Directory data to your Lion Server.

NOTE ► There is no need to back up an Open Directory replica's databases. In fact, restoring a replica can be dangerous, because it puts an outdated copy of the account information on the network. Because a replica is a copy of the master, the master effectively backs up the replica. If a replica develops a problem, you can just change its role to standalone server. Then you can set up that server as though it were a brand-new server, with a new host name, as a replica of the same master as before.

server18, server19, and server20 are no longer needed for the exercises. If you wish to keep using these servers as they were configured, you would need to:

► configure the Open Directory replica (server18) as a standalone server.

► configure server18 as a new replica of the Open Directory master.

► unbind the member servers (server19 and server20) and rebind them.

Troubleshooting

Because Open Directory includes several services, there are several log files used for tracking status and errors. You can use Server Admin to view status information and logs for Open Directory services. For example, you can use the password-service logs to monitor failed login attempts for suspicious activity, or use the Open Directory logs to see all failed authentication attempts, including the IP addresses that generated them. Review the logs periodically to determine whether there are numerous failed tries for the same password ID, which would indicate that somebody might be generating login guesses. It is imperative that you understand where to look first when troubleshooting Open Directory issues.

Accessing Open Directory Log Files

Generally, the first place to look when Open Directory issues arise is the log files. Recall that Open Directory comprises three main components: the LDAP database, the Password Server database, and the Kerberos Key Distribution Center. Lion Server's Server Admin tool allows for easy viewing of all server-related Open Directory log files with respect to these three components.

The main log files are:

► Open Directory Log
► Configuration Log
► Kerberos Server Log
► LDAP Log
► Password Service Server Log
► Password Service Error Log

To access these log files:

1 If necessary, open Server Admin, select server17.pretendco.com, and select Open Directory in the service list on the left.

2 Select Logs in the toolbar, and then choose the Password Service Server Log from the pop-up menu at the bottom of the window.

3 Enter the word networkuser1 in the search field in the upper right of the window.

Confirm that you can see lines that contain "Policy test failed" for networkuser1, from when you attempted to change the password in an earlier exercise, but the proposed password did not meet password policy requirements.

You should also see a line that contains "changed password for user" from when you successfully changed networkuser1's password.

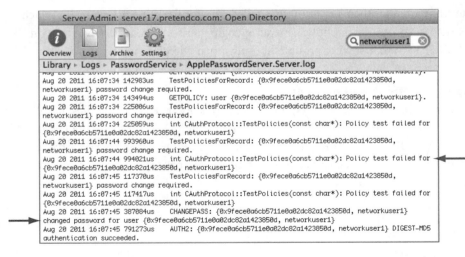

Interpreting log files can be a difficult task, and you may need the help of a more experienced system administrator. You can email the appropriate log file to the administrator. When you choose a log file from the pop-up menu, the path to the each log file is displayed below the toolbar.

Troubleshooting Directory Services

If Lion or Lion Server experiences a startup delay, or the login window displays a red status indicator with the text "network accounts unavailable," the computer could be trying to access an LDAP directory that is not available on your network.

There are several ways to begin troubleshooting when you are unable to connect to a directory service. These include:

▶ using Login Options in the Users & Groups preferences to confirm that the network server is available.

▶ using Directory Utility to make sure the LDAP and other configurations are correct.

▶ using the Network preferences to make sure the computer's network location and other network settings are correct.

▶ inspecting the physical network connection for faults.

If you can't modify the password of a user whose password is authenticated by Open Directory, or if you can't modify a user account to use Open Directory authentication, one of two things might be possible:

▶ You might not be authenticated as the directory administrator for that directory.

▶ Your administrator user account might not be configured for Open Directory authentication. If you have upgraded from an earlier version of Mac OS X Server, the account might have a crypt or shadow password rather than an Open Directory password.

Troubleshooting Kerberos

When a user or service that uses Kerberos experiences authentication failures, try these techniques:

▶ Ensure that the DNS service you use is resolving addresses correctly. This is especially important at the time you are promoting a server to Open Directory master. If the DNS doesn't resolve addresses correctly, the incorrect address will be written to the Kerberos configuration files. Kerberos tickets won't be usable.

▶ Kerberos authentication is based on encrypted timestamps. If there's more than a five-minute difference between the KDC, client, and server computers, authentication may fail. Make sure that the clocks for all computers are synchronized using the NTP service of Lion Server or another network time server.

▶ Make sure that Kerberos authentication is enabled for the service in question.

▶ Refer to the password-service and password-error logs for information that can help you solve problems. You can sometimes detect incorrect setup information, such as wrong configuration filenames, using the logs.

▶ View the user's Kerberos ticket. Kerberos tickets are visible in the Ticket Viewer application, which is found in /System/Library/CoreServices.

Preparing DNS Records (Optional)

NOTE ▶ Skip this section if you already have the appropriate DNS records available in your environment.

Open Directory services rely on forward and reverse DNS records for the computers hosting Open Directory services. You can use the exercises in this section to have your Lion server provide a common set of DNS records for the servers you will use to complete the exercises in this chapter.

In this section you will prepare a DNS zone, create appropriate DNS records, and configure your OS X computer to use this newly updated DNS service so you can get on with the task of configuring Open Directory services.

If you configure your OS X computer to use the DNS service hosted by your OS X server, you may experience delays with Server Admin, because there are not yet DNS records for your OS X computer.

Configuring DNS to Support Multiple Open Directory Servers

If no DNS records are available when you initially set up Lion Server, Server Assistant configures a DNS zone specifically for that one server. This is great, but you may eventually need to change your server's Network preferences to use a DNS service that offers a complete set of DNS records.

In this exercise, you will replace the automatically created and limited DNS zone with a DNS zone for your larger organization: pretendco.com. You will create machine records for two additional servers, and Server Admin will automatically create reverse DNS records for you. You will configure your Open Directory master (10.1.17.1) to host the DNS service, and you'll configure your other Lion servers to use the DNS service offered by your Open Directory master. If you already have a DNS service available on your network, or if you have only one server, simply read through this exercise.

The seemingly strange numbering scheme matches the scheme used in the classroom exercises, where each student has a number *n*, and they use server*n*, with IP address 10.0.0.*n*1; so server19 uses 10.0.0.191.

1　On your OS X computer, open Server Admin to connect to your Open Directory master at 10.1.17.1 as ladmin (password: ladminpw).

2　Select DNS in the list of services for 10.1.17.1.

3　Click Zones in the toolbar.

4　If necessary, at the warning, select the "Do not show this message again" checkbox.

　Be extra cautious with this exercise. Click OK.

5　Click the Add Zone pop-up menu, and choose Add Primary Zone (Master).

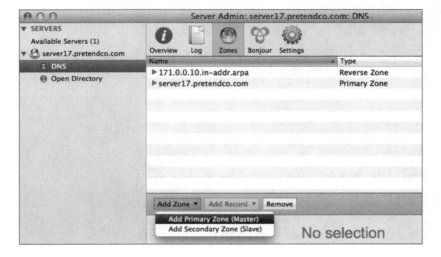

6　In the Primary Zone Name field, enter pretendco.com.

7　In the Admin Email field, type student17@pretendco.com.

8　Click the Add (+) button next to the Nameservers field.

　The Zone and Nameserver Hostname values are populated automatically.

Click Save to save the information for your new pretendco.com zone.

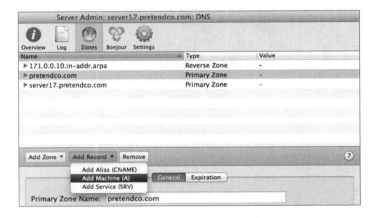

9 With pretendco.com still selected in the top pane, click Add Record and choose Add Machine (A).

10 In the Machine Name field, enter server17, and then press Tab.

Press Tab again to move to the IP Addresses field.

11 In the IP Addresses field, edit the IP address.

12 Change the IP address to 10.0.0.171, and then press Return to stop editing the IP address.

13 Click Save to save this new DNS record.

14 Ensure that pretendco.com is still selected in the top pane. Click Add Record and choose Add Machine (A).

15 In the Machine Name field, enter server18, and in the IP Addresses field, enter 10.0.0.181.

16 Click Save to save this record.

17 Click Add Record and choose Add Machine (A). Create a record for server19.pretendco.com at 10.0.0.191, and then click Save.

18 Click Add Record and choose Add Machine (A). Create a record for server20.pretendco.com at 10.0.0.201, and then click Save.

You now have records for server17, server18, server19, and server20.

To keep things simple, you will remove the primary zone and the reverse zone that Server Assistant automatically created when you set up the server at 10.0.0.171.

1 To help make sure you remove the correct item, use the disclosure triangle next to each zone to display less information.

2 Select the server17.pretendco.com zone. Be sure that you select the server17.pretendco.com zone, not the server17 machine record (which should be hidden if you performed the previous step).

3   With server17.pretendco.com selected, click Remove.

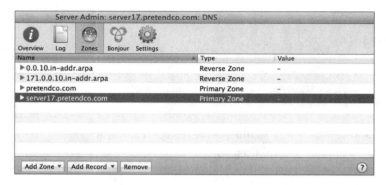

4   Select the 171.0.0.10.in-addr.arpa zone (not 0.0.10.in-addr.arpa), and click Remove.

This removes the reverse DNS zone that Server Assistant automatically created.

5   Click Save.

6   Click the disclosure triangles next to each zone to show more information.

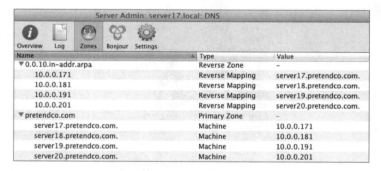

7   Confirm that you have the same zones and records as shown in the preceding figure.

8   Confirm that the DNS service is running. Look in the sidebar of Server Admin; if the status indicator for DNS is not green, click Start DNS in the lower-left corner of Server Admin.

Optionally, create an additional zone for use in Chapter 7, "Managing Web Services."

1   Click Add Zone, and choose Add Primary Zone (Master).

2   In the Primary Zone Name field, enter pretendco.lan.

3   Click the Add (+) button next to the Nameservers field.

4   Confirm that the Zone field contains "pretendco.lan".

5   In the Namserver Hostname field, replace the existing contents with server17.pretendco.com.

6   Click Save.

7   Click Add Record, and choose "Add Machine (A)".

8   In the Machine Name field, enter www.

9   Replace the IP Addresses field with 10.0.0.172.

10 Click Save.

11 Click Add Record, and choose "Add Machine (A)".

12 In the Machine Name field, enter ssl.

13 Replace the IP Addresses field with 10.0.0.173.

14 Click Save.

Now that you have configured your Open Directory master to also offer DNS services for pretendco.com, you need to configure your other servers to use that DNS service.

1   On your OS X computer, open Server Admin. Choose Server > Add Server, and connect to server18.pretendco.com as ladmin.

2   In Server Admin, select server18.pretendco.com and choose Server > Share Server's Screen. Authenticate as ladmin to connect.

3   On 10.0.0.181, open System Preferences and open Network.

4   Select the active interface, then click Advanced.

5   Click DNS.

6   Select any existing values in the DNS Server field, and click Remove (-).

7   In the DNS Server field, click Add (+) and then type 10.0.0.171.

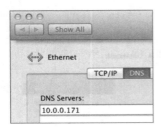

8   Click OK to dismiss the Advanced pane.

9   Click Apply.

Your server at 10.0.0.181 now relies on the DNS service offered by 10.0.0.171. If the server at 10.0.0.171 reboots or otherwise becomes unavailable, the server at 10.0.0.181 has no DNS service. In a production environment, you should have DNS service available from at least two DNS servers. However, it is outside the scope of this book to set up secondary DNS services to be hosted by Lion Server.

10 Use Launchpad to open the Network Utility in the Utilities folder, and perform a lookup for server18.pretendco.com.

Confirm that the Answer section contains the correct IPv4 address for server18 (10.0.0.181).

11 Perform a lookup for 10.0.0.181, and confirm that the Answer section contains server18.pretendco.com.

12 For the third and last check, perform a lookup for server17.pretendco.com, and confirm that the Answer section contains 10.0.0.171.

13 Log out of your server as ladmin.

14 Close the Screen Sharing window.

15 Repeat the preceding steps for server19 and server20 to assign 10.0.0.171 as the DNS service.

What You've Learned

▶ Directory services centralize system and network administration and simplify a user's experience on the network.

▶ Open Directory is Apple's extensible directory-services architecture.

▶ Directories store information in a specialized database that is optimized to handle a great many requests for information and to find and retrieve information quickly. Information may be stored in one directory or in several related directories.

▶ The Open Directory service uses OpenLDAP to provide the LDAP standard for directory access, enabling you to maintain information in a single location on the network rather than on each computer. It also uses Kerberos to provide secure authentication, and for those applications that do not yet use Kerberos, the Open Directory service provides the Password Server service.

▶ The Server app and the Open Directory service window of Server Admin let you configure how Lion Server works with directory information.

▶ Workgroup Manager enables you to create both local and network user accounts. Once you configure your server as an Open Directory master or an Open Directory replica, you can use the Server app to create network users and network groups only.

▶ The Users & Groups preferences is the primary method for binding to another directory service. To edit advanced options, use Directory Utility, which is available in /System/Library/CoreServices on both Lion and Lion Server, from the Tools menu of the Server app, and from the Join or Edit button in the Users & Groups preferences.

▶ You can use the Server app or Server Admin to configure your Lion Server to provide directory services as an Open Directory master.

▶ You can use Server Admin to configure your Lion Server to provide directory services as an Open Directory replica.

▶ You can use the Users & Groups preferences to configure your Lion Server to bind to another directory service regardless of whether or not the binding server is an Open Directory server itself.

▶ You can use the Server app to configure your Lion Server to bind to another directory service. Keep in mind that it first attempts to configure your Lion Server as an Open Directory master, before it allows you to bind to another directory service.

▶ After you bind your Lion Server to another directory service, you can use Server Admin to join another Kerberos realm.

▶ You should carefully choose which tools you use to create an Open Directory master and to create users, because the Server app performs extra steps involving the System keychain and Service Access Control Lists (SACLs).

▶ If you bind your Open Directory master to another directory service, you can use the Server app to import users and groups from another directory service, which automatically adds those users and groups to the appropriate SACLs.

▶ You can edit global password policy with the Server app and with Server Admin, and you can edit individual user password policy with Workgroup Manager.

References

The following documents provide more information about offering directory services with Lion Server. Additional resources are available at http://www.apple.com/macosx/server/resources/.

Lion Server Administration Guides

Lion Server: Advanced Administration
http://help.apple.com/advancedserveradmin/mac/10.7/

Lion Server: Upgrading and Migrating
http://images.apple.com/macosx/server/docs/Upgrading_and_Migrating_v10.7.pdf

Apple Knowledge Base Documents

You can check for new and updated Knowledge Base documents at http://www.apple.com/support/.

Document HT4696, "Lion Server: Changing opendirectoryd logging levels"

Document HT4789, "Lion Server: Locale-aware replica servers not added to the Default Locale"

Document TS3958, "Lion Server: When binding a Lion Open Directory Server using SSL, 'Unable to add server' appears"

Document TS3861, "Mac OS X v10.7: Unable to connect to a Mac OS X v10.6 Open Directory Server"

Document TS3896, "Lion Server: Server Admin does not show second level Open Directory Replicas status"

Document TS3898: "Lion Server: When binding to Open Directory, use System Preferences"

Document TS3889, "Unable to create automount on a Lion Server that is a member of Open Directory"

Books

Carter, Gerald. *LDAP System Administration* (O'Reilly Media, Inc., 2003).

White, Kevin. *Apple Pro Training Series: OS X Lion Support Essentials* (Peachpit Press, 2012).

Garman, Jason. *Kerberos: The Definitive Guide* (O'Reilly Media, Inc., 2003).

URLs

Heimdal Kerberos 5, PKIX, CMS, GSS-API, SPNEGO, NTLM, Digest-MD5 and, SASL implementation: http://www.h5l.org/

Designing an Authentication System: A Dialogue in Four Scenes: http://web.mit.edu/kerberos/www/dialogue.html

OpenLDAP: community developed LDAP software: http://www.openldap.org/

Lightweight Directory Access Protocol (v3): Technical Specification: http://www.rfc-editor.org/rfc/rfc3377.txt

SASL: Simple Authentication and Security Layer: http://asg.web.cmu.edu/sasl/

Chapter Review

1. What is the main function of directory services?

2. What standard is used for data access with Open Directory? What version and level of support is provided for this standard?

3. In terms of Open Directory, what four roles can Lion Server play?

4. What are the two methods of applying password policies, and where are they located?

5. When you create an Open Directory archive, is the sparse image created on the server that hosts the Open Directory service, or on the administrator computer from which you run Server Admin?

6. What criteria determines the Open Directory locale with which a Lion Open Directory client associates?

7. What log shows successful and failed attempts to authenticate against the password service?

8. What tool can you use to confirm forward and reverse DNS records?

9. What tool can you use to check the ability to obtain a Kerberos ticket?

Answers

1. Directory services provide a central repository for information about the computers, applications, and users in an organization.

2. Open Directory uses OpenLDAP and the Lightweight Directory Access Protocol (LDAP) standard to provide a common language for directory access. Open Directory uses LDAPv3 to provide read and write access to the directory data.

3. Lion Server can be an Open Directory master, a standalone server, connected to a directory system, and an Open Directory replica.

4. Per-user policies are defined in Workgroup Manager, and global policies are defined in Server Admin or the Server app.

5. The archive is created on the server that hosts the Open Directory service.

6. If a Lion computer's IPv4 address is in the range of a subnet associated with an Open Directory locale, that computer should use any of the Open Directory servers associated with that locale. Otherwise, it will use the default locale.

7. Password Service Server Log, located at /Library/Logs/PasswordService/AplePasswordServer.Server.log shows successful and failed attempts to authenticate.

8. You should use Network Utility to confirm forward and reverse DNS records before configuring as an Open Directory master or replica, or binding to another directory service.

9. Ticket Viewer is in /System/Library/CoreServices, and you can use it to confirm the ability to obtain a Kerberos ticket.

4

Time

This chapter takes approximately three hours to complete.

Goals

Configure Profile Manager

Construct management profiles

Deliver profiles

Install and delete profiles

Manage users, groups of users, devices, and groups of devices using profiles

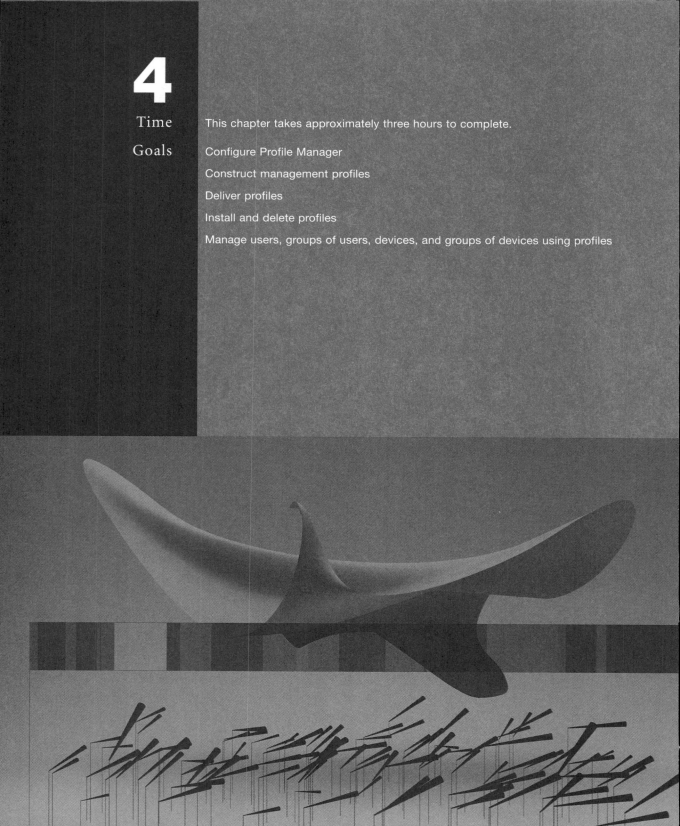

Chapter **4**
Managing Accounts

If you run an organization with several hundred users or even just a handful, how can you make sure you can manage their experience with OS X and iOS? In previous chapters you learned management techniques involving the user name, password, and home folder. There are many other aspects to user account management, and it is important to understand how these various aspects interact with each other.

OS X Lion Server provides a service called Profile Manager that allows you, as the administrator, to assign certain behaviors to the client devices such as computers and mobile devices.

Introducing Account Management

Account management was controlled by Workgroup Manager in Mac OS X 10.6 and earlier, but Lion introduces the concept of profiles that contain configurations and settings. By assigning profiles to users, user groups, devices, or groups of devices you can achieve control over your systems.

With effective account management, you can achieve a range of results, including the following:

▶   Providing users with a consistent, controlled interface

▶   Controlling settings on mobile devices and computers

▶   Restricting certain resources for specific groups or individuals

▶   Securing computer use in key areas such as administrative offices, classrooms, or open labs

▶   Customizing the user experience

▶   Customizing Dock settings

Profile Manager

Profile Manager is an account management tool that allows the development and distribution of configurations and settings to control the experience on Lion computers and iOS devices. The configurations and settings are contained in XML based text files called profiles. Profile Manager has three parts:

1   Profile Manager web tool

2   User Portal web site

3   Mobile Device Management Server

Profile Manager Web App

The web tool allows easy access to the Profile Manager functionality from any browser that can connect to the Lion Server with the Profile Manager service turned on. An administrator can utilize the web interface to create profiles for use on client machines. It is also used to create and manage device accounts and device group accounts. Users and Groups are created in the Server app, but are displayed in the Profile Manager web app. The Profile Manager is reached at https://*server.domain.com*/profilemanager/.

User Portal

The User Portal is a simple way for users to enroll devices, obtain profiles, and wipe or lock their devices. The User Portal is accessed via a web browser and lists the user's enrolled devices and available profiles. It is reached at https://*server.domain.com*/mydevices/.

Device Management

You can configure and enable the Mobile Device Management (MDM) functionality to allow you to create profiles for devices. When you or your users enroll Lion computers and iOS 4 or later devices, this allows over the air (OTA) management of devices including remote wipe and lock.

Levels of Management

Using Profile Manager you can apply profiles at various levels including:

▶   Individual Users

▶   Groups of Users

▶   Devices

▶   Device Groups

Not all management levels make sense for all purposes, so when setting policy you have to decide what is appropriate. For example, you might want to define printers by device groups, because a typical situation has a group of computers located geographically close to a specific printer. You may want to set VPN access via a group of users such as remote salespeople. And individuals might have specific application access rights granted to them.

Each level can have a default group of settings and then custom settings. Mixing and layering profiles with conflicting settings is not recommended.

Configuring Profile Manager

To allow assigning profiles, the Profile Manager service must be enabled. Using profiles is significantly different than managing clients in earlier versions of OS X Server. Note that the older method of using Workgroup Manager is still valid in Lion Server, but this book doesn't approach it. For information on OS X Managed Client , see Chapter 9, "Managing Accounts," in the book *Apple Training Series: Mac OS X Server Essentials v10.6.*

Terminology

In the context of device management, a Profile is basically a collection of settings. Configuration profiles define settings such as Wi-Fi settings, email accounts, calendar accounts, and security policies. Enrollment profiles allow the server to manage your device. A payload is what's inside a profile.

Preparations for Profile Manager

Prior to configuring Profile Manager, you'll need to set up a few items to make the process more streamlined.

▶ Configure your server to manage network users and groups. This is also referred to as creating an Open Directory Master.

▶ Obtain and install an SSL certificate. It is recommended to use one signed by a trusted certificate authority. You could use the certificate that was automatically generated when you configured your server to manage network accounts, but you first need to configure devices to trust that certificate. If you instead use your self-signed certificate, you won't be able to enroll iOS devices.

▶ Obtain an Apple ID for use when you request a push certificate from Apple through the http://appleid.apple.com website. Prior to using this ID, make sure you log in at that site under "Manage My Account" and verify the address. Otherwise, it is possible that you won't have success requesting the push certificate.

Enabling Profile Manager

In this section, you'll go through the steps to enable Profile Manager including the signing of a configuration profile.

1   Open Server app and select Profile Manager in the Server app sidebar.

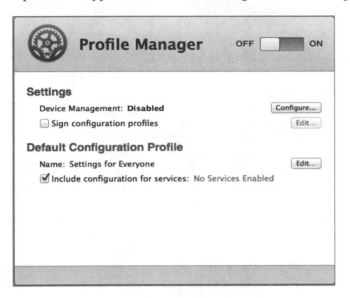

2   Click Configure, next to Device Management.

3 The service will gather some data and give a description of its capabilities. Click Next.

4 Choose your certificate. If you use your self-signed certificate, you will not be able to enroll any iOS devices.

5 Request an Apple Push Notification certificate using an Apple ID. If you do not have one, there's a link to obtain one under the credential fields. Make sure to verify the address at the http://appleid.apple.com site. Click Next.

6   A green circle will indicate that you succeeded. Click Finish.

7   Select the checkbox labeled "Sign configuration profiles," then choose the Code Signing certificate that was created when you created your network accounts.

By signing the profiles with a certificate, you provide a way to validate that the profiles came from where they are supposed to be from.

8   If you don't have any services running, use this time to configure and activate a few services, then click the On/Off switch to turn on Profile Manager.

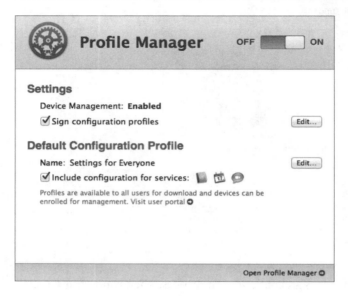

User Profile Portal

The User Profile Portal provides simple access for users to log in, apply profiles, and manage their devices. The portal is accessed via a web browser; by simply publishing the website, users anywhere in the world can enroll their devices–whether they be computers, iPhones or other iOS based mobile devices. It is through the portal that a user can lock or wipe their enrolled devices.

NOTE ▸ The example below is for OS X, but the iOS version is conceptually and visually similar.

1   Navigate to the site https://server17.pretendco.com/mydevices.

2   Through a series of redirects the user will be prompted for her credentials to log in.

3   The user is given tabs for Devices and Profiles. Devices is where the user can enroll the device. Profiles is where the various profiles made available to her will be displayed.

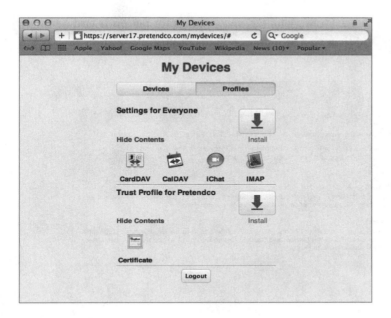

4 Click the Install Trust Profile. The profile will be downloaded, and the Profiles preferences will appear.

5 Click the Show Profile button to view the contents of the profile, then click Continue.

6   In the next window click Show Details to view more information regarding the certificates involved, and then click Install. Enter an administrator's credentials when prompted.

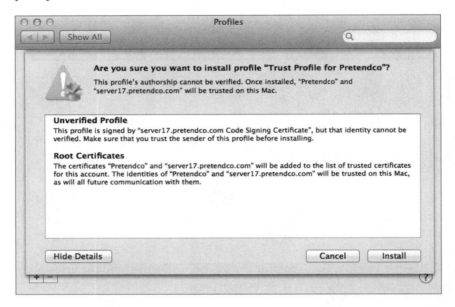

7 Navigate to the Devices tab and click Enroll. You will be brought back to the Profile preferences and asked if you want to enroll. View the profile and then click Install.

8 In the next screen, you will be asked to install Remote Management which allows the server to manage that machine. View the profile and click Continue. Enter an administrator's credentials when prompted.

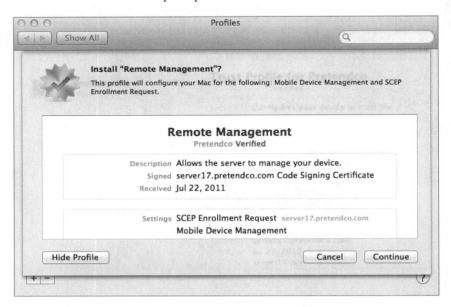

9 Now that the profile has been installed on the computer, refresh the view in the browser and notice that the computer is now listed under the Devices tab with choices to Lock or Wipe the computer. This allows the user to utilize any modern web browser to control those aspects of the computer remotely, if the machine were to get lost or stolen.

10 To lock the remote device, navigate to the site https://server17.pretendco.com/mydevices on a different computer and log in. Choose your test computer and lock it by clicking the Lock button and entering a 6 digit passcode. Click the Lock button again, and a confirmation box will appear. Once the confirmation has been given, the remote computer will reboot and then offer a dialog to unlock the machine via the passcode.

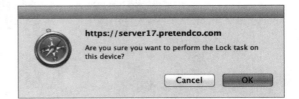

Managing Profiles Locally

Occasionally a profile will need to be viewed, added, or removed to make way for an updated profile or to simply stop management of the device. Managing the profiles local to a computer is done via the Profiles preference pane located in System Preferences. You added a profile to the computer in the previous exercise and now you will remove one.

To remove a profile local to an OS X computer:

1 Open the Profiles preference pane in System Preferences. The various profiles installed on the computer are listed along with their contents and purposes.

2 Pick the profile you wish to remove such as the remote management profile and click the Remove (-) button.

3   A confirmation dialog box will appear. Click Remove. Enter a local administrator's credentials, if prompted, and click OK.

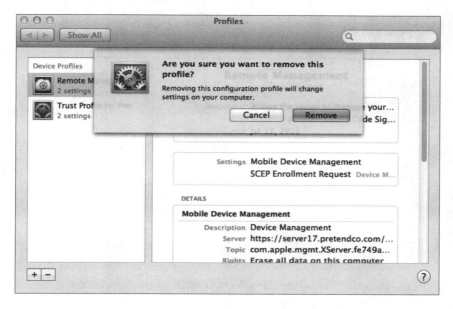

To remove a profile local to an iOS device:

1   Navigate to Settings/General/Profiles.

2   Tap the profile to show the details.

3   Tap the Remove button.

4   Confirm the removal by tapping the Remove button on the confirmation box.

5   Exit Settings.

Using Profile Manager

Once Profile Manager has been turned on, you access the actual management interface via a web application. The web application can be reached via web browser on any machine.

1   Navigate to the site https://server17.pretendco.com/profilemanager.

2   Log in to the Profile Manager web app with an administrator's credentials.

3   The layout is a column view where the selection made in the left column defines the content of the column to the right. Click on Devices under the Library and click an enrolled computer.

4   In the computers information pane, click Profile and then click Edit under Settings.

5 In the new window that opens, scroll down the list to the Mac OS X section, noting that there are sections for iOS and combined iOS and Mac OS X. Click Dock and then click Configure.

6 Change the settings to place the Dock on the Left and to automatically hide and show the Dock.

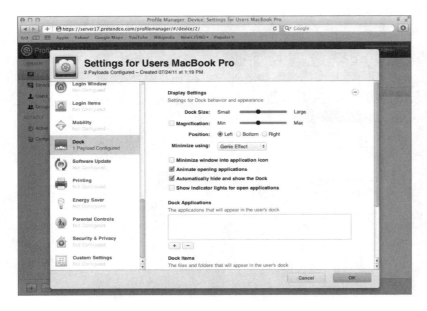

7 Scroll back to the top of the list in the left column and choose General. Under Profile Distribution Type select Manual Download. Click OK.

8 Note that the Dock preference is indicated in the settings for the computer. Click Save.

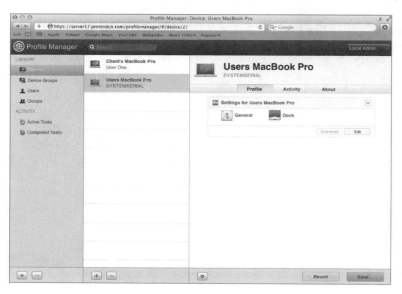

9 A warning that new settings might be pushed to the managed devices is presented. Click Save.

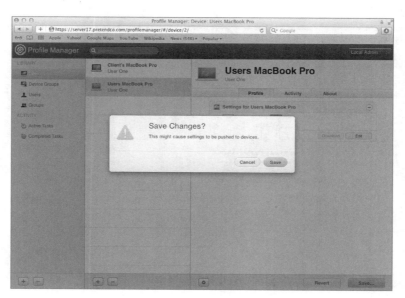

10 Under the Settings for the computer, click the Download button. A copy of the preferences is stored in the profile that has been downloaded to the machine Profile Manager is running on. Open the profile in TextEdit.app and view the contents. The profile is simply an XML text file.

11 Copy the file to your client computer and double-click on it to install. Choose Show Profile to view the contents of the profile.

12 Click Install and enter the local administrators password.

13 Log out and log back in. Notice the Dock is now hidden on the left side.

14 Open the Profiles preference pane in System Preferences. View the new profile. Remove the profile by clicking the Remove (-) button at the bottom of the left column. Acknowledge the removal and enter a local administrator's credentials. Upon logging out and back in, the original Dock location and behavior will be restored.

Delivering Profiles

Once created, profiles can be delivered to users and computers or iOS devices in a number of ways:

► Via the User Portal where users log in to the portal with their account credentials and they are presented with the profiles assigned to them.

► Emailed to users. The profile is a simple text file, so it is easily transported.

► Web link. The profile can be published on a website for users to visit and download.

► Automatic Push. The profile gets automatically pushed to the device with no user interaction (the device must be enrolled for this to work).

Remotely Locking or Wiping a Device

Once enrolled, a device or group of devices can be remotely locked or wiped. In this example, a remote lock will be performed. A remote wipe can be attempted, but only do it on a device you don't mind reconfiguring. The device can be locked via Profile Manager by an administrator or via the User Portal by the users themselves.

Upon requesting a lock, a confirmation pane will appear, a passcode will be requested, and the lock command will be sent. On Lion computers, the machine is shut down and an EFI passcode is set, so it needs to be entered to use the machine again. For iOS devices, the screen is locked and the passcode enforced.

► Profile Manager: Log into Profile Manager and select the device or group of devices to be locked. In the Action (gear) menu at the bottom of the right pane choose Lock.

► User Portal: Once users log in, each device they enrolled will be displayed in the Devices.

Managing User, Group, Device, and Device Group Accounts

You can create settings for four different types of accounts:

► User—Usually relates to a specific person. This is the account that the person identifies himself or herself with when logging in to the machine. A user's short name or UID number uniquely identifies the user on a system.

► Group—Represents a group of users, a group of groups, or a mixture of both.

► Device—Similar to a user account, it's the singular entity that represents a given piece of hardware. Device accounts are uniquely identified by their Ethernet ID, serial number, IMEI, or MEID.

► Device Group—Represents a group of computers or iOS devices, a group of device groups, or a mixture of both.

Which Preferences Can Be Managed?

In addition to various other settings for user, group, devices, and device group accounts, Profile Manager provides control over the preferences listed in Table 4.1. Table 4.2 describes the manageable preferences payloads for devices and device groups.

Table 4.1   Manageable Preferences Payloads for Users and Groups

Preference	OS X	iOS	Description
General	•	•	Profile distribution type, how the profile can be removed, organization, and description
Passcode	•	•	Define passcode requirements such as length, complexity, reuse, etc.
Email	•	•	Configure email settings such as servers, account name, etc.
Exchange	•	•	Configure Exchange ActiveSync settings
LDAP	•	•	Configure connection to LDAP server
CardDAV	•	•	Configure access to CardDAV server
CalDAV	•	•	Configure access to CalDAV server
Network	•	•	Configure network setting on the device, including wireless and wired
VPN	•	•	Configure VPN settings: L2TP, PPTP, IPSec (Cisco), CiscoAnyConnect, Juniper SSL, and F5 SSL
Certificate	•	•	Allows the installation of PKCS1 and PKCS12 certificates
SCEP	•	•	Define connection to Simple Certificate Enrollment Protocol (SCEP) server
Web Clips	•	•	Display defined Web Clips as application icons

Table 4.1 (continued)

Preference	OS X	iOS	Description
Restrictions	•	•	Define application and content restrictions (separate OS X and iOS versions)
Subscribed Calendars		•	Configure calendar subscriptions
APN		•	Configure carrier settings such as the Access Point Name (Advanced use only)
iChat	•		Configure connection to Jabber or AIM chat servers
Login Items	•		Specify applications, items and network mounts to launch at login
Mobility	•		Define mobility settings for OS X clients to allow cached credentials and portable home directories
Dock	•		Configure Dock behavior
Printing	•		Configure printing settings and access to printers or print queues
Parental Controls	•		Define settings for Parental Controls such as content filtering and time limits
Security and Privacy	•		Define whether or not to send diagnostic and usage data to Apple (might change in the future)
Custom Settings	•		Apply custom preferences for items not defined in other payloads. Similar to applying preference manifests in WGM

Table 4.2   Manageable Preferences Payloads for Devices and Device Groups

Preference	OS X	iOS	Description
General	•	•	Profile distribution type, how the profile can be removed, organization, and description
Passcode	•	•	Define passcode requirements such as length, complexity, reuse, etc.
Email		•	Configure email settings such as servers, account name, etc.
Exchange		•	Configure Exchange ActiveSync settings
LDAP		•	Configure connection to LDAP server
CardDAV		•	Configure access to CardDAV server
CalDAV		•	Configure access to CalDAV server
Network	•	•	Configure network setting on the device including wireless and wired
VPN	•	•	Configure VPN settings: L2TP, PPTP, IPSec (Cisco), CiscoAnyConnect, Juniper SSL, and F5 SSL
Certificate	•	•	Allows the installation of PKCS1 and PKCS12 certificates
SCEP	•	•	Define connection to Simple Certificate Enrollment Protocol (SCEP) server
Web Clips		•	Display defined Web Clips as application icons
Restrictions	•	•	Define application and content restrictions (separate OS X and iOS versions)
Subscribed Calendars		•	Configure calendar subscriptions
APN		•	Configure carrier settings such as the Access Point Name (Advanced use only)
Login Items	•		Specify applications, items, and network mounts to launch at login

Table 4.2 (continued)

Preference	OS X	iOS	Description
Mobility	•		Define mobility settings for OS X clients to allow cached credentials and portable home directories
Dock	•		Configure Dock behavior
Printing	•		Configure printing settings and access to printers or print queues
Parental Controls	•		Define settings for Parental Controls such as content filtering and time limits
Security and Privacy	•		Define whether or not to send diagnostic and usage data to Apple (might change in the future)
Custom Settings	•		Apply custom preferences for items not defined in other payloads (similar to applying preference manifests in WGM)
Directory	*		Configure binding to directory services
Login Window	*		Configure Login Window options, such as messages, appearance, access, and Login/LogoutHooks
Software Update	•		Define an Apple Software Update Server to be used by the computer
Energy Saver	•		Define Energy Saver policy such as sleeping, timed actions and, wake settings

Managing Preferences for Users in a Group

Although you can set up preferences individually for users with network accounts, it's more efficient to manage preferences for the groups to which they belong. Using groups allows you to manage users regardless of which devices they use.

Managing Device Group Accounts

A device group account is set up for a group of computers or iOS devices that have the same preference settings and are available to the same set of users and groups. You create and modify these device groups in Profile Manager.

When you set up a device group, make sure you have already determined how the devices are identified. Use descriptions that are logical and easy to remember (for instance, the description might be the computer name). This also makes it easier to find the devices to add them to the correct device group.

Creating a Device Account

There are two ways to set up a device account:

▶ During device enrollment the device account is created automatically.

▶ You can create a placeholder in Profile Manager, so when the user logs into the User Portal, predefined profiles are assigned to the device.

To manually create a placeholder in Profile Manager:

1   Click Devices in the Profile Manager Library.

2   Click the Add (+) button below the list of devices, and select Add Placeholder.

3   Give the placeholder a name and choose how to identify the device by Ethernet ID, serial number, IMEI, or MEID.

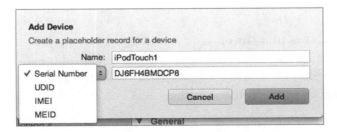

4   Click the Add button.

5 From the placeholder entry, you can add profiles and management that will be applied automatically once the device is enrolled.

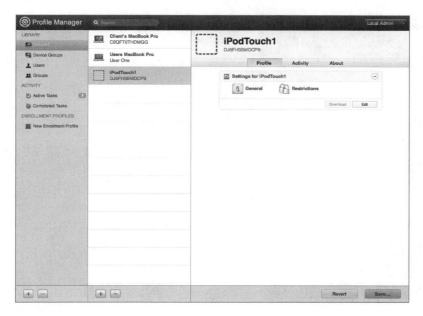

To import a list of placeholders in Profile Manager:

Lists of devices can be imported into Profile Manager via a comma separated value (CSV) file. The file needs to be structured as this:

name, serial number, UDID, IMEI, MEID

Leave a field empty if you're not using that value.

1 Click Devices in the Profile Manager Library.

2 Click the Add (+) button below the list of devices, and select Import Placeholders.

3 Choose the import file and upload.

Creating and Populating a Device Group

To create and populate a Device Group, Profile Manager is utilized:

1 Click Device Groups in the Profile Manager Library.

2   Click the Add (+) button below the list of device groups. This creates a new group that can be populated with the desired name.

3   To add devices to the device group, click the Add (+) button under the device group pane.

4   Click the device to add to the device group and then click Done.

5 To add device groups to the device group, click the Add (+) button under the device group pane.

6 Click the device group to add to the device group and then click Done.

7 Click Save.

Troubleshooting

Occasionally things won't work the way you expect, and you'll have to troubleshoot the situation. Even a robust service like Profile Manager can have an occasional issue.

Viewing Logs

The profilemanager.log is located at /Library/Server/ProfileManager/Logs and can be viewed with Console by double clicking. Errors may be reported and listed in the logs.

Viewing Profiles

If a device is not behaving as expected, look at the list of installed profiles on the device and see if the proper profiles have been installed. The solution may be as simple as applying the expected profile to the device.

Installing Profiles

If you're having problems installing a profile, you may have improper certificates. Review your SSL certificates for validity and make sure the trust profile has been installed on the device.

Problems Enrolling a Device

A trust profile must be installed prior to enrolling a device, unless you are using a certificate signed by a trusted certificate authority.

What You've Learned

▶ Account management encompasses fine-tuning the user experience by managing preferences and settings for users, groups, devices, and device groups.

▶ Profile Manager is the new management tool in Lion Server. It provides profile-based management of users, groups, devices, and device groups—from anywhere on your network or even across the Internet.

▶ A device group is a list of devices that have the same preference settings and are available to the same users and groups. You can create and modify device groups in Profile Manager web app.

▶ Preferences can be set for many built-in OS X options for users, workgroups, devices, or device groups. Other preferences can be managed if provided in a .plist format and applied via the Custom Settings profile payload.

References

The following documents provide more information about managing accounts on Lion Server. All these and more are available at http://www.apple.com/macosx/server/resources/documentation.html.

Administration Guides

Lion Server: Advanced Administration
https://help.apple.com/advancedserveradmin/mac/10.7/

Profile Manager Help
https://help.apple.com/profilemanager

Apple Knowledge Base Documents

You can check for new and updated Knowledge Base documents at http://www.apple.com/support/.

Chapter Review

1. What tool is used to create profiles?

2. Name at least three ways a profile can be delivered.

3. Why should a configuration profile be signed?

4. How is a profile removed from an OS X computer? From an iOS device?

5. What is a configuration profile? An enrollment profile?

6. What steps are involved with turning on the Profile Manager service?

7. What steps are involved with specifying that you want to sign your configuration profiles?

8. What three components comprise Profile Manager?

Answers

1. The Profile Manager web app is used to create profiles.

2. User portal, email, web page, manual delivery, or push to enrolled devices via the mobile device management capabilities of Profile Manager enable profile delivery.

3. A configuration profile should be signed to validate the contents of the profile.

4. In OS X 10.7 Lion, the profiles are managed in the Profiles preference pane within System Preferences. On an iOS device, navigate to Settings/General/Profiles to view and remove installed profiles.

5. A configuration profile contains settings and preferences to manage the user experience in a controlled device. An enrollment profile allows the device that it's installed on to be remotely controlled, performing such tasks as remote wipe and lock, and installation of other configuration profiles.

6. You can just click the On/Off switch in the Server app Profile Manager pane to turn on the Profile Manager service, but to enable device management (also known as Mobile Device Management), click Configure next to "Device Management," select a valid SSL certificate, and specify a verified Apple ID to obtain an Apple Push Notification Service certificate.

7. In the Server app Profile Manager pane, select the checkbox labeled "Sign configuration profiles," then choose a valid code signing certificate. Then when you create profiles with the Profile Manager web app, they are automatically signed.

8. The Profile Manager includes the Profile Manager web app, the user portal, and the optional device management (Mobile Device Management) service.

5

Time This chapter takes approximately three hours to complete.

Goals Understand the concepts of Netboot, NetInstall, and NetRestore

Create an image for deployment

Configure the NetBoot service

Configure clients to use NetBoot

Learn to troubleshoot NetBoot

Chapter **5**

Implementing Deployment Solutions

Knowing how to use time efficiently is a very important aspect of an administrator's job. When managing several hundred OS X computers, an administrator needs a solution that is both speedy and flexible for performing day-to-day management of computers. When computers need to be set up for the first time, what software should be installed? Should they have the latest software updates? Should they have a full complement of non-Apple software, such as Adobe Creative Suite or Microsoft Office? What about shareware programs and the necessary work-related files? Safety videos? Mandatory PDFs?

Before you can push out data to a computer, you must decide how to push out that data and in what state. Though there are several third-party tools that complete the tasks of image creation and deployment, Apple has several applications to assist you with this process. These helpful applications include System Image Utility, Apple System Restore (ASR), Apple Remote Desktop (ARD), and NetBoot.

With the advantage of these deployment software tools, you can build an automated system that needs very little user interaction to function. This chapter will focus primarily on the NetBoot service provided by OS X Lion Server.

Creating NetBoot images can be a lengthy process, but most of the time is spent waiting for the image to be processed. Because this chapter includes the creation of two images, you may wish to split this chapter over a couple days, or over a dinner break, at either of the two image-creation steps.

While you use the Server app to manage most Lion Server services, you use System Image Utility and Server Admin (installed with Server Admin Tools, which you can download from Apple) to create NetBoot images and configure the NetBoot service.

Deployment Issues

One significant challenge for OS X administrators today is the deployment of software to multiple computers. Whether it is operating system (OS) releases and updates or commercial applications, installing the software manually is a labor-intensive process. Lion Server provides services and technologies to aid in this deployment. The NetBoot service simplifies OS rollout and upgrades.

Managing Computers with NetBoot

Think about the ways in which you boot your computer. Most often, your computer starts up from system software located on the local hard drive. This local startup provides you with a typical computer experience of running applications, accessing information, and accomplishing tasks. When you perform an OS installation for versions of OS X prior to Lion, you could boot from a CD-ROM or DVD-ROM disc.

Managing a single standalone computer isn't much of an inconvenience. However, imagine managing a lab of computers. Every time you need to upgrade the operating system or install a clean version of OS X, you would need to boot each computer in the lab from the installation CD or DVD disc or from Lion Recovery. Even with a set of installation discs for each computer, it would still be time-consuming to update or refresh the entire lab.

Lion Server provides the NetBoot service, which simplifies the management of operating systems on multiple computers. With NetBoot, client computers start up using system software that they access from a server instead of from the client's local hard drive. With NetBoot, the client obtains information from a remote location. With other startup methods, the client boots off a local source, such as the internal hard drive or other device.

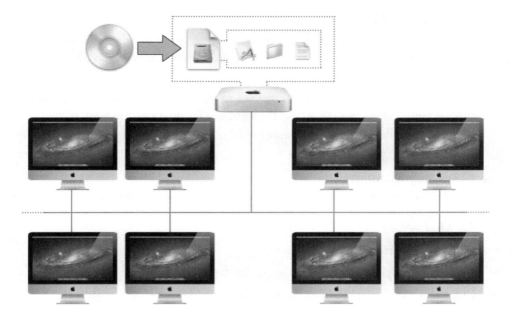

NetBoot is most effective in situations in which there is a high frequency of user turnover and in which a large number of computers are being deployed with a common configuration. The ability to deploy standard configurations across multiple computers makes NetBoot ideal for computing environments such as:

▶ Classrooms and computer labs: NetBoot makes it easy to configure multiple identical desktop systems and repurpose them quickly. With NetBoot, you can reconfigure systems for a different class simply by restarting from a different image.

▶ Corporate workstations: Using NetBoot to install system software allows you to reimage, deploy, and update workstations very quickly. Also, because installation is done over the network, it can even be done in place at the user's desk. A creative way to take advantage of this technology is to create a NetBoot image with various computer diagnosis and disk recovery software. Booting into a NetBoot rescue image at a user's desk could save a lot of time for a frustrated user.

▶ Kiosks and libraries: With NetBoot, you can set up protected computing environments for customers or visitors. For example, you can configure an information station with an Internet browser that connects only to your company's website, or set up a visitor kiosk that runs only a database for collecting feedback. If a system is altered, a simple restart restores it to its original condition.

- ▶ Computational clusters: NetBoot is a powerful solution for data centers and computational clusters with identically configured web or application servers. Similarly purposed systems can boot from a single NetBoot image maintained on a network-based storage device.

- ▶ Emergency boot disk: Netboot can be used to troubleshoot, restore, and maintain client computers. NetBoot can also help access computers whose boot drives have failed and whose Recovery HD is not available.

Hardware Requirements

For NetBoot to function properly, certain minimum hardware requirements must be met:

- ▶ 512 MB RAM on the client computer
- ▶ 100Base-T Ethernet (up to 10 clients)
- ▶ 100Base-T switched Ethernet (10 to 50 clients)
- ▶ 1000Base-T switched Ethernet (beyond 50 clients)

Apple has no official test results for configurations beyond 50 clients. Although there are some Mac computers that can use NetBoot over Wi-Fi, it is best to use Ethernet for NetBoot when possible.

Understanding NetBoot Startup Types

There are three types of NetBoot startup:

- ▶ A standard NetBoot startup (using a NetBoot boot image) provides a fairly typical experience, because clients start up using software that they access from a server.

- ▶ A Network Install, also known as NetInstall, startup sequence (using a NetBoot Install image) enables you to quickly perform fresh installations of your operating system. It also allows you to install applications or updates, or install configured disk images. The terms Network Install and NetInstall are used interchangeably in this chapter.

- ▶ NetRestore is aimed at deploying existing volumes. Another defining choice is the ability to define a restore image source other than the disk image embedded in the NetInstall set. This allows you to host the image on other servers.

Keep these three types of NetBoot in mind while you work through the remainder of this chapter.

With NetBoot, you create disk images on the server that contain OS X or OS X Server system software. Multiple network clients can use each disk image at once. Because you are setting up a centralized source of system software, you need to configure, test, and deploy only once. This dramatically reduces the maintenance required for network computers.

When you start up from a NetBoot image, the startup volume is read-only. When a client needs to write anything back to its startup volume, NetBoot automatically redirects the written data to the client's shadow files (which are discussed later in this chapter, in the section "Understanding Shadow Files"). Data in shadow files is kept for the duration of a NetBoot session. Because the startup volume is read-only, you always start from a clean image. This is ideal in lab and kiosk situations in which you want to ensure that users never alter the startup volume.

Stepping Through the NetBoot Client Startup Process

When a client computer boots from a NetBoot image, it performs a number of steps to start up successfully:

1. The client places a request for an IP address.

    When a NetBoot client is turned on or restarted, it requests an IP address from a DHCP server. While the server providing the address can be the same server providing the NetBoot service, the two services do not have to be provided by the same computer.

2. After receiving an IP address, the NetBoot client sends out a request for startup software. The NetBoot server then delivers the boot ROM (read-only memory) file ("booter") to the client using Trivial File Transfer Protocol (TFTP) via its default port, 69.

3. Once the client has the ROM file, it initiates a mount and loads the images for the NetBoot network disk image.

    The images can be served using Hypertext Transfer Protocol (HTTP) or Network File System (NFS).

4. After booting from the NetBoot image, the NetBoot client requests an IP address from the DHCP server.

    Depending on the type of DHCP server used, the NetBoot client might receive an IP address different from the one received in step 1.

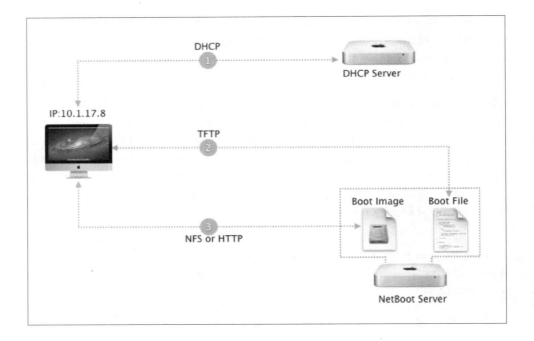

Using Home Folders with NetBoot

When you restart a client computer from a NetBoot image, the client computer receives a fresh copy of the system software and the startup volume. Users cannot store documents or preserve preferences on this startup volume, because it is a read-only image. If the administrator denies access to the local hard drive or removes the hard drive, users might not have any place to store documents. However, if you configure network user accounts to use network home folders, users can store documents and preserve preferences in their network home folders.

When a user logs in to a NetBoot client computer using a network user account, the client computer retrieves his or her home folder from a share point. Typically, this share point resides on a server other than the NetBoot server, although with a small number of clients, one could perform both duties from the same server.

> **TIP** ▶ The NetBoot service places high demands on a server. To prevent performance degradation, store home folders on a different, preferably dedicated, home folder server.

Creating Images with System Image Utility

System Image Utility is the tool you use to create all three types of NetBoot images. Located in the /Applications/Server folder on your Lion server computer, System Image Utility uses files from a mounted volume, disk image, or the "Install OS X Lion" application to create a NetBoot image. System Image Utility is included in the Server Admin Tools download available from the Apple website (http://support.apple.com/kb/DL1419). It is not available in the default software package supplied with OS X Server.

Each image requires an image ID, or index, which client computers use to identify similar images. If, when a client lists the available NetBoot images in the Startup Disk pane of System Preferences, two images have the same index, the client assumes that the images are identical and displays only one entry. If only one server will serve an image, assign it a value between 1 and 4095. If multiple servers will serve the same image, assign it a value between 4096 and 65535. System Image Utility generates a semi-random index between 1 and 4095, but you can change it if you customize the image.

When creating an image, you specify where to store it. For the NetBoot service to recognize the image, it must be stored in /<volume>/Library/NetBoot/NetBootSPn/imagename. nbi, where n is the volume number and imagename is the image name you entered when you created the image. If you have already configured the NetBoot service, the Save dialog includes a pop-up menu listing the available volumes. If you choose a volume from that pop-up menu, the save location changes to the NetBootSPn share point on that volume.

> **TIP** In a NetBoot environment, many clients booting from the same NetBoot server can place high demands on the server and slow down performance. To improve performance, you can set up additional NetBoot servers to serve the same images.

System Image Utility also enables you to customize your NetBoot, NetRestore, or Network Install configurations by adding any of the following Automater workflow items:

▶ Add Configuration Profiles

▶ Add Packages and Post-Install Scripts, which allows you to add third-party software or make virtually any customization you desire automatically.

▶ Add User Account, which will include additional users in your image. These users could include system administrator accounts or user accounts.

▶ Apply System Configuration Settings, which allows you to automatically bind computers to LDAP Directory servers, along with applying basic preferences such as the computer's host name.

▶ Automated Installation, which can assist in doing speedy deployments in which you're dealing with identical configurations and want to do hands-off installation.

▶ Disk partition support, which is built in to System Image Utility so you can add a partition automatically in your deployments.

System Image Utility contains a feature called Filter Computer Models that enables you to determine which system the image will boot. You can specify which model of hardware will be booted off which image. For example, if you wanted to configure a portable or desktop image, you could choose those models from a list for each image.

Creating NetBoot Image Types

With System Image Utility, you can create two distinct types of NetBoot images:

▶ A boot image is a file that looks and acts like a mountable disk or volume. NetBoot boot images contain the system software needed to act as a startup disk for client computers on the network. When creating a boot image, you can specify a default user account that the client can use to access the network disk image. You must specify a user name, short name, and password.

▶ An install or restore image is a special boot image that boots the client long enough to install software from the image, after which the client can boot from its own hard drive. Just as a boot image replaces the role of a hard drive, an install image is a replacement for Lion Recovery or an installation DVD.

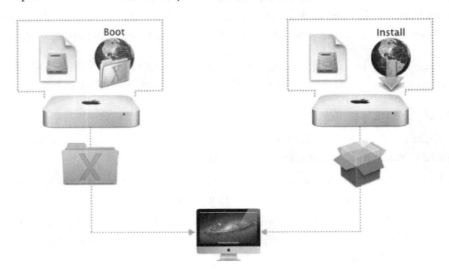

NOTE ▶ There is no real difference between the NetBoot, Net Restore, and Network Install processes: A boot image starts up and runs either the Finder or the Installer. The distinction is how the image file is tagged. The tag allows the user to visually differentiate between image file types in utilities such as Startup Disk in System Preferences.

Using Network Install

Network Install is a convenient way to reinstall the OS, applications, or other software onto local hard drives. For system administrators deploying large numbers of computers with the same version of OS X, Network Install can prove very useful. All startup and installation information is delivered over the network. You can perform software installations with Network Install using a collection of packages or an entire disk image (depending on the source used to create the image).

TIP ▶ For installing small packages rather than entire disks, it might be easier to use ARD, because not all packages require a restart. If NetInstall is chosen to deploy a package, the client system has already been restarted once to actually boot off the NetBoot server.

When creating an install image with System Image Utility, you have the option to automate the installation process to limit the amount of interaction from anyone at the client computer. Keep in mind that responsibility comes with this automation. Because an automatic network installation can be configured to erase the contents of the local hard drive before installation, data loss can occur. You must control access to this type of Network Install disk image, and you must communicate to users the implications of using these images. Always instruct users to back up critical data before using automatic network installations. When configuring your NetBoot server, you will be warned about this even if you aren't doing automated installs.

NOTE ▶ Set the default NetBoot image on every server. Images that normal users can select should probably be NetBoot images, not Network Install images. You may also turn off the NetBoot service when you don't need it.

Creating NetBoot Images

When creating NetBoot images, specify a source for the image in System Image Utility. System Image Utility, included with the OS X 10.7 Server Admin Tools download, should only be used to build images of Mac OS X v10.7. You can use Lion Server to serve images of any version os OS X, but if you wish to make images of earlier OS X versions, you should use the respective version of OS X and its version of System Image Utility to build the image. You can create images the following sources:

▶ "Install OS X Lion" as downloaded from the Mac App Store

▶ Disk images: Instead of using a configured hard drive as a source, you can use Disk Utility to create a disk image of a configured hard drive, and then use the disk image as a source for creating NetBoot images.

▶ Mounted volumes: When a mounted volume is selected as a source, the entire contents of the volume—including the operating system, configuration files, and applications—are copied to the image. When a client computer starts up from an image created from a mounted volume, the boot experience is similar to that of starting up from the original source volume. A copy of the source volume is written to the client computer's disk drive. A benefit of using volumes for image sources is that the image creation is much faster than when using discs. In addition, installations that use images created from volumes are faster than installations that use disc-created images.

When creating the images, you have the option of adding additional software to the image. For example, you may need to include an update to the operating system with an image created from the installation discs. You specify additional software to be installed, in the form of an installer package, in the Other Items field.

> **TIP** Use the latest version of the operating system when creating NetBoot images. If you are creating OS X 10.7 images, use the imaging tools from OS X 10.7 Server. If you are creating OS X 10.6 images, use the imaging tools on OS X 10.6 or OS X Server 10.6.

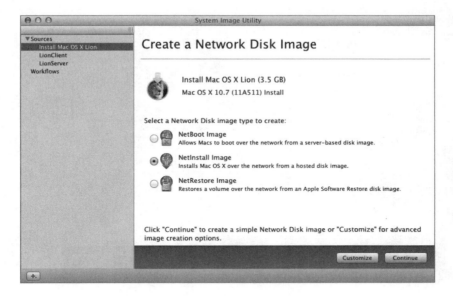

When adding new computers to the NetBoot environment, you may need to update the NetBoot image to support them. Check the OS software version that accompanied the new computer.

To create a Network Install image from the "Install OS X Lion" application as downloaded from the Mac App Store, follow these steps:

1   Copy the "Install OS X Lion" application into the /Applications folder.

2   Open /Applications/Server/System Image Utility.

3   In the Sources list on the left, select "Install Mac OS X Lion."

4   Select the NetInstall Image button.

5   Click Continue.

6   Change the Image Name to My NetInstall v1.

7   Change the Description to NetInstall of OS X 10.7 Version 1.

   TIP ▶ Give your images unique identifiers to help you keep track of which image is which. This process often involves multiple attempts and updates, which you'll want to be able to track.

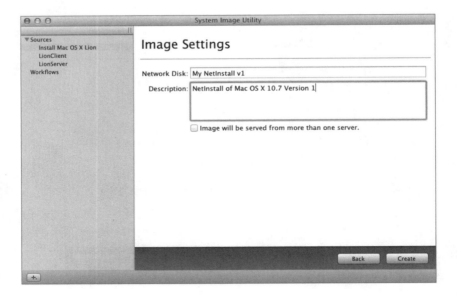

8 Click Create.

9 Agree to the software license agreement.

10 When prompted where to save the image, select your desktop or select the /Library/NetBoot/NetBootSP0 folder and click Save.

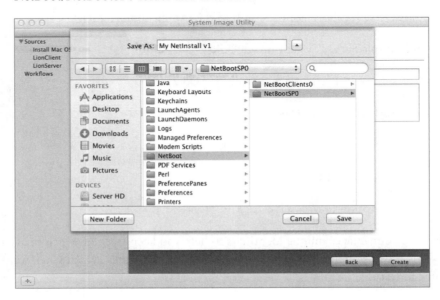

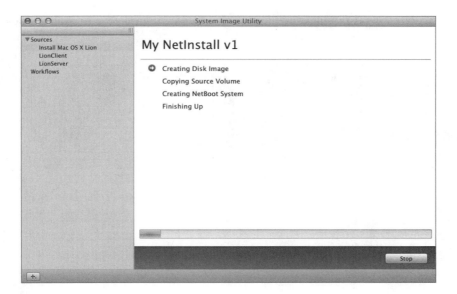

Creating an image can take from 15 minutes to a few hours depending on the size of the source image and the speed of the computer. In the meantime, you'll continue by configuring your server.

Creating a NetRestore image is very similar to creating a NetInstall image, but you start with an existing computer image or by connecting a preconfigured computer via Target Disk Mode and picking it as the image source. For more information refer to the deployment guide available on the Apple website.

Specifying a Default Image and Protocol

The NetBoot service is configured in Server Admin. Within Server Admin, the Images pane lists the available NetBoot images on the server, which can host up to 25 different disk images. Each image can be enabled, allowing client computers to use the image to boot, or each image can be disabled, preventing client computers from accessing the image. While you can have several images, you must specify one of the NetBoot images as the default image. When you press the N key on a client computer at startup, if the client has never started up from that NetBoot server before, the server will provide the default image to start up the client; hold down Option-N to use the current default.

For each image, you can also specify which protocol, NFS or HTTP, is used to serve the image. NFS continues to be the default and the preferred method. HTTP is an alternative that enables you to serve disk images without having to reconfigure your firewall to allow NFS traffic.

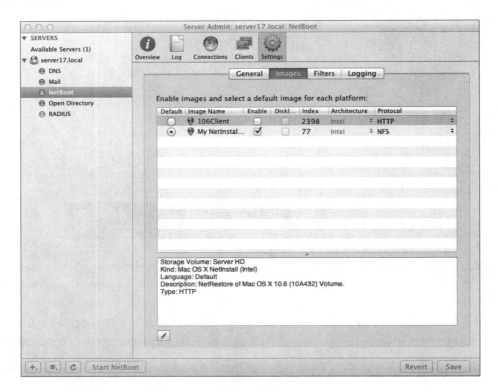

TIP ▶ Remember that image files can be very large and can take up a significant amount of disk space on the server. Consider using a second volume to hold the images and keep them off the boot volume.

Understanding Shadow Files

Many clients can read from the same NetBoot image, but when a client needs to write anything (such as print jobs and other temporary files) back to its startup volume, NetBoot automatically redirects the written data to the client's shadow files, which are separate from regular system and application software files. These shadow files preserve the unique identity of each client during the entire time the client is running off a NetBoot image. NetBoot also transparently maintains changed user data in the shadow files, while reading unchanged data from the shared system image. The shadow files are re-created at boot time, so any changes that the user makes to the startup volume are lost at restart.

This behavior has important implications. For example, if a user saves a document to the startup volume, the document will be gone after restart. This preserves the condition of the environment the administrator set up, but it also means that you should give users accounts on a network server if you want them to be able to save their documents.

For each image, you can specify where the shadow file is stored using the Diskless checkbox in the NetBoot image configuration in Server Admin. When the Diskless option for an image is disabled, the shadow file is stored on the client computer's local hard drive at /private/var/netboot/.com.apple.NetBootX/Shadow. When the Diskless option is enabled, the shadow file is stored in a share point on the server named NetBootClientsn in /<volume>/Library/NetBoot, where n is the number of the client using the shadow file. With the Diskless option enabled, NetBoot enables you to operate client computers that are literally diskless.

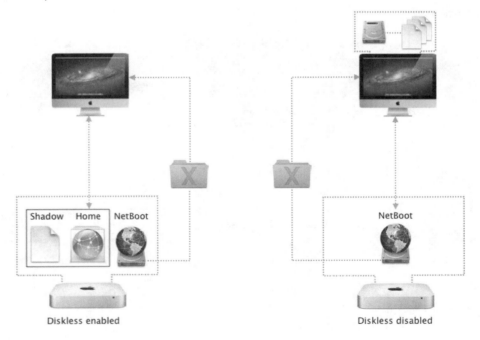

Diskless enabled   Diskless disabled

TIP Make sure you consider the storage need for shadow files when configuring your server. When running diskless, users may experience delays, since writes to the shadow files take place via the network and not locally.

Configuring a NetBoot Server

You need to configure your server to offer NetBoot images to your client computers. This, like many other services, is done through Server Admin.

1   Open /Applications/Server/Server Admin and connect to your server.

2   Select the NetBoot service in the left column.

If the NetBoot service isn't visible, add it by clicking the Add (+) button and choosing "Add Service" from the pop-up menu.

3   Click the Settings button in the toolbar.

4   In the General pane, enable the Ethernet port.

5   Select your server's storage hard drive to serve both Images and Client Data.

6   Click Save.

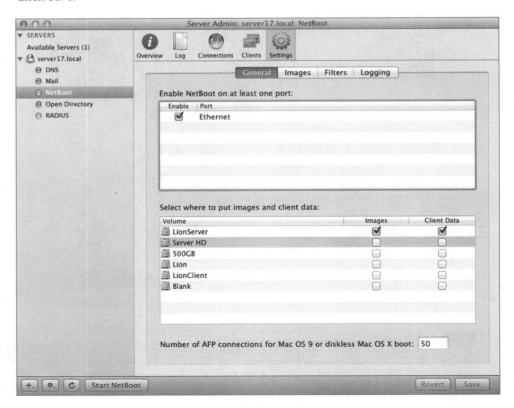

Verifying the Share Points

Your NetBoot service is now partially configured. The action of selecting a hard drive to serve the images should have automatically configured two share points for you. You should verify this now. Running AFP is only needed if you will host diskless NetBoot.

1   Open Server app.

2   Click the File Sharing service in the list.

3   Review the Share Points list.

Notice the addition of two share points: NetBootClient$n$ and NetBootSPn. These share points are used for the shadow files and NetBoot images, respectively. However, only the NetBootClients$n$ share is available over AFP by default. Additionally, this process may not start the file-sharing services, so you should do that now.

Configuring NetBoot to Serve an Image

Before we can start the NetBoot service, it has to have an image it can serve, and be configured to use it.

1   After the image is created, copy your NetBoot image (NBI) to the NetBootSP0 folder if it isn't already there. Do so by dragging the entire My NetInstall v1.nbi folder to the NetBootSP0 folder.

2   After it has copied over, return to Server Admin.

3   Select the NetBoot service in the left column.

4   Click the Settings button in the toolbar.

5   Click the Images tab.

You should see your My Install image listed. Note when you select it that it was assigned an image ID index, and that the description you typed when creating the image is visible in the bottom pane. This is the only place where the description is shown, and it can be useful to describe certain aspects of the image. Users will not see this description.

6   Enable the image by selecting the Enable and Default checkboxes.

7   Click Save.

8   Click the Start NetBoot button.

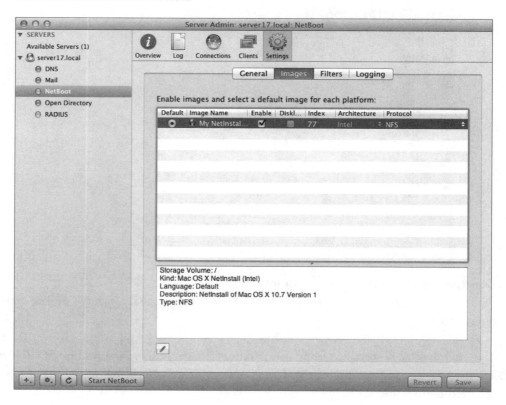

Configuring a NetBoot Client

As long as your client computer has the latest version of its firmware and is a supported client computer, you don't need to install any other special software. The Extensible Firmware Interface (EFI) (Intel) boot code contains the software used to boot a computer using a NetBoot image.

There are three ways to cause a computer to use NetBoot at startup:

▶ Press the N key on the keyboard until the blinking NetBoot globe appears in the center of the screen. This method allows you to use NetBoot for a single startup. Subsequent reboots return the computer to the previous startup state. Your client computer will then boot from the default NetBoot image hosted by the NetBoot server.

▶ Select the desired network disk image from the Startup Disk pane in System Preferences. The version of the Startup Disk pane included with OS X v10.2 and later presents all available network disk images on the local network. Notice that NetBoot and Network Install disk images maintain unique icons to help users differentiate between the two types of images. With the desired network disk image selected, you can reboot the computer. The computer then attempts to use NetBoot on every subsequent startup.

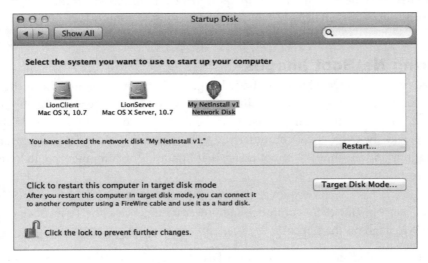

▶ Hold down the Option key during startup. This invokes the Startup Manager, which presents an iconic list of available system folders as well as a globe icon for NetBoot. Click the globe icon and click the advance arrow to begin the NetBoot process. This option doesn't allow you to pick which image you want to boot from. As when holding down the N key, you will get the default image.

It is important to note a couple of things that can upset the NetBoot process:

▶ If no network connection exists, a NetBoot client will eventually time out and look to a local drive to start up. You can prevent this by keeping local hard drives free of system software and denying users physical access to the Ethernet ports on a computer.

▶ Zapping the parameter random-access memory (PRAM) resets the configured startup disk, requiring you to reselect the NetBoot volume in the Startup Disk pane of System Preferences.

We'll try starting up your client computer with NetBoot now.

1   Shut down your OS X computer.

2   Turn on the computer while holding down the N key on the keyboard until the blinking NetBoot globe appears.

It should boot into the OS X Installer from the NetInstall image you just created and enabled. Because we don't actually want to reinstall your computer, just shut down the computer. We'll be booting the computer into Target Disk Mode in the next section, so just leave it turned off.

Configuring NetBoot Images

The NetInstall image you created is a very basic image used for the same purpose as the OS X installation media. In most NetBoot situations in which people are working off the network image, you'll probably want to create a customized environment for them. In this example, you'll take the OS X client computer you've been working on and use it as your template computer for creating a NetBoot image that hundreds of computers could boot and operate from.

1   Hold the T key on your client computer and power it on. Release the T key once you see a FireWire logo on the screen.

This boots your client computer into Target Disk Mode, effectively turning the computer into an external FireWire disk enclosure.

2   Plug a FireWire cable between your client and server computers.

You should see your client computer's hard drive appear on your server's desktop. If you don't, you may need to change the Finder preferences to display External Disks.

3   On your server, open System Image Utility.

4   Click the Customize button, and then Agree when the license agreement appears.

This opens a window containing Automator Library actions related to System Image Utility. This is a feature that allows you to create complex workflows for creating NetBoot images, and save them for later repeated use if desired.

5   In the Define Image Source action in the window, select NetBoot, and identify the Source as your computer's hard drive.

6   Drag the Add User Account action to the workflow.

7   Configure the Add User Account action as follows:

- ▶   Name: NetBoot Admin
- ▶   Short Name: nbadmin
- ▶   Password: nbadmin
- ▶   Allow user to administer this computer.

If desired, you could add additional local accounts by adding more Add User Account actions to the workflow.

8   Drag the Apply System Configuration Settings action item to the workflow and configure it as follows:

- ▶   Generate unique Computer Names starting with Chapter7.
- ▶   Change ByHost preferences to match client after install.

This last setting may or may not be desired in your environment. Certain settings are saved in preference list (plist) files that include the MAC (Media Access Control) address of your computer in the filename. If you'd like those files to be renamed to the MAC address of the target computer, you should use this option.

9   Drag the Create Image action to the bottom of the workflow and configure it as follows:

- ▶   Save To: NetBootSP0. Because we're on the server and it already knows we're running NetBoot, it allows you to save the image directly in the correct location, /Library/NetBoot/NetBootSP0.
- ▶   Image Name: The Boot
- ▶   Installed Volume: Will already be filled in.

▶ Description: This is the boot image made from a target mode computer.

▶ Index: Pick a number below 4095 that is different from the index of your first image, such as 432.

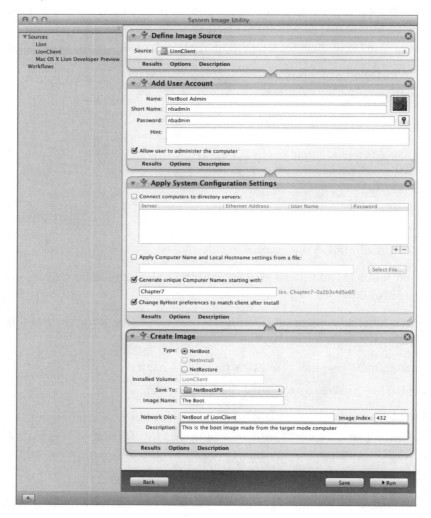

10 Click Run. Enter the administrator account credentials to create the image.

If you'd like to see more information about what's happening, you can choose View > Show Log.

After the image is created, you must enable it.

Configuring NetRestore Images

NetRestore image building is much the same as making a NetBoot or NetInstall image. The main difference is that the image you create will be restored to the hard drive of the computer you are NetBooting. This is a great way to deploy preconfigured images. There are additional features available, including external image sources such as a network share or ASR multicast streams. For more information refer to the deployment guide available on the Apple website.

Filtering NetBoot Clients

The NetBoot Filters pane permits you to allow or deny access to NetBoot services based on the client computer's hardware, or MAC, address. Once you enter a list of hardware addresses, you can either limit NetBoot access to just the listed computers or prevent the listed computers from using NetBoot (and allow all others to use it). This allows NetBoot and non-NetBoot clients to coexist in harmony. Filtering removes the risk of allowing non-NetBoot clients to access unlicensed applications or to accidentally perform a network installation. By maintaining accurate Filters settings, you can seamlessly integrate NetBoot into traditional network configurations.

NetBoot access is controlled through a list of hardware addresses. If you know a computer's hardware address, you can click the Add Hardware Address (+) button and type it in. Alternatively, if you enter a computer's DNS name in the Host Name field and click the Find button, Server Admin retrieves the hardware address, which you can add by clicking the Add (+) button next to the Hardware Address field.

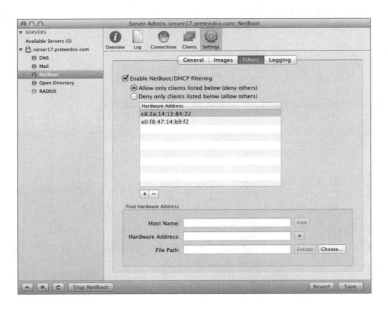

You also have the ability to set NetBoot filters on a per-image basis in addition to the per-server filters. This could be particularly useful if you have one server for multiple Mac classrooms. Each classroom could be configured with its own NetBoot image, and use per-image filters to limit which classrooms can access which image.

1   Open Server Admin on your server computer.

2   Click the Edit Image (pencil) icon at the bottom of the Images pane.

This pane allows you to perform per-image filters based on hardware type and/or specific Ethernet hardware addresses. It's important to differentiate between the per-image filters and the NetBoot servicewide filters.

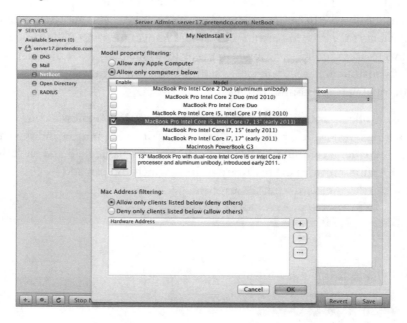

3   Select "Allow only clients listed below," and select your client computer hardware type in the list.

4   Click OK to dismiss the Edit Image dialog.

5   Click Save.

6   If you still have your client computer connected to the server, drag your client computer's drive icon to the Trash to eject it from your server.

7 Turn off your client computer and remove the FireWire cable attaching it to your server.

8 Boot your client computer normally and log in.

9 Open System Preferences.

10 Click Startup Disk.

11 Select NetBoot image with the filters.

12 Restart your client computer.

It should boot from the NetBoot image you just created. Try logging in using the nbadmin account you specified when creating the image.

Monitoring NetBoot Clients

You can monitor NetBoot usage with Server Admin. The NetBoot Clients pane provides a list of client computers that have booted from the server. Note that this is a cumulative list—a list of all clients that have connected to the server—not a list of currently connected computers only. By selecting a given computer in the list, you can also see additional information about that client, such as its system type, client name, the name and index of the NetBoot image it booted from, and the last time it booted.

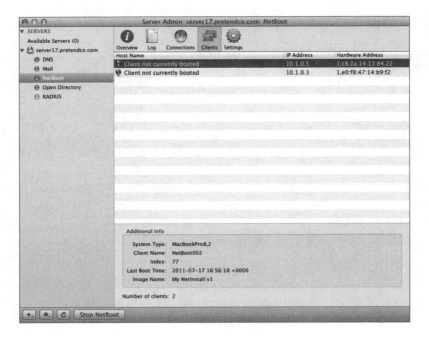

Additionally, the NetBoot logs can be useful when monitoring the progress of a NetBoot in action. You can access your NetBoot server logs using these steps:

1   Open Server Admin and connect to your server.

2   Select the NetBoot service on the left.

3   Click the Log button in the toolbar.

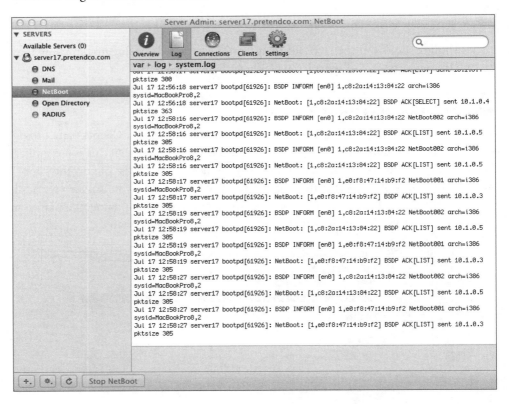

By picking the Connections tab in the NetBoot service, you can monitor the current connections to the NetBoot service. It will report the computer's hostname, IP address, its progress in percentages and status.

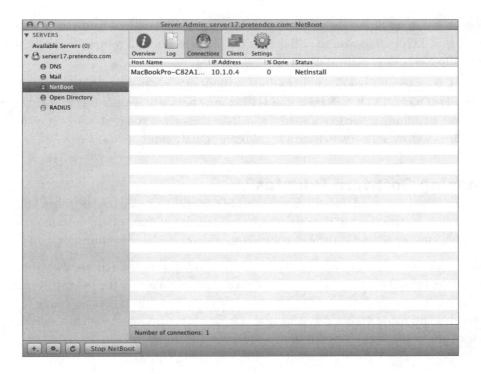

Troubleshooting NetBoot

NetBoot is a fairly straightforward process. If a client does not successfully start up from a NetBoot server, you can troubleshoot the issue by looking into the following areas:

▶ Check the network. The client must have an IP address obtained through DHCP.

▶ Check the server logs for bootpd messages, since the underlying process that serves NetBoot is bootpd. These logs can also identify if you mistyped an Ethernet hardware address or selected the wrong type of hardware for a filter.

▶ Press and hold the Option key as you boot the client, which will indicate whether you have a firmware password configured for the computer. A firmware password requires that a password be entered before any alternate boot sources are used, such as a Netboot image. A firmware password is applied if a lock command was ever sent to an OS X client.

▶ Check the disk space on the server. Shadow files and disk images may be filling the server's hard drive disk space. You may want to add bigger hard drives or more of them to accommodate these files.

▶ Check for server filters. Do you have filters enabled for IP address, hardware address, and model type? If so, you should disable the filters to allow all computers on the network to NetBoot or NetInstall.

▶ Check your server firewall configuration. NetBoot requires that a combination of DHCP/BOOTP, TFTP, NFS, AFP, and HTTP ports be open. Temporarily disabling the firewall or adding a rule to allow all traffic from the subnet you're starting up with NetBoot will indicate if you have a firewall configuration problem.

Managing Software Updates

With Lion Server, you have the option of mirroring Apple's Software Update servers on your local server. This has two distinct advantages. The first is that you can save Internet bandwidth, and the second is you can control the updates available to your users.

When using Software Update Server all of your client computers will retrieve their software updates from the server on your local network rather than over the Internet, which will also result in faster downloads for your users. Controlling which updates can be downloaded and made available to your users can be particularly useful when a software update might be incompatible with some software you're using.

Setting up your software update server is easy. Here's how:

1 From your Lion computer, open Server Admin and connect to your server.

2 Click the Add (+) button in the lower-left corner, and choose Add Service to add the Software Update service on your server. Click Save.

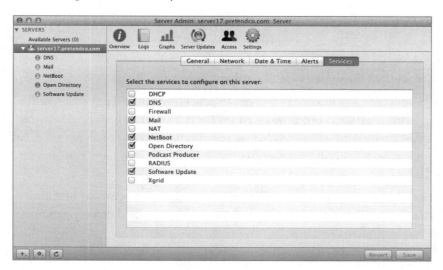

3   Click the Software Update service on the left side of the Server Admin window.

4   Click the Settings tab.

5   Configure the settings as follows:

▶   Do not select "Limit user bandwidth to."

▶   Set "Provide updates using port" to 8088 (the default).

▶   Select "Copy all updates from Apple."

▶   Select "Automatically enable copied updates."

▶   Select "Delete outdated software updates."

TIP ▶ If you have a slow network connecting your client and server computers, or if you have a large number of clients, you may want to limit the user bandwidth.

TIP ▶ You can change the location of the update packages. If you have another storage volume, you may want to consider doing this, as the default location is on your boot drive and the updates can take a considerable amount of room on the volume.

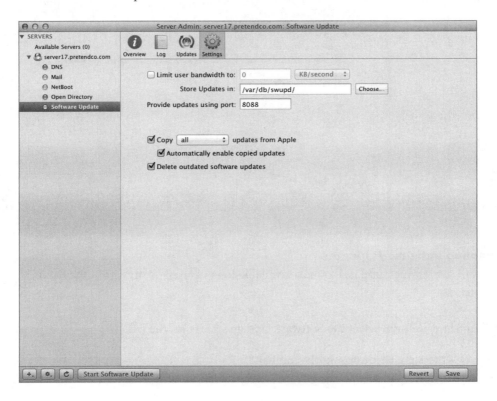

6 Click Save.

7 Click the Start Software Update button at the bottom of Server Admin.

8 Click the Updates button in the toolbar.

This will begin mirroring the software updates from Apple. If you have a slow Internet connection, this initial sync will take quite some time, possibly a number of hours.

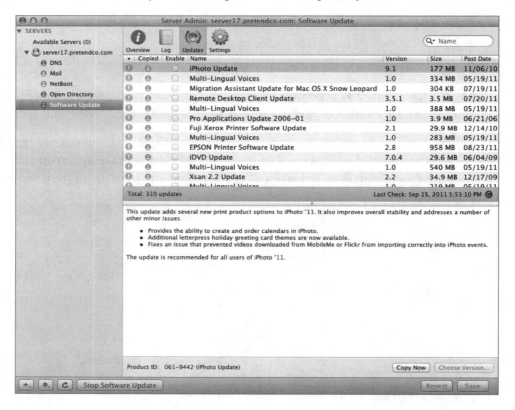

Enabling Individual Updates

You can select which updates to make available to your users from within the list of updates.

1 In Server Admin, select the Software Update service on the left.

2 Click the Updates button in the toolbar.

This screen lists all the updates currently available from Apple's servers.

3   Select which updates you want to be enabled.

If the list of updates is empty, it is still being copied down from Apple.

NOTE ► The update must be copied down before you can enable it.

4   Click Save.

Configuring Computers for Your Software Update Service

As with other settings, you'll be using profiles to tell your computer to utilize your local software update server instead of Apple's. This preference can be set at the device or device group level. Refer to Chapter 4, "Managing Accounts" for more information on how to build profiles.

If you are not using Profile Manager, you can use the defaults command in Terminal to point unmanaged client computers to a Software Update server. You must be an administrator to use the defaults command:

sudo defaults write /Library/Preferences/com.apple.SoftwareUpdate CatalogURL *URL*

Replace *URL* with the URL of the Software Update server, including the port number and the name of the catalog file:

sudo defaults write /Library/Preferences/com.apple.SoftwareUpdate CatalogURL "http://updates.pre-tendco.com:8088/index.sucatalog"

Troubleshooting Software Update Service

If Software Update Service (SUS) doesn't work as expected, you can troubleshoot the issue by looking into the following areas:

► Check the network. The client must be able to contact your SUS server and be able to communicate with it over the port you configured (8088 by default).

► Are the updates listed in SUS? If the updates haven't been downloaded, they won't be available to the client devices.

► Is the SUS profile installed on the device? If the computer doesn't have a profile containing the SUS information, it won't know to look for your SUS server.

► Is the specific update enabled? Check in the list of updates.

What You've Learned

▶ Deployment options are available to keep multiple desktops up-to-date.

▶ NetBoot, NetRestore, and Network Install are server-based methods of deploying.

▶ You can create images from optical media, hard drives, or disk images.

▶ You can add servicewide or per-image filters based on hardware type or Ethernet hardware address.

▶ Software Update Service can mirror the Apple updates on your local server and provide the updates to devices configured to utilize it.

References

The following references provide more information about topics discussed in this chapter. (Additional resources are available at http://www.apple.com/server/documentation.)

Administration Guides

Lion Server: Advanced Administration
https://help.apple.com/advancedserveradmin/mac/10.7/

Apple Knowledge Base Documents

You can check for new and updated Knowledge Base documents at http://www.apple.com/support.

Document HT1159, "Mac OS X versions (builds) for computers"

URLs

Apple System Imaging List: http://lists.apple.com/mailman/listinfo2/system-imaging

Chapter Review

1. What are the advantages of using NetBoot?

2. What are three ways to configure the network startup disk?

3. Which network protocols are used during the NetBoot startup sequence? What components are delivered over each of these protocols?

4. What is a NetBoot shadow file?

5. What are the major differences between NetBoot, NetInstall, and NetRestore?

Answers

1. Because NetBoot unifies and centralizes the system software that NetBoot clients use, software configuration and maintenance are reduced to a minimum. A single change to a NetBoot image propagates to all client computers on the next startup. NetBoot also decouples the system software from the computer, decreasing potential time invested in software troubleshooting.

2. A client can select a network disk image via the Startup pane within System Preferences, by holding down the N key at startup to boot from the default NetBoot image, or using the Option key.

3. NetBoot makes use of DHCP, TFTP, NFS, and HTTP during the NetBoot client startup sequence. DHCP provides the IP address, TFTP delivers the boot ROM ("booter") file, and NFS or HTTP is used to deliver the network disk image.

4. Because the NetBoot boot image is read-only, anything that the client computer writes to the volume is cached in the shadow file. This allows a user to make changes to the boot volume, including setting preferences and storing files; however, when the computer is restarted, all changes are erased.

5. NetBoot allows multiple machines to boot into the same environment. NetInstall provides a convenient way to install operating systems and packages onto multiple machines. NetRestore provides a way to clone an existing image to multiple machines.

6

Time
Goals

This chapter takes approximately three hours to complete.

Configure Lion Server to share files with iOS devices and Mac and Windows clients over the network

Configure Lion Server to control access to files based on user and group accounts, standard POSIX permissions, and access control lists (ACLs)

Offer Time Machine services

Troubleshoot file services on Lion Server

Chapter **6**
Providing File Services

It is quite simple to use Lion Server to share files across a network for your users, whether they are using Mac, Windows, or iOS devices. The four basic steps are:

- ▶ Plan
- ▶ Configure accounts
- ▶ Configure the File Sharing service
- ▶ Monitor the server

In this chapter you will explore the challenges associated with file sharing and the issues to consider when setting up file sharing. The main focus of the chapter is on setting up shared folders, also called share points, with appropriate access settings based on standard POSIX permissions and access control lists (ACLs). This chapter also addresses automatic network mounts, which provide a network destination for Time Machine backups, and general file-sharing troubleshooting issues to consider when enabling file services on Lion Server.

You will learn how to use the Server app to add and configure individual share points, and you'll use the Console application while logged in to the server to monitor logs.

Addressing the Challenges of File Sharing

When planning to offer file services, there are a number of issues to consider. The obvious questions are:

▶ What content will you will share?

▶ What types of clients will be accessing your file server?

▶ What protocols will the client computers or devices use?

▶ What levels of access do your various users and groups require?

At first glance, these questions might seem relatively easy to answer, but in practice, especially in dynamic organizations, requirements can get very complex, and it can be difficult to facilitate your users' access to the things necessary to remain productive, without constant intervention from an administrator.

When accessing a file server, a user typically has to authenticate, and then he sees a choice of valid share points available to mount. When he navigates inside a mounted share point, folders' badges (small icons displayed on the lower-right corner of the folder icon) display a red do-not-enter sign for folders he is not authorized to access, and a blue arrow for folders to which he has write-only access to. This is a combination of authorization for accessing the file sharing service, as well as authorization for accessing individual files and folders.

Authorization is a constant occurrence; every time a user accesses a file, the computer checks file permissions against the user's account information to see if the user is authorized to use the file.

After completing this chapter you will be in a good position to carefully consider your file sharing needs before you implement file sharing on your Lion Server.

Understanding File Sharing Protocols

Lion Server includes a number of ways to share files. The method you select depends largely on the clients you expect to serve (although security is another factor to consider). You can use the Server app to enable the following file-sharing services:

▶ Apple Filing Protocol (AFP): This protocol is useful mainly for sharing files with Mac clients, both older Mac OS 9 clients and the latest OS X clients.

▶ Windows file service: Server Message Block (SMB) is the native file-sharing protocol for Windows, but is also used in UNIX environments.

▶ Web-based Distributed Authoring and Versioning (WebDAV): This protocol is an extension to the web service protocol (HTTP), and enables various clients, including iOS applications, to access files hosted by your Lion Server.

Lion Server has a completely new implementation of SMB, based on Microsoft's open specifications. When Windows clients use NetBIOS to browse for network file servers, a computer running Lion Server with file sharing enabled appears just like a Windows server with file sharing enabled appears.

NOTE ▸ Lion Server works with SMB clients that use UNICODE and extended security, including Mac OS X v10.6 Snow Leopard or later and Windows XP or later. Mac OS X v10.5 or earlier clients should use AFP instead of SMB.

From an iOS device, with an app that supports WebDAV, a user can specify the URL in the form of http://*your server's host name or IP address*/webdav (or https://*your server's host name or IP address*/webdav if the web service is configured to use SSL). If you do not provide a specific share point in the URL, all WebDAV-enabled share points will appear. Even without the benefit of SSL, the traffic for authentication is encrypted via WebDAV digest.

You can share a folder over several different protocols simultaneously. When you create a share point in the Server app:

▸ The share point is automatically shared over AFP.

▸ The share point is automatically shared over SMB.

▸ The share point is not enabled for guest users.

If you want to share it over WebDAV, you must explicitly enable that service for that share point by selecting the checkbox labeled "Share with iOS devices (WebDAV)." Here is an example of using Keynote on an iPhone to connect to a WebDAV share point:

Lion Server also provides file service with protocols that are outside the scope of this book; there are knowledge base articles in the References section at the end of this chapter regarding the following:

▶   File Transfer Protocol (FTP) – This file-sharing protocol is lightweight in the sense that it is simple and does not have all the features available in the other file-sharing services. FTP allows you to transfer files back and forth between client and server, but you cannot, for example, open a document over an FTP connection. The primary benefit of FTP is that it is ubiquitous: It is hard to find a Transfer Control Protocol (TCP)–capable computer that does not support FTP.

▶   Network File System (NFS) – NFS is the traditional method of file sharing for UNIX-based computers. NFS has its heritage in research facilities and academia in the 1980s. While it can be very convenient and flexible, and can be used with Kerberos provide robust security, when used with legacy clients it can suffer from some security issues that do not affect the other protocols. The primary use for NFS is to provide files to NetBoot clients and UNIX or Linux computers. Although OS X has a core based on NetBoot clients and UNIX, you should normally use AFP for Mac clients.

Comparing File-Sharing Protocols

This table gives a short comparison of file-sharing protocols. There really isn't one best protocol. Instead, think of the protocols as different tools at your disposal to give different types of access.

	AFP	**SMB**	**WebDAV**
Native platform	Mac OS	Windows	Multi-platform
Security	Authentication is normally encrypted	Authentication is normally encrypted	Uses clear text passwords but can be protected with SSL via https
Browsable	Bonjour	Bonjour and NetBIOS	Not Browsable
Example URL	afp://server17. pretendco.com/ Users	smb://server17. pretendco.com/ Public	https://server17. pretendco.com/ webdav

AFP and SMB are both full-featured file-sharing protocols with reasonably good security.

WebDAV uses WebDAV-Digest to encrypt authentication, but if you use the Server app to configure the Web service to use an SSL certificate, WebDAV is available only via HTTPS, which encrypts WebDAV file sharing traffic.

Planning File Services

When setting up file services on Lion Server, proper initial planning can save you time in the long run. Follow these guidelines when you first start planning to implement file services.

Plan Your File-Server Requirements

Determine your organizational requirements:

▶ How are your users organized?

▶ Is there a logical structure to follow for assigning users to groups that best address workflow needs?

▶ What types of computers will be used to access your file server?

▶ What share points and folder structures will be needed?

▶ Who needs what access to various files?

▶ How will users interact with one another when accessing these share points?

▶ How much storage space do you currently have, how much storage space do your users currently need, and at what rate will their need for storage grow?

▶ How will you back up and archive your storage?

These answers will dictate the file services you configure, as well as how you might organize groups and share points.

Use the Server app to Configure Users and Groups

The main goal is to end up with a group structure that best matches your organizational needs and allows easy maintenance over time. Setting up users and groups at the beginning is trivial. But, setting up users and groups that continue to work as the organization goes through natural changes over time is not as simple as it first appears. Nevertheless, having a logical group structure that can be used to allow and deny access to your server file system will save you from continually adjusting file-service access later on. Lion Server supports groups within groups and setting access-control lists on folders.

TIP For testing of groups, share points, and ACLs, you do not need to have all users entered. You may decide to test with a skeletal set of users and groups that meet the business requirements of your organization. After verifying the groups and share points, you can then enter or import the full set of users.

Use the Server App to Start and Configure the File Sharing Service

The Server app is the main application you use to

▶   start and stop the file sharing service.

▶   add new share points.

▶   remove share points.

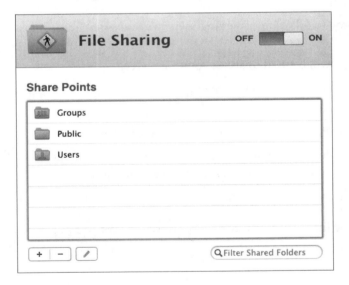

For each share point, you can

▶   configure ownership, permissions, and the access control list (ACL) for the share point.

▶   enable or disable AFP for the share point.

▶   enable or disable SMB for the share point.

▶   enable or disable WebDAV for the share point.

▶   allow or disallow guest access to the share point.

▶   make the share point available for network home folders.

Adjust Settings over Time

After you start the file sharing service, you'll need to perform regular maintenance. You will probably use the Server app to perform the following maintenance tasks as your needs change:

▶ Use the Users pane to add users to groups, groups to users, and groups to groups.

▶ Use the Users pane to modify the allowed services for each user.

▶ Use the File Sharing pane to add and remove share points.

▶ Use the File Sharing pane to modify ownership, permissions, and ACLs for share points.

▶ Use the Storage pane to modify ownership, permissions, and ACLs for folders and files.

Monitor Your Server for Problems

Monitoring server usage is a valuable method to keep track of workflow. You can view graphs and watch for usual traffic patterns, usage spikes, and low-usage periods that you could use to plan backups or perform server maintenance.

There are several ways to monitor your server:

▶ Use the Server app's Stats pane to monitor processor usage, memory usage, and network traffic.

▶ Use Server Admin's Overview pane to monitor graphs of CPU use, network throughput and available disk space.

▶ Use Server Admin's Overview pane to monitor the number of Connected Users (this displays to users connected via AFP).

The following figure is from the Overview pane of Server Admin (which was covered in more detail in Chapter 1, "Installing and Configuring OS X Lion Server").

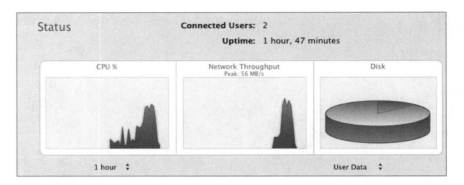

Be aware that if your server offers services other than file sharing, then those other services could also affect resources such as network throughput, so you need to be careful interpreting the graphs.

Use the Console to view the AFP Error Log

If you log in at the server, you can use the Terminal application to view the AppleFileServiceError.log.

1 Log in on your Lion Server.

2 Click Launchpad in the Dock, click the Utilities folder, and open Console.

3 If there is no sidebar with a log list, click Show Log List in the toolbar.

4 If necessary, click the disclosure triangle to view the content of /Library/Logs, then click the disclosure triangle to view the content of AppleFileService.

5 Click the AppleFileServerError.log.

This log displays events such as the AFP service stopping.

You might use additional software, such as Terminal, or third-party software to monitor your server.

Creating Share Points

After determining server and user requirements and entering at least a sample set of users and groups that represents the organizational structure, the next step in sharing files is to configure your share points. A *share point* can be any folder, drive, or volume that is mounted on the server. When you create a share point, you make that item and its contents available to network clients via the specified protocols. This includes deciding what items you want to give access to and organizing the items logically. It requires using your initial planning and knowledge of your users and their needs. You might decide that everything belongs in a single share point and use permissions to control access within that share point, or you might set up a more complex workflow. For example, you could have one share point for your copywriters and a separate share point for the copy editors. Perhaps you would also have a third share point where both groups could access common items or share files. Setting up effective share points requires as much knowledge of your users and how they work together as it does the technology of share points.

It is also important to keep in mind that different protocols handle issues like filename case-sensitivity differently. For this reason, it's usually best to limit your file-sharing protocols to those needed by the clients that are connecting to your file sharing service. For example, if you have only OS X clients connecting to a share point, it will simplify things to use only the AFP service and disable SMB sharing for that share point.

Exploring File Sharing

To help you understand the tools and options available for file sharing, explore the File Sharing pane of the Server app. If you've been following along with the exercises in the book, you have already turned on file sharing during authentication exercises.

1   If necessary, on your administrator computer, open the Server app, choose Manage > Connect to Server, choose your Lion Server, and authenticate as your local administrator (username: ladmin and password: ladminpw).

2   If necessary, select File Sharing in the Server app sidebar, and turn on File Sharing.

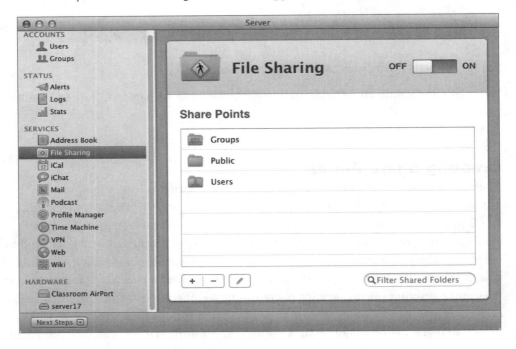

This is a very simple interface that includes:

▶   the On/Off switch.

▶   a list of share points.

▶   buttons to Add (+) and Remove (-) share points.

▶   an edit button to edit a selected share point.

▶   a text filter field to limit the share points displayed.

Understanding the Default Share Points

If you enabled File Sharing on Lion before you installed Lion Server, you will have the same share points that your Lion computer had. If you are working with a new installation of Lion Server, your server automatically shares the following folders:

Groups (/Groups)

Public (/Shared Items/Public)

Users (/Users)

Additionally, you may see a share point for each local user that was created with the Users & Groups preference; the Public folder of their home folder is a share point. The name of the share point is based on the local user's Full Name. In the following example, someone with administrator credentials used the Users & Groups preferences to create a user named "Temporary Local User" for testing purposes, and Lion Server automatically created a share point for this user, as shown in the figure below.

If you edit a group and select the checkbox "Give this group a shared folder," the Server app creates a folder for that group in the /Groups folder of your boot volume, whether or not Groups is a share point, and creates an access control entry (ACE) that gives the members of the group full access over their group folder.

Although these default share points are convenient, you are free to remove them.

Adding and Removing Share Points

It's pretty simple to add a shared folder. You can use the Server app to select an existing folder, or even create a new folder to share. Use the following steps to create a test share point in the Shared Items folder, which is a convenient place for you to create new shared folders.

1   On your administrator computer, Click Add (+).

2   Select your boot volume, then select the Shared Items folder.

3   Click New Folder.

4   Name the folder Accounting and click Create.

5   Select the new Accounting folder you just created, and then click Choose. Note that this step is often overlooked.

    If you forget to choose the new folder, and click Choose, you make the Shared Items folder a share point. If that happens, don't worry, you can remove Shared Items as a share point. Removing a share point does not remove its contents.

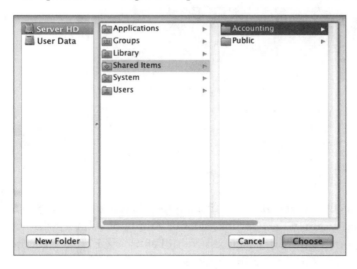

You just created a new folder, and made that folder a share point.

Removing a share point is just as easy. When you remove a share point, you don't remove the folder or its contents from the file system, you just stop sharing it.

6   Select the Accounting share point, and click Remove (-).

7   Click Remove at the confirmation pane.

If someone using a Mac has a share point from Lion Server mounted, and you stop the file sharing or remove that share point, then the user will see a message indicating that the share point is no longer available. This is the message that is displayed to a user using Lion:

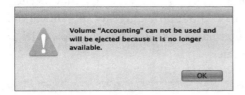

Configuring Individual Share Points

In the next section, you will look at what kinds of changes you can make to a share point.

1   Select the Public share point.

2   Click the Edit button (looks like a pencil), or just double-click the share point.

3 Click Cancel to return to the list of share points without making any changes.

The editing pane includes the full path to the shared folder (like/Shared Items/Public), as well as the following elements which you will learn about in this chapter:

▶ The Access pane that includes standard POSIX ownership and permissions, and can also include access control list (ACL) information

▶ Checkboxes to enable and disable sharing over various protocols

▶ A checkbox to enable or disable guest access

▶ A checkbox to "Make available for home directories over" (AFP or SMB)

Note that there is a checkbox labeled "Allow guests users to access this share." This checkbox affects both AFP and SMB services, so when you use the Server app to enable guest access for AFP, you also enable guest access for SMB. Users from Mac or Windows client computers can access guest-enabled share points without providing any authentication. When users on Macs click your server's computer name in their Finder window sidebar's Shared section, they automatically connect as Guest.

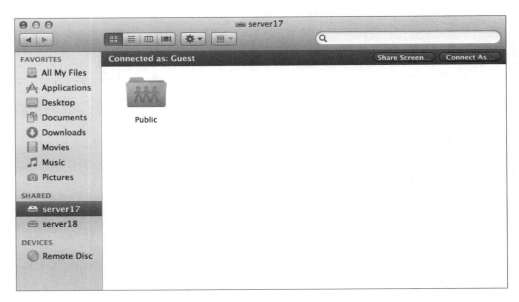

Now that you are familiar with the protocols you can enable, and the basics of creating, removing, and editing share points, it's time to get into more detail about the Access pane and the other things you can edit for a share point.

Configuring Access to Share Points and Folders

Once you've created a share point and determined the protocols you will use, you can begin to address levels of access within that share point. You need to consider POSIX privileges (UNIX-based ownership and permissions) as well as file-system access control lists (ACLs). Using this very flexible system, you can apply complex access settings to any folder or file.

You can configure access for your shared folders with the Server app File Sharing pane, and configure access for any folder or file with the Server app Storage pane. Be aware that these two panes display information differently.

Configuring Access with the Server App File Sharing Pane

To configure access settings for a share point, use the Access pane when viewing that share point. The standard POSIX settings are listed with the owner's Full Name, followed by the word "owner" in parentheses; the Full Name of the group associated with the folder; followed by the words "primary group" in parentheses and "Everyone Else."

In the figure below, the System Administrator (the root user, who has access to every file on the system) is the owner, and the group named Administrators is the primary group associated with the Users share point.

If there are any access control entries (ACEs) in that folder's access control list (ACL), these ACEs will appear above the POSIX entries. In the figure below, there is an ACE for the network group Workgroup, and the Access pane is not large enough to display the standard POSIX permissions for Everyone Else. If you scroll down, you will see the row for Everyone Else.

To change the standard POSIX owner, double-click the name of the current owner; to change the group, double-click the name of the current primary group. Once you start typing, a menu with names that match what you have typed appears.

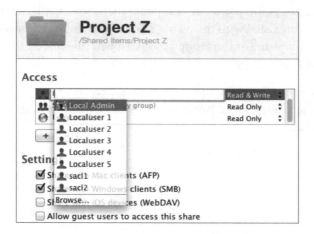

From there, you can either choose a name, or click Browse. If you click Browse, choose a user (or group) and then click OK. Once you choose a name, the Full Name appears in the owner or primary group field.

To change permissions, click the pop-up menu on the right, and choose any of the four options, and then click Done:

► Read & Write

► Read Only

► Write Only

► No Access

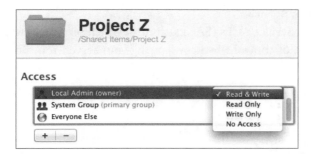

NOTE ▶ After making permissions changes, be sure to click Done to save your changes. If you select a different pane in the Server app, or quit the Server app, your changes might not get saved.

Once the user is authenticated, file permissions control access to the files and folders on your server. One setting should be called out with respect to permissions: the *Others* permissions, which is displayed as "Everyone Else" when editing permissions with the File Sharing pane. When you set Others permissions, those permissions apply to everyone who can see the item (either a file or folder) who is neither the owner nor a member of the group assigned to the item.

Guest access can be very useful, but before you enable it, be sure you understand its implications in your permissions scheme. As the name implies, guest access lets anyone who can connect to your server use its share points. A user who authenticates as Guest is given Others permissions for file and folder access. If you give read-only access to Others on a share point that allows guest access, everyone on your network (and, if your server has a public IP address and is not protected by a firewall, the entire Internet) can see and mount that share point, a situation you might not intend to allow.

If a user using guest creates an item on an AFP share point, the owner of that item is set to "nobody."

If a folder is buried deep within a file hierarchy where guests can't go (because the enclosing folders don't grant access to Others), then guests can't use the Finder to browse to that folder.

TIP ▶ The best way to validate permissions is by logging in from client computers and testing access from valid user accounts.

Configuring Access to the File Sharing Service

File ACLs control file-system access. Service ACLs (SACLs) control which services a user can access and provide an extra level of control when configuring your server. You can edit SACLs:

▶ in Server Admin per service.

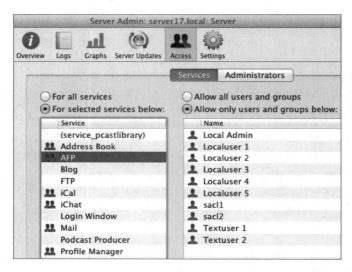

▶ in Server Admin, globally for all the services on your server.

▶ in the Server app Users pane for each user's access to a list of services.

Review who has access to connect to each of your file-sharing services, AFP and SMB. This access is controlled through the use of SACLs, a topic described in more detail in Chapter 2, "Authenticating and Authorizing Accounts." SACLs require explicit permission to connect to your file server. Each user, or a group to which the user belongs, will need to be registered as being allowed to use a given service. After confirming SACLs, review the file system permissions on the folders that are your share points. The permissions of the folders that are your share points will control what share points are listed on the client when they connect to your server. In many cases, you should also review the permissions of the enclosed folders because a larger group will often have access to the share point than will have access to all of its subfolders.

Keep in mind that even if you carefully remove users from a SACL, when you use the Server app to create a new user, the Server app automatically adds the user to the SACL for a number of services. Because of this, it may be important in your organizations' situation to always use the same tool, either the Server app or Workgroup Manager, to create new users.

Understanding POSIX Ownership, POSIX Permissions, and ACLS

For access to files and folders, Lion Server uses basic file permissions in addition to optional access control lists (ACLs) to make authorization decisions about access to files and folders. In Lion and Lion Server, every file and every folder has a single user account assigned as its "owner," a single group associated with it, and an optional ACL. Access permissions are assigned for the owner, for the group, and for everyone else, and the optional ACL adds additional permissions information.

When a file sharing client uses the file sharing service, she must authenticate as a user (or as a guest if you enabled that for the share point). A remote user has the same access to files over file sharing that she would have if she logged in locally with the same user credentials she provided to mount the share point.

Understanding POSIX Ownership and Permissions

In the POSIX permissions model, which Lion and Lion Server use, every file and every folder is associated with exactly one "owner" and exactly one "group." As an administrator, you can change the POSIX owner and the POSIX group, but keep in mind that every file must have one and only one owner, and one and only one group as part of the POSIX ownership. For more information, see "Understanding File System Permissions" in Chapter 3, "File Systems" in the book *Apple Pro Training Series: OS X Lion Support Essentials*.

When planning to share files over various file sharing protocols, it helps to understand how the POSIX ownership and permissions model comes into play with various file sharing protocols. Here's the easy part: When you copy an item within a single volume, that item always retains its original ownership and permissions.

In contrast, when you create a new item on a shared folder mounted via AFP or WebDAV, or copy an item from one volume to another volume, Lion and Lion Server use the following rules for ownership and permissions for the new file or folder:

▶   The owner of the new item is the user who created or copied the item.

▶   The group is the group associated with the enclosing folder; in other words, the newly copied item inherits its group from the enclosing folder.

▶   The owner is assigned read and write permissions.

▶   The group is assigned read-only permissions.

▶   "Others" (also displayed as "Everyone Else") is assigned read-only permissions.

The variable that controls the permissions for newly created files is called the umask (changing the umask from the default value is outside the scope of this book). Under this model, if you create an item in a folder in which the group has read/write permission, the item will not inherit that permission. Without using ACLs, if a user wants to let other group members edit the new item, she must change its permissions manually, using the Finder's Get Info command, or using chmod in the command line, or some third party tool to modify permissions. This is required for every new item, so this addition to a user's workflow is one reason to use ACLs.

Understanding POSIX Permissions with SMB

When you create a new file or folder via SMB, no matter what the permissions are of the enclosing folder, the following is the same as with AFP:

▶ The owner of the new item is the user who created or copied the item.

▶ The group is the group associated with the enclosing folder; in other words, the new item inherits its group from the enclosing folder.

▶ The owner is assigned read and write permissions.

However, there are two big differences:

▶ The group is assigned "No Access" permissions.

▶ "Others" (also displayed as "Everyone Else") is assigned "No Access" permissions.

The umask doesn't come into effect at all for files and folders created over SMB. Just like the situation with AFP, a user who wants to share documents with other members of her group needs to modify permissions for each new item if she creates or copies from another volume into the share point. Again, using ACLs is a good strategy to help your users.

Understanding POSIX Permissions with WebDAV

When you create a new file via WebDAV from an iOS device:

▶ The owner of the new item is the user who created or copied the item.

▶ The group is the group associated with the enclosing folder; in other words, the new item inherits its group from the enclosing folder.

▶ The owner is assigned read and write permissions.

▶ The group is assigned read-only permissions.

▶ "Others" (also displayed as "Everyone Else") is assigned read-only permissions.

Comparing How Sharing Protocols Assign POSIX Ownership and Permissions

This table gives a short comparison of how POSIX permissions are assigned for new items (files and folders) that are added to a shared folder via a file-sharing protocol. This includes items that a user creates, as well as items that a user copies to a shared folder from a different volume.

	AFP	**SMB**	**WebDAV**
Owner	The owner of the new item is the user who created or copied the item.		
Group	The group is the group associated with the enclosing folder.		
Owner Permissions	The owner is assigned read and write permissions.		
Group Permissions	Read Only	No Access	Read Only
Others (Everyone) Permissions	Read Only	No Access	Read Only

Understanding Access Control Lists

Because of the limitations of the POSIX permissions model, you will probably use ACLs to help control access to folders and files. Apple's ACL model maps to the Windows ACL model, so Windows users experience the same permissions for folders and files that Mac users do.

In this section you'll learn about applying ACLs with the Server app, with the File Sharing pane, which presents a simplified interface, and also with the Storage pane, which offers more flexibility. You'll learn how ACL inheritance works, and why it is so powerful.

NOTE ▶ You can apply ACLs on only Mac OS Extended volumes.

Distinguishing Between the Uses of UID, GID, and GUID

You have learned that POSIX owners and groups are determined by user and group IDs (UIDs and GIDs). Because UIDs and GIDs are simple integers, it is possible for users to have duplicate user IDs. Usually this is an error, but sometimes an administrator will want the POSIX UID to be identical on two separate users.

ACLs are much more complex and require a unique identification of a user or group. For this purpose, every user and group has a globally unique ID (GUID). This is not normally exposed in Workgroup Manager or the Server app because there should be no reason to change it. Every time a user or group is created, a new 128-bit string (as shown in the following figure) is randomly generated for that user or group. In this way, users and groups are virtually guaranteed unique identification in ACLs and SACLs.

When you create an ACE for a user or group, the GUID of that user or group is stored, rather than the user name, user ID, group name, or group ID. This is why if you see a GUID instead of a full name in an ACL or in a SACL, it is probably because an account that used to have an entry in the ACL or SACL was deleted with a method other than using Server app or Workgroup Manager.

Here's an example of an exposed GUID from the Server app:

If you see this, without knowing what account corresponds to the GUID, you could either leave the entry in place or remove the entry. If you happen to re-import the account in a way that also imports its GUID, then that entry will be associated with the user or group again. However, if the account associated with the GUID is truly gone forever, you can remove the entry; highlight the entry and click Remove (-).

Configuring ACLs with the Server App File Sharing Pane

In Lion Server, you use the Server app to configure access control lists (ACLs). An ACL is made up of one or more access control entries (ACEs). Each ACE includes the following:

▶   The globally unique ID (GUID) of the one user or group for which this ACE applies

▶   Whether the ACE allows access or denies access (the Server app creates only allow entries and displays a checkbox to indicate that a rule specifies allow or deny)

▶   The permission the ACE allows (see the section "Configuring Complex Permissions for an ACE")

▶   The inheritance rules for the ACE (see the section "Understanding ACL Inheritance")

▶   The folder or file to which the ACE applies

You can add as many access control entries (ACEs) for an item as you like, and you have a much larger range of permission types available than with standard POSIX permissions.

Use the following steps to create a new folder and to add an access control entry (ACE) to that folder's ACL to allow all members of the group Workgroup to have Read & Write access to files and folders.

1   If necessary, on your administrator computer, connect to your Lion Server as a local administrator.

2   Click File Sharing in the Server app sidebar.

3   Click the Add (+) button, navigate to the Shared Items folder on your boot volume, click New Folder, and name the folder FileSharingPaneExample. Click Create to create the folder.

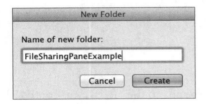

4   Select FileSharingPaneExample, then click Choose.

    NOTE ▶ Be sure to select the folder you just created before you click Choose. Otherwise, you will create a share point for the enclosing folder, instead of the folder you just created.

5   In the File Sharing pane, double-click the share point named FileSharingPaneExample.

6   Click the Add (+) button, and start typing Workgroup.

7   Choose Workgroup from the list.

8   Confirm that the permission for Workgroup is set to Read & Write.

9 Click Done to save the change.

NOTE ▶ The inherited ACE for Spotlight allows Spotlight to maintain an index of the files on your Lion Server. Do not disable this ACE or you may experience unexpected behavior.

Configuring ACLs with the Server App Storage Pane

The Storage pane of the Server app offers a little more flexibility than the File Sharing pane for configuring ACLs, particularly the ability to:

▶ set complex permissions for an ACE, more than just Read & Write, Read, or Write.

▶ set the inheritance for ACLs.

▶ set an ACL for an individual file, not just for folders.

Use the following steps to create a new shared folder and to add an access control entry (ACE) to that folder's ACL to allow all members of the group Administrators to have full control over files and folders.

1 If necessary, on your administrator computer, connect to your Lion Server as a local administrator.

2 Click File Sharing in the Server app sidebar.

3 Click the Add (+) button, navigate to Shared Items folder on your boot volume, click New Folder, and name the folder StoragePaneExample.

4 Select the StoragePaneExaple folder, and click Choose to make this folder a share point.

5 Click your server in the Server app sidebar, and then click the Storage pane.

6 Navigate to /Shared Items on your boot volume, select StoragePaneExample and choose Edit Permissions from the Action pop-up menu.

7 Click the Add (+) button, and start typing Administrators.

8 Choose Administrators (admin).

9 Click the Permission pop-up menu for Administrators, and choose Full Control.

10 Click all the disclosure triangles to display all the permissions that you have enabled.

You'll learn more about these 17 options later in the next section.

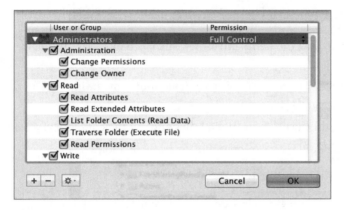

11 Click OK to save the change.

Configuring Complex Permissions for an ACE

When you edit an ACE with the Storage pane of the Server app, you can use the disclosure triangles to show the details for the ACE. You have four broad categories for which you can apply allow rules:

► Administration

► Read

► Write

► Inheritance

For the first three (Administration, Read, and Write), if you enable a checkbox, you allow access for the user in the ACE. If you disable a checkbox, this does not deny access, it just doesn't explicitly allow access.

For the category of Administration, you can select or deselect to allow permissions for:

▶ Change Permissions (User can change standard permissions.)

▶ Change Owner (User can change the item's ownership to himself or herself.)

For the Read set of permissions, you can select or deselect to allow permissions for:

▶ Read Attributes (User can view the item's attributes, such as name, size, and date modified.)

▶ Read Extended Attributes (User can view additional attributes including ACL and attributes added by third party software.)

▶ List Folder Contents (Read Data) (User can read files and see the contents of a folder.)

▶ Traverse Folder (Execute File) (User can open file, or traverse a folder.)

▶ Read Permissions (User can read the POSIX permissions.)

For the Write set of permissions, you can select or deselect to allow permissions for:

▶ Write Attributes (User can change POSIX permissions.)

▶ Write Extended Attributes (User can change ACL or other extended attributes.)

▶ Create Files (Write Data) (User can create files, including changing files for most applications.)

▶ Create Folder (Append Data) (User can create new folders and append data to files.)

▶ Delete (User can delete file or folder.)

▶ Delete Subfolders and Files (User can delete subfolders and files.)

With just these 13 checkboxes, you have a large amount of flexibility to allow additional permissions beyond what you can configure with just POSIX permissions.

Because the Server app does not allow you to create Deny rules, if you need to deny access, a good strategy is to set the standard POSIX permissions for Others to No Access, and then configure an ACL to build up rules to allow appropriate access for various groups.

Understanding ACL Inheritance

One powerful feature of ACLs is inheritance: When you create an ACE for a folder, from that point on when a user creates a new item in that folder, the operating system assigns that same ACE to the new item. In other words, the ACE is inherited. For each ACE in the folder's ACL, you can control how that ACE is inherited; when you edit an ACE, you can enable or disable each of the following checkboxes (By default, all four "Applies to" options are enabled.):

▶ Apply to this folder: This ACE applies to this folder.

▶ Apply to child folders: This ACE will be assigned to new folders inside this folder, but not necessarily to new folders that are created inside the child folders of this folder, unless "Apply to all descendants" is also selected.

▶ Apply to child files: This ACE will be assigned to new files inside this folder, but not necessarily to files that are inside the child folders of this folder, unless "All descendants" is also selected.

▶ Apply to all descendants: This makes the two preceding options apply to items in an infinite level of nested folders in this folder.

When an ACE is inherited from a folder, it appears dimmed as in the figure below (you can inspect an inherited ACE but not edit it):

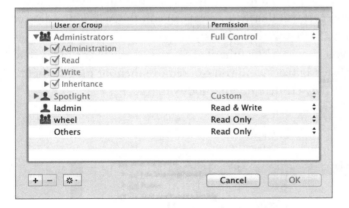

If an inherited ACL doesn't meet your needs, first consider why the ACL model didn't work in this case: Do you need a different share point, a different group, or maybe a different set of ACEs in the ACL? In any event, you can click the action pop-up menu (looks like a gear) and choose one of these two actions to change the inherited entries:

▶   Remove Inherited Entries

▶   Make Inherited Entries Explicit

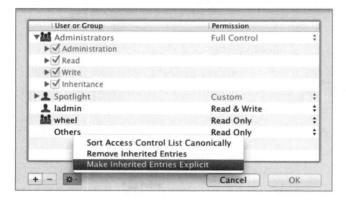

Remove Inherited Entries removes all the inherited ACEs, not just one ACE that you might have selected. The inherited ACL could be an aggregation of inherited ACEs from more than one parent folder.

Make Inherited Entries Explicit applies all the inherited ACEs as if they were applied directly to the ACL. Once you perform this action, you can edit the ACEs, including editing or removing individual ACEs that were previously greyed out. The following figure illustrates what happens if you choose Make Inherited Entries Explicit: The ACEs that were listed in grey are now listed in black, and you can remove them or modify them. The ACE for Spotlight is automatically created; do not modify that ACE.

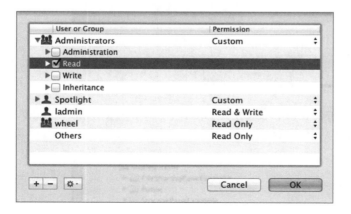

When you use the Server app 's File Sharing pane to update a folder's ACL that has inheritance rules, the Server app automatically updates the ACL for items in the folder that have already inherited the ACL (this is not the case if you update the ACL using the Storage pane).

Understanding ACL Portability

Because ACLs are applied when a file or folder is *created*:

▶ If you *move* an item from one location to another *on the same volume*, the ACL for that item (if one exists) does not change, and is still associated with the item.

▶ If you *copy* an item from one location to another, the item's ACL does not get copied; the copied item will inherit, from its enclosing folder, any ACEs that are appropriately configured to be inherited.

However, what happens if you update an existing ACL, or create a new ACL, after files have already been created? You'll need to propagate the ACL, which is the topic of the next section.

Understanding Propagating Permissions

When you use the Storage pane to update an ACL for a folder, or create an ACL for a folder, this action doesn't affect the files and folders that already exist inside that folder, so you have to *propagate* the ACL, which copies the updates to the ACL to child objects, also referred to as sub folders and files, according to the inheritance rules. Don't worry about overwriting explicitly defined ACEs for child objects, because propagating an ACL does not affect any explicitly defined ACEs for sub folders and files.

After you've modified an ACL, choose Sort Access Control List Canonically, especially if there are any Deny ACEs in the ACL, close the Edit Permissions window, and then from the Action menu, choose Propagate Permissions. The figure below illustrates that the default is to propagate the ACL, but you can also choose to update different combinations of standard POSIX ownership and permissions to sub folders and files.

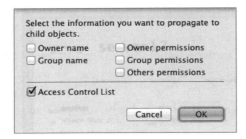

Understanding Group Membership and ACLs

When working with ACLs, it is important that you plan your setup properly to avoid conflicting permissions settings, such as having a user be a member of two groups, one with read permissions on a folder and one with no access permissions on the same folder. These types of conflicts can occur if you do not plan your ACL permissions models well.

Using ACLs to control access to server resources can be extremely valuable, as long as you take care up front to organize your user and group accounts appropriately. The recommended way to approach this management is to take advantage of using smaller groups to correctly reflect the needs of your organization, including nesting groups within groups. Use these group accounts to manage access on a more granular basis.

Understanding Multiple Groups

The standard POSIX permissions work well in a single desktop mode such as Lion. Yet when the system becomes more complex, the standard POSIX permissions model does not scale well.

Complex workflows might require more than just the User, Group, and Others classes available with the standard POSIX permissions model. In particular, having a single group is very limiting. The POSIX owner must be an individual user account (it can't be a group), and granting permission to Others usually opens up the files to a wider audience than you want. Adding an ACL permits you to assign multiple groups to a folder, and assign each a unique permissions setting. Because ACLs can assign different permissions to multiple groups, you must carefully plan what your group structure is going to look like to avoid any confusion. This is a common requirement in any environment that has multiple groups collaborating on a single project.

Understanding Nested Groups

In addition to assigning multiple groups to a single folder, Lion Server allows groups to contain other groups. Breaking groups down into subgroups can make your access easier to understand as an administrator. You can use nested groups to reflect the structure of your organization.

While nested groups are powerful, they should be used with care. If you build a deep, complex hierarchy, you may find that access is harder—rather than easier—to understand. Mirroring your organizational structure is usually safe and useful. However, be wary of ad hoc groups that don't relate to any external structure. They may be a quick way to give access to some users, but later on may make it more difficult to understand your access.

Understanding POSIX Permissions vs. ACL Settings

It is important to understand how the POSIX permissions model and the file system ACLs behave, and how they behave together, in order to accurately configure share points to behave as you intend.

Understanding How File-System ACLs Work

When you use the Server App to define ACLs, you are creating individual access control entries (ACEs). These entries and lists are specific to a file-system location. Each ACE contains the following information:

▶ User or group associated with this entry

▶ Type of entry (Allow or Deny)

▶ Permissions (Full Control, Read & Write, Read, Write, or Custom, along with inheritance settings)

> **NOTE** ▶ The Server app does not distinguish between Allow and Deny. You simply see a checkbox. When you assign a new ACE, it is assumed that you are assigning an Allow rule. However, when you look at an ACE that has Deny, such as the ACE for a user home folder for Everyone to Deny Delete, you can't tell whether this rule is an Allow or a Deny rule.

The order of entries is important because lists are evaluated top to bottom by Lion Server.

Allow and deny matches work differently for ACLs. When evaluating ACLs, the operating system starts with the first ACE and moves downward, stopping at the ACE that applies to the user and matches the operation, such as reading, being performed. The permission (either to allow or to deny) for the ACE is then applied. Any ACEs further down in the list are then ignored. Any matching Allow or Deny ACE overrides standard POSIX permissions.

Understanding POSIX and ACL Rules of Precedence

When a user attempts to perform an action that requires authorization (read a file, or create a folder), Lion Server will allow this action only if the user has permission for that action. Here is how Lion Server combines POSIX and ACLs when there is a request for a specific action:

1. If there is no ACL, POSIX rules apply.

2. If there is an ACL, the order of the ACEs matters. You can sort the ACEs in an ACL in a consistent and predictable way: In the Server app Storage pane, select an ACL, then from the Action pop-up menu (labeled with a gear and a down arrow) choose Sort Access Control List Canonically. This is especially important if you add an ACE to an ACL that contains an ACE that denies access.

3. When evaluating an ACL, Lion Server evaluates the first ACE in the list and continues on to the next ACE until it finds an ACE that matches the permission required for the requested action, whether that permission is Allow or Deny. Even if a deny ACE exists in an ACL, if a similar allow ACE is listed first, the allow ACE is the one that is used, because it is listed first. This is why it is so important to use the Sort Access Control List Canonically command.

4. A POSIX permission that is restrictive does not override an ACE that specifically allows a permission.

5. If no ACE applies to the permission required for the requested action, the POSIX permissions apply.

For example, if Localuser 1 attempts to create a folder, the requested permission is Create Folder. Each ACE is evaluated until there is an ACE that either allows or denies Create Folder for Localuser 1 or a group that Localuser 1 belongs to.

Even though this is an unlikely scenario, it illustrates the combination of an ACL and POSIX permissions: If a folder has an ACE that allows Localuser 1 full control, but the POSIX permission defines localuser1 as the owner with no access, then Localuser 1 effectively has full control. The ACE is evaluated before the POSIX permissions.

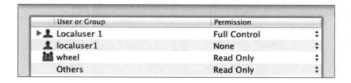

As another example, consider a folder with an ACL that has a single ACE that allows Localuser 2 read permission, and the folder's POSIX permission defines Localuser 2 as the owner with read-and-write permission. When Localuser 2 attempts to create a file in that folder, there is no ACE that specifically addresses the Create Files (Write Data) request, so no ACE applies to that request. Therefore, the POSIX permissions apply, and Localuser 2 can create the file.

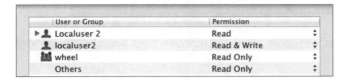

Configuring Access Control

In this section, you will create a folder hierarchy and a means of controlling access to facilitate the workflow of the users and groups on your server. Using standard POSIX permissions and file-system ACLs, you will follow the path of an example project from development to review. You will discover that the ability to manipulate a file can be determined by where the file is located in the system, rather than by who created or owns the specific file.

To properly configure your server, you will need to understand the intended workflow of your users. Here is the scenario: A company uses a share point for design production projects. The two designers need to be able to read and write documents in the share point, including documents that the other designer created. No one else in the organization should be able to see the files, except the Vice President (VP) of Sales (rather than using real names for this exercise, you will use descriptive names).

Even though you *could* start out by configuring the Design group as the primary group and assign it read-write permissions to the folder, any new items created will be automatically have a POSIX permission of read-only for the primary group, so instead, you need to create an ACE for the Design group to allow them read-write access. You will also need to create an ACE for the VP of sales to allow read access.

As part of this scenario, after you get the users, groups, and share points configured, be prepared for management to assign another request, which you will cheerfully fulfill.

First, clean up the example share points you created earlier in the chapter.

1   If necessary, on your administrator computer, open the Server app and connect to your Lion Server as a local administrator.

2   Select File Sharing in the Server app sidebar.

3   Select the FileSharingPaneExample share point, and click Remove (-).

4   Click Remove at the confirmation pane.

5   Select the StoragePaneExample share point, click Remove (-), and click Remove at the confirmation pane.

Create some users for the exercise, and create a Designers group for the two designers.

1   If necessary, on your administrator computer, open the Server app and connect to your Lion Server as a local administrator.

2   Click Users in the Server app sidebar.

3   Add the following users:

Full Name: Designer 1
Account Name: designer1
Password: design

Full Name: Designer 2
Account Name: designer2
Password: design

Full Name: Sales VP
Account Name: salesvp
Password: sales

4   Click Groups in the Server app sidebar.

5   Create the following group:

Full Name: Designers
Group Name: designers

6   Double-click the Designers group, and add Designer 1 and Designer 2 to the Members list.

7   Click Done to save the changes.

Next, create a shared folder for the Designers group, and configure its permissions so that:

▶ members of the Designers group have read & write access to all items.

▶ the Sales VP has read-only access to all items.

▶ no one else can see the contents.

1 Click File Sharing in the Server app sidebar.

2 Click the Add (+) button.

3 Navigate to the Shared Items folder on your server's boot volume.

4 Click New Folder.

5 Name the folder Designs, and then click Create.

6 Select the new Designs folder you just created, and then click Choose.

7 Double-click the Designs share point.

8 Scroll down to the Everyone Else entry, click the pop-up menu for permissions, and choose No Access.

Note that the owner and primary group are inherited from the enclosing folder (Shared Items). Don't worry about that; the owner of new items will be the user that creates the item. Also, remember that over AFP, new items will get read-only access applied to the primary group, so you need to use an ACL to provide Read & Write access to the Designers group.

9   Click Add (+).

10   Start typing Designers, and then choose Designers.

Confirm that the permission is automatically set to Read & Write for the Designers group.

11   Click the Add (+) button, start typing salesvp, and choose Sales VP.

12   Set the permissions for Sales VP to Read.

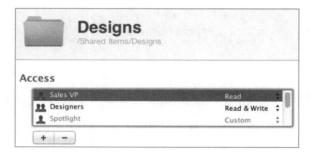

13   Click Done to save these settings.

Even though the permissions do not allow the local administrator to view or edit files, you can still use the Server app's Storage pane to inspect ACLs on items in the folder.

Confirm that Designer 1 and Designer 2 can create and edit items in the design share point, and that Sales VP cannot create, edit, or remove items.

1   On your administrator computer, in the Finder, choose File > New Finder Window.

2   If there is an Eject button next to your server in the sidebar, click it to eject any mounted volumes from that server.

3   If your server appears in the Finder sidebar, select your server.

Otherwise, if there are enough computers on your network that your server does not appear in the Shared section of the Finder sidebar, click All, double-click your server, and then click Connect as.

4   In the upper-right corner of the Finder window, underneath the toolbar, click Connect As.

5   In the authentication window, provide credentials for designer1 (password: design).

Do not select the checkbox to remember the password, otherwise you will need to use Keychain Access to remove the password before you can connect as a different user.

After you successfully authenticate, you see all the share points that the user Designer 1 has access to read.

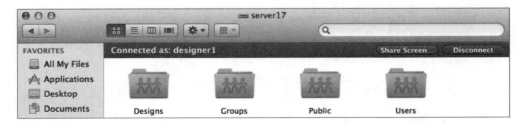

6   Open the Designs folder.

7 Press Command-Shift-N to create a new folder, enter the name "Folder created by designer1."

8 Press Return to stop editing the folder name.

You won't do anything else with this folder in the exercise, but you confirmed that Designer 1 has permission to create a folder.

9 Click Launchpad in the Dock, and select TextEdit.

10 If you do not see a new blank document, choose File > New.

11 Enter the following text, "This is a file started by Designer 1."

12 Choose File > Save.

13 If necessary, click the triangle next to the Save As field to reveal more options.

14 Select your server in the Shared section of the sidebar, then select Designs.

15 In the Save As field, name the file Designer 1 Text File.rtf and click Save.

16 Choose File > Close.

17 If there is no Finder window still open, in the Finder press Command-N to open a new Finder window.

18 Click Eject next to your server in the Finder sidebar.

19 Select your server, then click Connect As.

20 At the authentication window, provide credentials for Designer 2 (password: design).

Do not select the checkbox to remember the password.

21 Open the Designs folder.

22 Open the Designer 1 Text File.

23 Add another line at the end of the text file: "This was added by Designer 2."

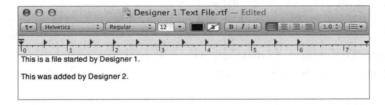

24 Choose File > Save a Version.

25 Choose File > Close.

If you see a message about the volume not being able to access older versions of the document, click Close.

26 Click Eject next to your server in the Finder sidebar.

Confirm that you cannot edit a file in the Designs folder as the salesvp user.

1 Click Connect As.

2 At the authentication window, provide credentials for salesvp (password: sales).

3 Open the Designs folder.

4 Open the Designer 1 Text File.

5 Confirm that you can read the text, and that the toolbar contains the text "Locked," indicating that you cannot save changes to this file.

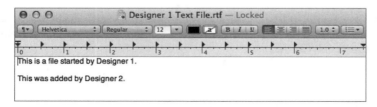

6 Choose TextEdit > Quit Textedit.

Confirm you cannot create a new folder in the Designs folder as the salesvp user.

1 In the Finder window, confirm that you are viewing the Designs folder.

2 Choose File > New Folder.

3 You see the message "Finder wants to make changes. Type your password to allow this." Provide local administrator credentials (name: ladmin and password: ladminpw) and click OK.

You are not able to create a new folder on the network volume, even after providing administrator credentials, because the user salesvp has only read permissions.

4 Because you effectively have read-only permission, you see a message that you don't have permission. Click OK at the message.

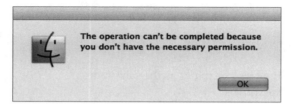

Confirm you cannot delete an item in the Designs folder as the Sales VP user.

1 Select the text file and choose File > Move to Trash.

2 At the "Are you sure" message, click Delete.

3 You see the message "Finder wants to make changes. Type your password to allow this." Provide local administrator credentials and click OK.

You are not able to delete this file on the network volume, even after providing administrator credentials, because the user Sales VP has only read permissions.

4 Because you effectively have read-only permission, you see a message that you don't have permission. Click OK at the message.

Confirm that a different user cannot view items in the Designs folder.

1 Click the Eject icon next to your server in the Finder sidebar.

2 At the authentication window, provide credentials for Localuser 1 (password: local).

Do not select the checkbox to remember the password.

3 Confirm that there is no Designs folder visible.

NOTE ▶ If you authenticate as an administrator, then you will see that there is a shared folder named Designs, but you will not be able to see the contents of the folder.

4 Click Disconnect in the upper-right corner of the Finder window, or if you selected a shared folder, click the Eject icon next to your server in the Finder sidebar.

You have successfully managed users and groups, created a share point, and managed the POSIX permissions and ACL for the share point to provide the access that management requested.

However, the company just added a new Marketing Vice President, who also wants read access to the files.

Rather than adding another individual user to the ACL, it makes more sense to create a group for vice presidents, add appropriate users to that group, and then add an ACE to allow read access for that group. To prevent confusion in the future, you will also remove the original ACE for the Sales VP; keeping the original ACE for the Sales VP is unnecessary because that user is part of a group that has an ACE.

1   If necessary, on your administrator computer, open the Server app and connect to your Lion Server as a local administrator.

2   Click Users in the Server app sidebar and add a new user:

Full Name: Marketing VP

Account Name: marketingvp

Password: marketing

3   Click Groups in the Server app sidebar and add a new group:

Full Name: Vice Presidents

Group Name: vps

Click Done to create the group.

4   Double-click the Vice Presidents group, click Add (+), add Marketing VP and Sales VP to the list of members, and click Done.

5   Click File Sharing in the Server app sidebar.

6   Double-click the Designs share point.

7   Highlight the Sales VP ACE and click Remove (-).

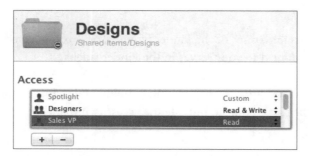

8   Click Add (+), enter vps, and choose Vice Presidents from the list.

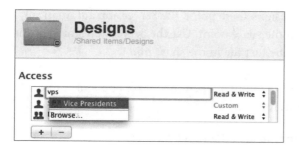

9 Choose Read for the permission for Vice Presidents.

10 Click Done.

11 In the Finder, if there is no Finder window visible, choose New > New Finder Window.

12 Select your server in the sidebar.

13 Click Connect As, and authenticate as marketingvp (password: marketing).

Do not select the checkbox to remember the password.

After you authenticate you see a list of share points that you can access.

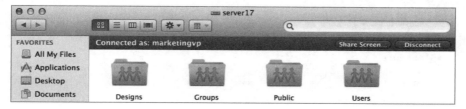

14 Open the Designs folder, and open the Designer 1 Text File.

15 Confirm that the toolbar has the text "Locked" to indicate that you cannot make changes to the file.

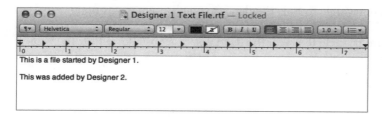

When you updated the ACL for the Designs share point, the Server app automatically propagated the change to the items in the share point. Use the Server app storage pane to inspect the ACL for the folder and the text file in the share point.

1 If necessary, on your administrator computer, open the Server app and connect to your server as a local administrator.

2 Click your server in the Server app sidebar, then click Storage.

3 Navigate to the Shared Items folder of your server's boot volume.

4 Select the Designs folder, then choose Edit Permissions from the Action pop-up menu.

5 Click the disclosure triangle to reveal the permissions allowed for the Designers group.

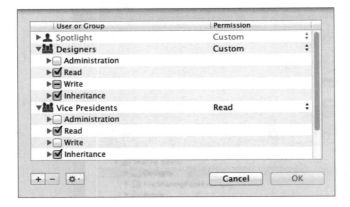

The Designers group has full Read access, and partial Write access (the Delete permission is not allowed, but Delete Subfolders and Files is enabled, so anyone in the Designers group can effectively delete any item except the Designers share point itself).

6 Click the disclosure triangle to hide the detail for the Designers group.

7 Click the disclosure triangle to reveal the Read permissions allowed for the Vice Presidents group.

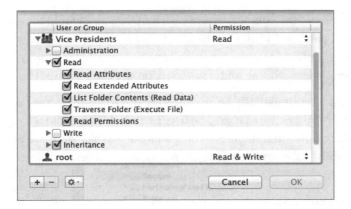

The Vice Presidents group has full read access, and this ACE gets inherited to all new items created in this folder.

8 Scroll down to view the standard POSIX permissions.

9 Click the disclosure triangle to hide the detail for the Vice Presidents group.

The POSIX permissions for Others is None ("Others" appears as "Everyone Else" in the File Sharing pane of the Server app), so unless a user is root, in the system group named wheel, or in the Designers or Vice Presidents group, that user will not be able to examine files in this share point. This includes the local administrator; even while logged in at the server as the local administrator, you cannot open that folder in the Finder. Of course you could add an ACE to allow the Administrators group to have some sort of permission to the shared folder, if that action matches the security requirements of your organization.

Preparing for a Network Home Folder

By default, when a person uses a Lion computer that is bound to an Open Directory server hosted on a Lion Server and logs in as a network user, she gets a home folder created in the /Users folder of that client computer's boot volume. One challenge, however, is that if the user moves from one computer to another, her home folder does not move with her; the documents she edited on the first computer are not available on the second computer. One solution to this problem is to provide a network home folder for a network user; when a network user logs in to a bound Mac, the computer retrieves the account information from a shared directory domain. The Mac uses the value of the location of the user's home folder, stored in the account, to mount the home folder, which resides physically on a home folder server.

TIP ▶ In previous versions of Mac OS X Server, a new network user would have no home folder defined by default, and would not be able to log in on a client Mac without a home folder defined. This is not necessary with Lion Server; a user without a network home folder simply gets a home folder in /Users on the client computer.

You can set up any share point to automatically be available for you to assign as the location for a network home folder for a network user. The user's network home folder can reside in any AFP or SMB share point that the user's computer can access. The share point must be automountable—it must have a network mount record in the directory domain where the user account resides.

An automountable share point ensures that the home folder is automatically visible in /Network/Servers when the user logs in to a Mac configured to access the shared domain. Because AFP is the native file-sharing protocol for Mac OS X, and allows Mac OS X clients to reconnect to the AFP service after a temporary network disconnection without errors, Apple recommends storing home folders in AFP share points.

NOTE ▶ The home folder doesn't need to be stored on the same server as the directory domain containing the user's account. In fact, distributing the task of providing directory services and file sharing services for home folders among multiple servers can help you balance your servers' workload.

Configuring Network Mounts

Next, you'll configure a new share point to be used for network home folders. This allows an administrator to configure a network user's home folder to be hosted on your server.

If you have not configured your server as an Open Directory master, you cannot perform these exercises; if this is the case, you can go back and perform the "Configuring Lion Server as an Open Directory Master" exercise from Chapter 3, or just read through the exercise.

1   If you have turned on Fast User Switching, you may encounter errors, which will prevent users from logging in to the Network account if they switch from a local account. If necessary, log off all users on your administrator computer except your initial administrator account.

2   On your administrator computer, if necessary, open the Server app and connect to your server as the local administrator.

3 Click File Sharing in the Server app sidebar.

4 Click Add (+) and navigate to the Shared Items folder on your server's boot volume.

5 Click New Folder.

6 Name the new folder Nethomes and click Create.

7 Select the Nethomes folder and click Choose.

8 Double-click the Nethomes share point to edit it.

9 Select the checkbox for "Make available for home directories."

10 Confirm that AFP is chosen in the protocol pop-up menu (the protocol pop-up menu is not available for Lion Server version 10.7.1 or earlier.).

11 Click Done to save the changes.

> **NOTE** ▶ The Server app does not actually make any changes if you select "Make available for home directories" on a server that is not an Open Directory master. It is outside the scope of this book to assign a user a network home folder that is hosted on a server other than the server that is the Open Directory master that defines that user's account.

Configuring Users to Use Network Home Folders

In addition to configuring the file server to share /Shared Items/Nethomes for network home folders, you must set each user account to indicate the share point that contains their home folder. To set up a home folder for a network user in the Server app, follow these steps:

1   Click Users in the Server app sidebar.

2   Click Add (+) and create a new user:

Full Name: Nethome 1

Account Name: nethome1

Password: net

3   Double-click the Nethome 1 user to edit that user.

4   Select the pop-up menu for Home Folder, and choose Nethomes.

5   Click Done to save the changes.

Now log in as this new user, and confirm that your home folder is on the network share point.

1   On your administrator computer, open the Users & Groups preferences, then click Login Options to verify that you are still bound to your server.

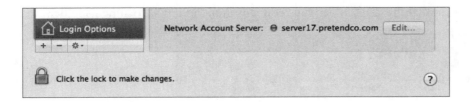

2   On your administrator computer, log out as ladmin.

3   On your administrator computer at the login window, click Other, then log in as Nethome 1 (password: net).

4   After you log in, choose Go > Home in the Finder to open your home folder.

5   Command-click the nethome1 icon in the title bar of the Finder window, and verify that the hierarchy displays that your home folder is located on the network share point rather than directly in the /Users folder on your Mac OS X computer, as shown in the figure below.

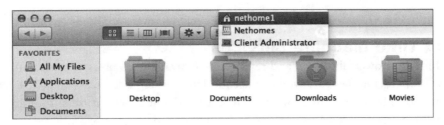

6   Open the Documents folder, press Command-Shift-N to create a new folder in Documents, and name the folder Test1.

7   Log out as Nethome 1.

Verify that a new home folder is created in the /Users folder on your server computer.

1   Log in to your administrator computer as ladmin, open the Server app, connect to your server, and authenticate as ladmin.

2   Select your server in the Server app sidebar, click Storage, and navigate to /Shared Items/Nethomes/nethome1/Documents on your server's boot volume.

3 Confirm that the Test1 folder you created is in nethome1's Documents folder.

Offering Time Machine Services

Time Machine is a powerful backup and restore service available to users of Macs with Lion, Snow Leopard, and Leopard; you can use the Time Machine service with your Lion Server to provide a backup destination on your server to Time Machine users. You can offer any volume attached to your Lion Server, but it's a good idea to use a volume that you dedicate to Time Machine only, because, by design, Time Machine will eventually fill the volume with backup files.

The File Sharing service must be turned on in order for clients to use the Time Machine service.

> **TIP** The Server app provides no warning that if you turn off the File Sharing service, you will interrupt active Time Machine backups or restores; so, if you offer the Time Machine service, be sure to not turn off the file sharing service until you have confirmed that no client computers are actively backing up or restoring with the Time Machine service.

After you choose a backup disk, the Server app automatically starts the Time Machine service and the File Sharing service, if they were not already on. On the backup disk, Lion Server automatically creates a Shared Items folder on the root of the backup volume, and creates a folder named Backups in that folder. Each client computer gets its own sparse disk image (a sparse disk image can grow in size) inside the Backups folder, and there is an automatically configured ACL to prevent anyone from deleting Time Machine files from the sparse disk image.

If you later change the backup volume, users who use your Lion Server's Time Machine service will automatically use the new volume. However, Lion Server does not automatically migrate existing backup files, and the next time Time Machine performs a backup on a client computer, it will back up all the files that are configured to be backed up, not just files that have changed since the last time Time Machine ran, so it may take a long time, depending on how much data is backed up.

Remember that you can use the Server app Users pane to configure individual user access to the Time Machine service (Control-click a user and choose Edit Access to Services, then select or deselect the checkbox for Time Machine).

Configuring a Time Machine Destination

It's really simple to make a volume available as a Time Machine destination. If you use an external USB, FireWire, or ThunderBolt drive, take precautions to ensure that it does not accidentally become disconnected.

If you attach a volume after you open the Server app, quit the Server app and open it again in order to see the newly attached volume in the list of disks to use for the Time Machine service.

1   Quit the Server app.

2   On your server, attach an external volume.

3   On your administrator computer, open the Server app and connect to your Lion server as a local administrator.

4   In the Server app sidebar, click Time Machine.

5   Next to Backup destination, click Edit to open a window that displays the available volumes.

6   Choose the volume to offer to Time Machine Users.

The message "This disk drive may not support Time Machine backup over the net-work" is displayed for external drives. "More information" is a link to knowledge base document TA24910 with more details about using external volumes (most fundamentally, you need to know not to eject an external volume used for Time Machine).

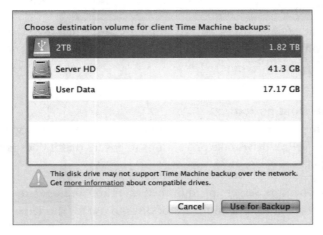

7   Click Use For Backup.

8   Note that the Server app displays which volume is used as the backup destination, and how much space is available on that volume.

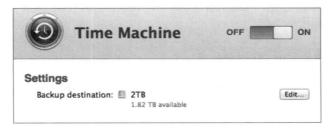

Configuring a Lion Computer to Use the Time Machine Destination

Verify that the network-based Time Machine works. Configure your administrator computer to use the Time Machine service.

1 On your administrator computer, open System Preferences.

2 If the lock in the lower-left corner of System Preferences is locked, click it and provide administrator credentials.

3 Click Time Machine.

4 Click Select Disk.

5 Select the item named Backups with your Lion Server's computer name. Note that no matter what the volume is actually named, the item appears with the name Backups.

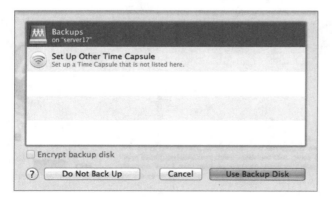

6 Click Use Backup Disk.

7 Provide credentials for a user on the server (either a local user or a network user) and click Connect.

Excluding System Files from the Time Machine Backup

Since this is a learning environment, you can reduce the amount of space required for a Time Machine backup by excluding System Files, such as the system applications and UNIX tools.

1 Click Options.

2 Click Add (+) to add a folder to be excluded.

3 Select the System folder and click Exclude.

4 At the notice that you've excluded the System folder, click All System Files.

5 Click Save.

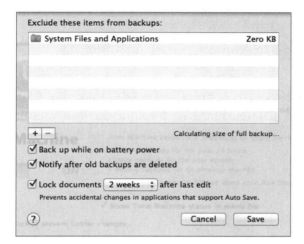

6   From the Time Machine menu, choose Back Up Now.

Restoring From the Network Time Machine Destination

To simulate accidentally deleting a file and using Time Machine to restore it, use the following steps to create a file with TextEdit, initiate a Time Machine backup, delete the file, empty the Trash, and then restore the file using Time Machine.

1   Open Launchpad from your Dock and click TextEdit.

2   Enter some text, like "This file will be deleted and then restored."

3   Press Command-S to save the file.

4   Press Command-D to choose the Desktop as the location to save the file.

5   Name the file DeleteMe (TextEdit automatically adds an appropriate extension such as .rtf or .txt) and click Save.

6   From the Time Machine menu, choose Back Up Now.

7   Wait until the backup has completed (the Time Machine icon stops spinning when the backup is done).

Delete the file and empty the Trash.

8   Drag the DeleteMe file to the Trash (or select DeleteMe and then press Command-Delete to send it to the Trash).

9   Click the Trash in the Dock.

10 If there are any files you do not wish to permanently erase, drag them to your Desktop or otherwise remove them from the Trash.

> **NOTE** ▶ Time Machine does not back up your Trash, so once you empty the Trash, you will not be able to restore files that were in the Trash before you made your first Time Machine backup.

11 From the Finder menu, choose Empty Trash (or press Shift-Command-delete to empty the Trash).

12 At the "Are you sure" message, click Empty Trash.

To enter Time Machine and restore the text file:

1   From the Time Machine menu, choose Enter Time Machine.

2   If the Finder window shows your home folder, open your Desktop folder.

3   Click the arrow to go backwards in time until you see your DeleteMe file.

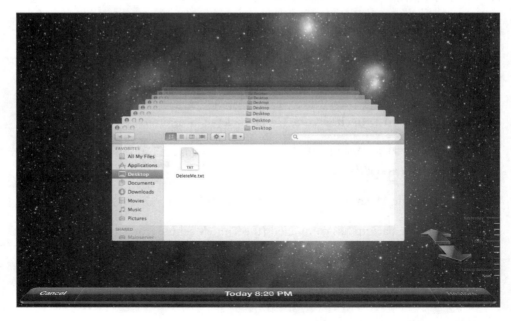

4   Select the DeleteMe file, and click Restore in the lower-right corner.

5   Open the DeleteMe file to confirm that this was the file you originally created.

6   Quit TextEdit.

7   Delete the DeleteMe file and empty the Trash.

Cleaning Up

Since this is a test environment, stop using Time Machine from your Lion Server.

1   On your administrator computer, open System Preferences.

2   If the lock in the lower-left corner of System Preferences is locked, click it and provide administrator credentials.

3   Click Time Machine.

4   Click Select Disk.

5   Click Do Not Back Up.

6   Quit System Preferences.

Now, configure the Time Machine service to stop using your external volume.

1   On your administrator computer, if necessary, open the Server app and connect to your server as a local administrator.

2   Click Time Machine in the sidebar of the Server app.

3   Next to Backup destination, click Edit.

4   Select None.

5   Click Use for Backup.

The Server app automatically stops the Time Machine service.

Troubleshooting File Services

Whether you're using AFP, SMB, or WebDAV, troubleshooting file services on Lion Server typically involves the following considerations:.

▶ Service availability: Is the service turned on? For Time Machine, the File Sharing service must be turned on.

▶ User access: What users or groups should have access to the specific files and folders on the server, and are their appropriate permissions set correctly?

▶ Platform and protocol access: From which clients, such as Macs, Windows, or iOS devices, are users trying to access the server? What protocols are they using when accessing the server?

▶ Special needs: Are there any special circumstances, such as users needing access to files in a format not native to the system they are using?

▶ Concurrent access: Is there a possibility that in your users' workflow, there could be multiple clients simultaneously accessing the same files, regardless of the file-sharing protocol(s) being used?

While the different sharing protocols (AFP, SMB, WebDAV) support multiple platforms, it can be tricky to provide concurrent access to the same files, especially with the new Auto Save and Versions document management features in Lion. Concurrent access means that multiple users are trying to access or modify the same files at the same time. Many times this is dependent on the specific cross-platform applications knowing how to allow multiple users to access the same file. Because Lion Server includes support for ACLs and these ACLs are compatible with those from the Windows platform, permissions mapping between Windows clients will be in line with what Windows users expect to see.

Understanding Case-Sensitivity Issues in File Sharing

Case sensitivity becomes an issue if you are copying files between two computers and only one of them has a case-sensitive file system. You can use Disk Utility to format a volume with a case-sensitive format, to handle legacy web content, for example. Suppose you have two files, Makefile and makefile, in the same folder on a case-sensitive volume shared by Lion Server. If you were to copy those files to a Lion computer, which is by default not case sensitive, you would run into problems. The Lion computer would attempt to overwrite one file with the other. When you copy files from a case-insensitive file system to a case-sensitive file system, you might have a problem with executable files.

More specifically, Apple's implementation of SMB in Lion has a distinct preference for lowercase filenames. For example, if your share point contains the files RUNSCRIPT and runscript, and you mount that share point from a Lion client over SMB, you will see runscript but not RUNSCRIPT in the Finder. If you move runscript to a different folder, afterwards you will see RUNSCRIPT. If you then move runscript back, you'll see runscript and RUNSCRIPT. If you then attempt to move RUNSCRIPT, you'll actually move runscript instead.

Not much can be done to synchronize case-sensitive and case-insensitive systems; you and your users need to work around the incompatibility. Given that AFP is a case-sensitive protocol, mounting a share point using AFP enables you to see the different case-sensitive files and download whichever one you'd like.

Accessing Logs for File Sharing Services

You can use the Console application on your server to inspect the logs related to AFP and WebDAV.

1   On your administrator computer, if you are not already connected to your server with the Server app, open the Server app, press Command-N to connect to a server, select your server, and authenticate to your server with the username ladmin and the password ladminpw.

2   Select your server in the Server app sidebar, and click Settings.

3   Click the arrow next to "Enable screen sharing and remote management."

4   At the Screen sharing authentication window, provide your local administrator credentials and click Connect.

5   On your server, if you aren't already logged in as your local administrator, log in with your local administrator credentials (Name: ladmin and Password: ladminpw).

Use the Console application to view the AFP logs.

1   In the Console window sidebar, click the disclosure triangle located to the left of /Library/Logs.

    If File Sharing has been providing AFP services on the server, there should be a section titled AppleFileService.

2   Click the disclosure triangle located to the left of the AppleFileService section, and inspect the file(s) inside by selecting each one and viewing their contents in the log detail area, on the right side of the window.

The WebDAV service also has a log that might contain information useful in gathering information for troubleshooting.

1   In the Console window sidebar, open /Library/Logs/userwebdav.log.

2   Stay logged in on your server computer.

Cleaning up

To keep the interface clean for the next chapters, remove the share points, users, and groups you created.

1   If necessary, on your administrator computer, log out as the nethome1 user and log in as ladmin.

2   Open the Server app and connect to your server.

3   Select Users in the Server app sidebar.

4   Select Designer 1 and click Remove (-). Click Delete to confirm.

5   Remove the following users:

Designer 2

Marketing VP

Nethome 1

Sales VP

6   Remove the following groups:

Designers

Vice Presidents

7   Select File Sharing in the Server app sidebar.

8   Select the Designs share point and click Remove (-). Click Remove to confirm.

9   Remove the Nethomes share point.

There are still files in the Shared Folder. You could log in on the server to remove those folders in the Finder while logged in on the server.

1   If you do not already have a Screen Sharing session open with your server, from the Tools menu, choose Screen Sharing, enter the host name of your server, authenticate as a local administrator, and click Connect.

2   On your server, if necessary, log in as a local administrator.

3   On your server, in the Finder, choose Go > Go to Folder, enter /Shared Items, and click Go.

4   Press and hold the Command key while you select the Designs, FileSharingPaneExample, NetHomes, and StoragePaneExample folders.

5   Choose File > Move to Trash.

6   Provide authentication as a local administrator if necessary.

7   Log out of your server.

8   On your administrator computer, quit Screen Sharing.

What You've Learned

▶   The four steps when implementing file-sharing services are to plan, configure user and group accounts, configure the file service, and then monitor your server.

▶   A share point is any folder, drive, or volume that you make available to network clients. You create and configure share points with the Server app.

▶   A share point can be shared over AFP, SMB, or WebDAV.

▶   Access control lists (ACLs) can be used to set very flexible restrictions on share points and folders.

▶   You can configure ACLs with the File Sharing and Storage panes of the Server app.

▶   You can make a share point available to host network home folders for network users.

▶   Rather than assign file system permissions for individual users, it is best to assign users to groups, and then assign permissions to groups.

▶   A globally unique identifier (GUID) is used to identify a user or a group in ACLs and service access control lists (SACLs).

▶   You can configure a share point on an Open Directory master to be available for network home folders over AFP or SMB, and then you can configure a user or users to use that share point for their network home folder.

▶   You can specify a volume to be used for the Time Machine service; clients can use the Time Machine preferences to choose an item named Backup, along with your Lion Server's computer name.

▶   The File Sharing service must be enabled in order for the Time Machine service to be running.

References

The following documents provide more information about topics in this chapter. Additional resources are available at http://www.apple.com/macosx/server/resources.

Lion Server Administration Guides

Lion Server: Advanced Server Administration

http://help.apple.com/advancedserveradmin/mac/10.7/

Apple Knowledge Base Documents

You can check for new and updated Knowledge Base documents at http://www.apple.com/support.

Document HT3275, "Time Machine: Troubleshooting backup issues"

Document HT4695, "Lion Server: How to configure NFS exports"

Document HT4698, "Lion Server: SMB file server works with Mac OS X v10.6, Windows XP or later"

Document HT4700, "Lion Server: Connecting to legacy AFP services"

Document HT4704, "Lion Server: Enabling the FTP service"

Document HT4727, "Lion Server: Connecting an iOS device to a WebDAV enabled share point hosted by Lion Server"

Document HT4745, "Lion Server: Configuring the NetBoot service enables NFS"

Document HT4283, "iWork for iOS: Using a WebDAV service"

Document HT4829, "Mac OS X: Mounting shared folders using an smb:// URL or the mount_smbfs command"

Document TA24910, "Mac OS X Server 10.5: About using drives for network Time Machine backups"

Document TS2938, "Lion Server: AFP users unable to authenticate with Kerberos after upgrading"

Document TS3838, "Lion Server: createhomedir command may not create homes for Active Directory users"

Document TS3859, "Lion Server: Guest access option applies to all shares"

Document TS3883, "Lion Server: Finder Sidebar may not connect via SMB if the computer's name contains certain characters"

Document TS3888, "Authentication issues when connecting to a Lion SMB server"

Document TS3889, "Unable to create automount on a Lion Server that is a member of Open Directory"

URLs

Welcome to WebDAV Resources: http://www.webdav.org/

Microsoft Open Specifications: Workgroup Server Protocol Program: http://www.microsoft.com/openspecifications/en/us/programs/wspp/default.aspx

Chapter Review

1. Name three file-sharing protocols supported by Lion Server and their principal target clients.
2. How does Lion Server support browsing for Windows clients?
3. When does an access control entry (ACE) for a folder's access control list (ACL) get propagated to items in the folder?
4. What two actions are necessary to perform in order to provide a network home folder for a network user?

5. What permissions can you choose for an ACE in the File Sharing pane of the Server app?

6. What permissions can you specify for an ACE in the Storage pane of the Server app?

7. In the Storage pane of the Server app, what 4 rules for inheritance can you apply to an ACE?

8. How do you remove an inherited ACE?

9. What might it mean if you see a GUID rather than a user name in an ACL?

10. What URL should you use from an iOS device to save to a WebDAV-enabled share point hosted by the Lion Server at server17.pretendco.com, if the web service on the Lion Server uses an SSL certificate?

11. Do both the File Sharing and the Time Machine services need to be turned on in order to offer Time Machine services to your users?

Answers

1. AFP for Mac clients; SMB for Windows clients; and WebDAV for iOS devices are three file-sharing protocols supported by Lion Server.

2. Lion Server uses NetBIOS to advertise its presence to Windows clients; Windows users see Lion Server in their Network Neighborhood or Network Places.

3. An ACE of a folder's ACL is propagated to a new item that is created in that folder, or copied into that folder from another volume, if the inheritance options for the ACE apply. Also, an administrator can select a folder in the Storage pane of the Server app, select "propagate permissions" from the Action pop-up menu, select the Access Control List checkbox, and click OK. Finally, if you use the File Sharing pane to modify an ACL that has been inherited, the changes will be propagated.

4. You need to first edit a share point and select the checkbox "Make available for home directories." Then you can edit a user, and select that share point in the Home Folder pop-up menu.

5. In the File Sharing pane of the Server app, when you edit an ACE, you can choose Read & Write, Read, or Write.

6. In the Storage pane of the Server app, when you edit an ACE, you can select checkboxes for 13 kinds of permissions. The categories include Administration, Read, and Write.

7. There are four inheritance rules, to apply to: folder, child folders, child files, and all descendants.

8. In the Storage pane of the Server app, navigate to the item that has an ACL, click the Action pop-up menu, choose Edit Permissions, click the Action pop-up menu, and choose Remove Inherited Entries.

9. If you see a GUID instead of a user name, it could mean that you removed a user or a group from your Lion Server, and the ACE is displaying that user or group's GUID because it cannot map the GUID to a user or a group.

10. In the iOS application that supports WebDAV, you would use the URL https://server17.pretendco.com/webdav. Depending on the application, you will see a list of share points that support WebDAV.

11. Yes, both File Sharing and Time Machine need to be on in order to offer the Time Machine service to your users.

7

Time   This chapter takes approximately three hours to complete.

Goals   Define OS X Lion Server's web engine

Understand how to manage the web service

Control access to websites

Configure multiple websites and locate site files

Examine website log files

Locate and use secure certificates for websites

Chapter 7
Managing Web Services

This chapter helps you understand, manage, and secure the various aspects of Apple's web services, including managing high-bandwidth connections, sharing files, and locating log files for access, viewing, and troubleshooting.

OS X Lion Server's web service is based on Apache, open source software commonly used in a variety of operating systems. Apache can be enhanced by the use of modules (think of them as plug-ins), and Apple has included several additional modules with Lion Server to extend the abilities of Apache. Unlike previous versions of OS X Server, managing modules is not done via the server management tools. Module management through command line tools is still possible, but beyond the scope of this book.

As of this writing, the version installed in Lion Server is Apache 2.2.20.

Understanding Basic Website Concepts

Before you manage any websites, it is important to know where critical Apache and website files are stored. All Apache and Apple configuration files for web services are located in /private/etc/apache2/, which is normally hidden from view in the Finder. Apache modules—including Apple-specific modules—are located in /usr/libexec/apache2/, which is also normally hidden from view in the Finder. The default location for Lion Server's website is located in /Library/Server/Web/Data/Sites/.

> **NOTE** ▶ This location for the site files is new in Lion Server. The old location at /Library/WebServer/Documents still exists but is not used in the default web service configuration.

As in prior versions, each user added to OS X Server (regardless of whether the users were added to the local directory or the shared LDAP directory also known as network users) had a home folder created and received a folder for a default webpage that anyone can access when web services and appropriate modules are enabled. These individual websites can be placed in the Sites folder in the user's home folder on Lion Server.

> **NOTE** ▶ User websites are made available once Web Sharing is turned on in the Sharing Preference Pane.

The URL to reach a Lion Server's webpage is its IP address, or fully qualified domain name (FQDN), such as http://10.0.0.171 or http://server17.pretendco.com. To access any user's website, a forward slash, a tilde (~), and the short name of the user are added to either the IP address or the FQDN (for example, http://10.0.0.171/~ladmin). While on the local subnet, the hostname and Bonjour address can also be used.

All website files and the folders in which they normally reside must be at least read only for Everybody or the www user or group, otherwise users won't be able to access the files displayed by their web browsers when they visit your site.

Enabling and Disabling Websites

When managing websites on Lion Server, you use the Server app. You also use the Server app to manage file and folder permissions, thus allowing or restricting access to folders that are to be seen by web browsers, such as Safari.

Because Lion Server has preconfigured web services for the default website, all you need to do to start exploring is turn on the web service.

To disable a website, you simply remove it from the list of websites in the Server app. This does not remove the site files, just the reference to the site in the web service configuration files.

Starting the Web Service in the Server app

To start the web service, you must first enable it as a service in the Server app.

1   Open Server.app and select Web in the list of services on the left.

2   Click on the On/Off switch at the top of the window to turn on the service.

3   Open Safari on OS X, and connect to http://10.0.0.171. Observe the page, then enter the FQDN (http://server17.pretendco.com), and make sure you can observe the page again. Refresh the page if necessary.

NOTE ▶ Notice that you did not configure the website in any way. Lion Server's web service is set to serve up the default webpage automatically.

4   Quit Safari by pressing Command-Q or choosing Quit from the Safari menu.

You will now examine some basic options for managing websites on Lion Server.

Managing Websites

You can manage many websites with Lion Server. Each website can be distinguished by a different IP address, domain name, or port over which everyone accesses the site. Before you change any parameters on your existing site, or add a new site, it's worth learning how Apple configures the defaults for the original site.

> **NOTE ▸** If you followed the examples in Chapter 4, "Managing Accounts," andstarted the Profile Manager service, then your server's default web site will use port 443 instead of port 80.

Viewing Website Parameters

While not editable, understanding what parameters Lion Server sets for the default website is helpful, as you will often want to adjust or change some of them on your other sites.

1 Select the web service in the list of services displayed on the left side of the Server app.

2 Choose the default website, and click the edit button in the toolbar below the Web Sites box.

3 Although you are looking at the default non-editable website, items to be defined and entered for any new websites would include:

▸ Domain Name: Fully qualified domain name defined when creating the site in the Server app.

▸ IP Address: IP address of the site as available in the pull down menu.

NOTE ▶ Lion Server can have multiple IP addresses on a single interface, or more than one Ethernet interface. Therefore, it is important to distinguish IP addresses as mapped to certain sites. Entering this information limits the site to just the entered parameters.

▶ Port: Logical port value that users visiting the site may need to know in order to access the site. Ports 80 and 443 are known by most browsers and do not require additional typing when entering the address.

NOTE ▶ Port 443 assumes SSL access to a site, which we will enable later.

▶ Store Site Files In: The location of the files served up by the selected site.

▶ Who Can Access: Allows the site to require authentication for access.

▶ View Document Root Contents: Opens a Finder window at the location where the site files are stored.

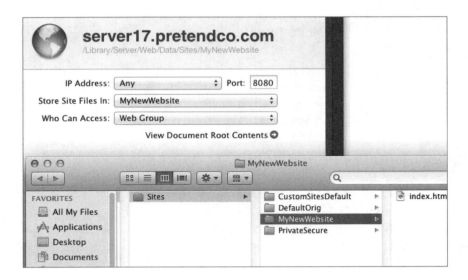

Domain Name, IP Address, and Port are used to separate sites from one another. For example, you can have two sites on the same IP address as long as their ports are different. You can also have two sites with the same IP address and different domain names. By editing and ensuring that one of these three parameters is unique, you are logically separating your sites.

Creating a New Website

Now that you have viewed the general parameters, you will create a secondary website based on a second IP address, FQDN, and port number.

1 On your server, add a second IP address (10.0.0.172) to the Ethernet port.

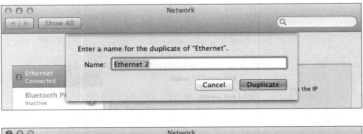

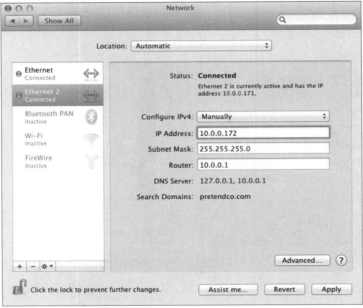

2 Open TextEdit and create a new document. In the document, add the text "My New Website!" and save as an html file named "index.html."

3 Use the Finder to navigate to /Library/Server/Web/Data/Sites and make a new folder called "MyNewWebsite."

4   Copy index.html into /Library/Server/Web/Data/Sites/MyNewWebsite.

5   Create a new folder called "Protected" in /Library/Server/Web/Data/Sites/MyNewWebsite.

6   Make a second document with the text "My Protected Website" and save it as an html file named "index.html."

7   Copy index.html into /Library/Server/Web/Data/Sites/MyNewWebsite/Protected.

8   In the Web service, click the Add (+) button to create a new site, and enter the following information, :

▶   Domain Name: server17.pretendco.com

▶   IP Address: Any

▶   Port: 8080

▶   Store Site Files In: Click Choose and navigate to /Library/Server/Web/Data/Sites/MyNewWebsite.

▶   Who Can Access: Anyone

Click Done.

9 Within Safari, enter http://server17.pretendco.com:8080 in the address bar and press Return to contact the site.

You should see your edited webpage from your directory over the port you chose, 8080.

NOTE ▶ You can see the proper site because you have defined a different port from the default server website.

10 If you try accessing http://www.pretendco.com, you'll see it defaults back to the original Lion Server default page.

Modify the website so that it responds to a different host name. The section "Preparing DNS Records" in Chapter 3, "Using Open Directory," contains directions for creating the appropriate DNS records for www.pretendco.lan at 10.0.0.172.

1   Click the Edit button for the website and change the following:

▶   IP Address: 10.0.0.172

▶   Port: 80

Click Done.

2   Within Safari, enter http://www.pretendco.lan in the address bar and press Return to contact the site.

You should see your edited webpage from your directory. This works because you have defined a specific IP for that site to respond to and a DNS record that responds with that IP address when using the FQDN for www.pretendco.lan.

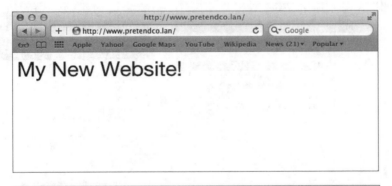

3   Quit Safari.

Verifying Folder Access

For proper web site behavior, it is imperative that folder permissions (and file permissions, to some extent) be set up with adequate access, as well as appropriate controls. At a minimum, the Everyone group must have read access for Apache to serve the files. It is also acceptable for the www user or group to have read-only access.

To check if permissions are read only for All:

1   Open the Server app and navigate to the Web service.

2   With your site selected, click on the Edit button, and then click on the View Document Root Contents. This will open a Finder window at the site folder.

3   View the standard permissions on the folder via Get Info (Command-I or right click) in the lower half of the window. Notice that for everyone, permissions are set to Read Only. This allows all users, including www, to access that folder.

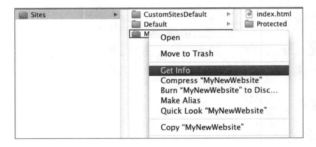

Managing Website Access

Lion Server provides a mechanism to control access to a whole web site or portions of the site that can only be accessed by certain users or groups.

Controlling access can be incredibly useful when dealing with websites that contain sensitive information or sections of a site that should only be accessible to one person or group. For example, you could set up a website so that only those users in a given group can access the site. You could also set up a portion of the site so that only a department has access to those particular pages. In most cases, access limitations are set up after users and groups are created, because the access to certain web directories is based on users and/or groups.

For this exercise a group called Web Group has been created along with two users, Web User and No Web User. Web User is a member of Web Group.

1   Select the website from the prior exercise. Click the Edit button and change the following:

▶   Who Can Access: Web Group

Click Done.

2   Within Safari, enter http://www.pretendco.lan in the address bar and press Return to contact the site.

You should be prompted for authentication. Members of Web Group will be able to access the site.

3   To protect an area within the website, select the website again in the Server app. Click the Edit button and change the following:

▶   Who Can Access: Customize

▶   Protected: Web Group (Click Save)

Click Done.

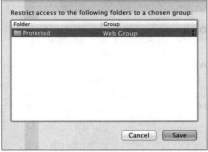

4 Within Safari, enter http://www.pretendco.lan in the address bar and press Return to contact the site. You should see your normal site. Enter http://www.pretendco.lan/Protected in the address bar and press Return. You should be prompted for authentication. Members of Web Group will be able to access the protected portion of the site. Users not part of the allowed group will be returned to an authentication prompt.

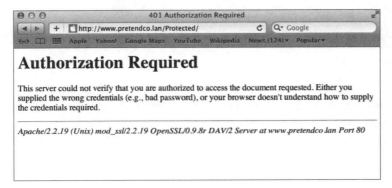

Securing Your Website

Most web traffic travels across the network in clear text, meaning that the content can be viewed by anyone who captures the web data. For many situations this is acceptable, but any time sensitive information is sent across the wire a method of protection is required.

It's very easy to encrypt the web traffic using SSL (Secure Sockets Layer) and a certificate.

Using SSL

Lion Server makes it easy to turn on SSL for a website. During the process of turning on SSL, the default port of the website changes from 80 to 443. In Lion Server, websites using SSL will automatically redirect a request for the site using http (port 80) to https (port 443). You will create a new website using the host name ssl.pretendco.lan. The section "Preparing DNS Records" in Chapter 3, "Using Open Directory," contains directions for creating the appropriate DNS records for ssl.pretendco.lan at 10.0.0.173.

1   On your server add another IP address (10.0.0.173) to the Ethernet port.

2   Quit the Server app, then open the Server app and connect to your server again.

3   Open TextEdit and create a new document. In the document, add the text "My New SSL Website!" and save as an html file named "index.html."

4   Use the Finder to navigate to /Library/Server/Web/Data/Sites and make a new folder called "MyNewSSLWebsite."

5   Copy index.html into /Library/Server/Web/Data/Sites/MyNewSSLWebsite.

6   In the Web service, click the Add (+) button to create a new site, and enter the following information:

▶   Domain Name: ssl.pretendco.lan

▶   IP Address: 10.0.0.173

▶   Port: 80

▶   Store Site Files In: Click Choose and navigate to /Library/Server/Web/Data/Sites/MyNewSSLWebsite.

▶   Who Can Access: Anyone

Click Done.

7   Within Safari, enter http://ssl.pretendco.lan in the address bar and press Return to contact the site. You should see your edited webpage from your directory.

   NOTE ► You should notice that the site isn't protected by SSL quite yet as you haven't provided an SSL certificate for the website to use.

8   Within Server app, pick your server under the Hardware heading in the left column. Click on the Settings tab.

9   Click on Edit next to SSL Certificate. Find the ssl.pretendco.lan site in the list and pick a certificate to use. Click OK.

   NOTE ► In the example shown a self-signed certificate that was automatically generated by the server is being used, but this will cause a certificate warning to appear in users' browsers since it is untrusted. To prevent this, consider buying a certificate from a known certificate authority.

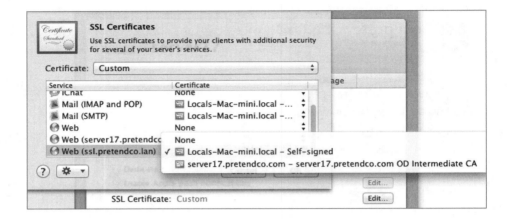

10 View the details of the ssl.pretendco.lan website in Server app, and you will see that the port has been changed to 443 from 80.

11 If you try accessing http://ssl.pretendco.lan, you will see that even though you entered in http:// you were automatically redirected to https://. Click on the lock in the upper right corner of Safari, and you will be presented with the details of the certificate used to secure the website.

Monitoring Web Services

When administering a website, it is important to understand how Lion Server handles Apache log files, where they are stored, and how to view them.

Viewing Apache Log Files

Apache has excellent logging capabilities and uses two main files when logging website information: the Access log and the Error log. The log files can store all kinds of information, such as the address of the requesting computer, amount of data sent, date and time of transaction, page requested by the visitor, and a web server response code.

Log files, named access_log and error_log, are located inside /var/log/apache2/ and are readable via the Console app.

To view Apache log files for a given site:

1   Open /Applications/Utilities/Console and navigate to /var/log/apache2 in the left-hand column and click on the disclosure triangle to view the access and error logs. You might need to click the Show Log List at the upper left corner of the Console window to view the various log locations.

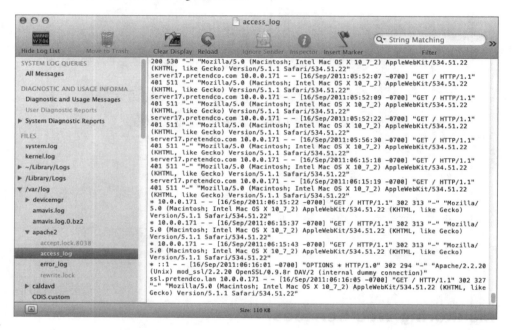

2   On your OS X computer, open /Utilities/Terminal and type

ab –n 10000 –c 50 http://server17.pretendco.com/

then press Return.

This is an Apache test tool that tells your Mac OS X computer to ask for 10,000 (the -n parameter) requests run concurrently by 50 (the -c parameter) pretend users' concurrent connections.

3   Click the Reload button in the Console toolbar to see the number of requests increase.

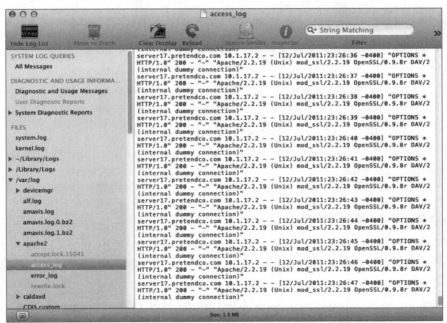

4   On your OS X computer, open Safari and type

http://server17.pretendco.com/nada.html

This page does not exist; therefore, it will log an error.

5 Using Console, check the error_log for the error by searching for "nada." You will see an error generated by the bad request.

Troubleshooting

To troubleshoot web services, it helps to understand how the service works and what pieces control what aspects of the service. Here are some areas to investigate:

▶ Check if Web service is running by verifying that there is a green dot next to the service in Server app.

▶ Check that the web site is pointing to the location where the web site files are stored.

▶ Verify that the web site files and directory can be read by _www or the group "everybody."

▶ Check if there are site restrictions as to who can access the site.

▶ Check that the appropriate networking ports aren't blocked to the server (80 for http, 443 for https and any others that may have been defined for a specific website).

▶ Check that the proper IP address has been set for the web site.

▶ Use Network Utility to check that DNS resolves properly for the web sites fully qualified domain name (FQDN).

What You've Learned

▶ The web service for both Lion and Lion Server is based on Apache.

▶ Apache uses modules to extend its functionality that are not manageable via the Server app.

▶ Permissions on website folders are crucial to visitors gaining access to portions of the site.

▶ Access can be controlled to restrict areas of a site to certain groups.

▶ Lion Server can host multiple websites over a single IP address.

▶ The Server app is used to manage the web service.

▶ You can see the logging of access and errors for your websites using Console.

References

The following references provide more information about topics discussed in this chapter. (Additional resources are available at http://www.apple.com/server/macosx/resources/.)

Administration Guides

Lion Server: Advanced Administration
https://help.apple.com/advancedserveradmin/mac/10.7/

URLs

Apache Organization site: http://httpd.apache.org

Apache log formatting information: http://httpd.apache.org/docs/2.2/logs.html, http://httpd.apache.org/docs/2.2/mod/mod_log_config.html

Enabling Name Based Web Hosting: http://support.apple.com/kb/HT4838

Chapter Review

1. On what software is Lion Server's web service based?
2. Which permissions are necessary on a web folder to ensure that visitors to the site can access the pages?
3. What are access controls?
4. Where is the default location for the Apache log files?
5. What is the advantage of using SSL on a website?

Answers

1. Lion Server's web service is based on Apache, the open source web server software.
2. The everyone or www group must have read access to the web files.
3. Access controls are paths to folders that can be restricted based on group.
4. The default location for Apache log files is /var/log/apache2/access_log and /var/log/apache2/error_log.
5. SSL helps protect the traffic traveling to and from the website by encrypting the data.

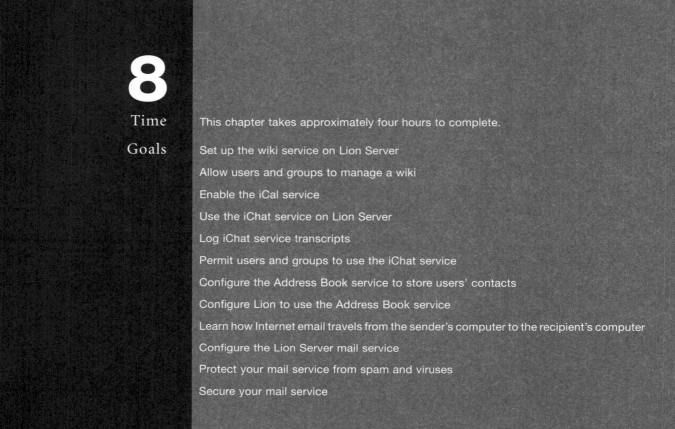

8

Time

Goals

This chapter takes approximately four hours to complete.

Set up the wiki service on Lion Server

Allow users and groups to manage a wiki

Enable the iCal service

Use the iChat service on Lion Server

Log iChat service transcripts

Permit users and groups to use the iChat service

Configure the Address Book service to store users' contacts

Configure Lion to use the Address Book service

Learn how Internet email travels from the sender's computer to the recipient's computer

Configure the Lion Server mail service

Protect your mail service from spam and viruses

Secure your mail service

Chapter 8

Using Collaborative Services

Lion Server has several services that offer a collaborative environment for users. These services allow for the sharing of contacts, information, events, and schedules, as well as chatting and blogging. They form the core of what is known as collaborative services. They are the:

▶ Wiki service

▶ iCal service

▶ iChat service

▶ Address Book service

▶ Mail service

With these services, users can chat in approved groups in a secure environment about internal projects, schedule appointments and meetings, permit others to manage their calendars, set up a wiki to document the progress of projects, and blog about their projects. They can also access these services from multiple computers and devices, and create projects with the wiki service without your intervention.

Utilizing Administrative Tools

In Lion Server, you use the Server app with the Address Book, iCal, iChat, and Web services for management. The Server app is also used for setting Service Access Control Lists (SACL's) for each of the services to control.

Locating the Data Stores

Each service stores its data on the boot volume at:

Address Book:	/Library/Server/Calendar and Contacts/
iCal:	/Library/Server/Calendar and Contacts/
iChat (archives):	/Library/Server/iChat/Data/message_archives/
Wiki:	/Library/Server/Wiki
Incoming Mail:	/Library/Server/Mail/Data/mail
Outgoing Mail:	/Library/Server/Mail/Data/spool

Understanding and Managing a Wiki

A wiki is a collaborative web-based tool that allows users and groups to post information in a manner that promotes the logical progression of an idea, project, theme, or any other focal point of discussion within an organization. Wikis are central to the idea of all users within a given group being able to post, edit, review, and discuss material without interference from other groups or departments within an organization. This can benefit the group whose wiki is hosting a confidential project or sensitive information. Lion Server wikis also keep a detailed history of a group's posts, so you can retrieve older information if necessary.

Wikis have a few layers of access control. You can administratively control the users and groups you allow to create wikis. Once a user creates a wiki, he or she can specify who can read it and who can edit it, all without any intervention from an administrator.

Once users have access to a wiki, they can post articles, images, and files for downloading, link pages together, and format the pages to their liking. Media such as images, movies, and audio are presented right on the webpage and do not need to be downloaded by the user.

Similar to wikis are blogs. Blogs permit users and groups to catalog their experiences surrounding a project or theme. Whereas wikis are collaborative, blogs tend to be singular in nature and organized in a chronological format; however, with group blogging, shared experiences may be posted together.

The wiki service integrates with the iCal service, which the next section covers.

Enabling a Wiki in the Server App

Enabling the wiki service on Lion Server is simply done by turning on the service in the Server app.

In this exercise, you will enable the service, and then limit who can create wikis. You will ensure that your site uses SSL to protect it.

> **NOTE ▶** Make sure you have a group called Wiki Group with Wiki User as a member. From Chapter 7 you should still have other users available; we will use No Web User in this exercise.

1   Open the Server app and select Wiki in the list of services on the left. Turn the service on by clicking the On/Off switch in the upper right corner of the window.

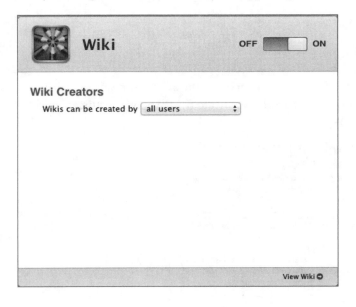

2   In Safari, navigate to server17.pretendco.com to view the default site, then click Wikis to see the interface. This connection isn't protected by SSL.

3   To protect the site with SSL, select your server in the Server app sidebar, click Settings, and click Edit next to the SSL Certificate field. Apply a certificate to the Web Service and click OK.

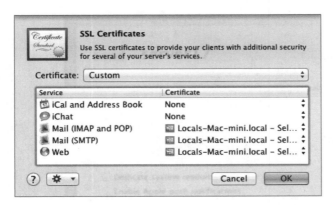

4 In Safari navigate to server17.pretendco.com to view the default site again, but notice that you are presented with a certificate dialog since a self-signed certificate was used. You will not see this if you use a certificate signed by a known certificate authority. Click Continue, then click Wikis to see the interface.

NOTE ► When the site was configured with an SSL certificate, it also set up an automatic redirect, so web requests for http will be sent to https.

5 At this point, all users can create a wiki. Log in as any user, click the Create pop-up menu (+) at the top of the page, and notice that you are given the choice to create a wiki. Log out when done.

6 To limit which users or groups can make a wiki, click the menu in the Wiki service in the Server app, and choose "Only Some Users." This will open a dialog box that will allow you to pick one or more users or groups to allow to make a wiki. Click the Add (+) button at the bottom of the pane, and then start typing "Wiki Group." As you type, you will be presented with choices, and Wiki Group will be available. You can also pick individuals in addition to groups. Click OK when done.

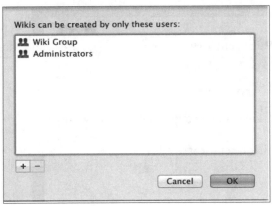

7   In Safari, navigate to server17.pretendco.com to view the default site again. Click the Wikis icon and then click the lock in the upper-right corner of the page to log in as Wiki User. Click the Create pop-up menu (+) and notice you are given the ability to create a new wiki. This is possible because Wiki User is a member of the allowed Wiki Group. Log out of the wiki.

8   Click the lock at the upper right of the page to log in as Not Web User. Click the Create pop-up menu (+) and notice you are not given the ability to create a new wiki. This is because Not Web User is not a member of the allowed Wiki Group. Log out of the wiki.

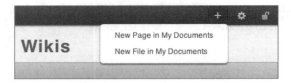

Creating Wikis

Users that you authorized to create wikis can begin the process of creating a wiki. Because wikis are web based, you can use any browser on any platform to authenticate users to start the process of wiki creation. In this exercise, you'll use network user credentials to create a wiki, manage access to it, and create some content.

1   From your OS X computer, open Safari, enter https://server17.pretendco.com, and then press Return.

The default webpage for your Lion Server appears.

2   Click the lock button in the navigation toolbar to get to the login window.

3   Log in as wikiuser with the password you set for it.

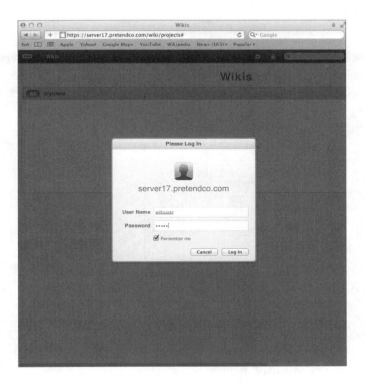

4   Click "wikis."

5   Click the Create pop-up menu (+) and choose and "New Wiki."

6   Enter the name Project A. In the Description field, enter This is the wiki for Project A.

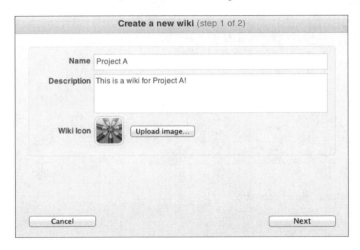

7 Click Next.

8 In the "Set wiki access" window, you could make the site public, yet still require users to log in to read or log in to write or both. However, you will make this site private and accessible only to some users and groups.

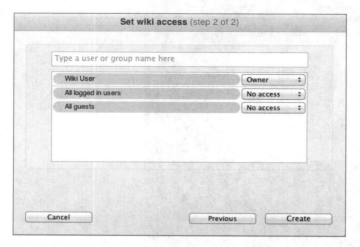

9 In the "Type a user or group name here" field, you must type a name and select from the list that appears. Enter Wiki, and then choose Wiki Group.

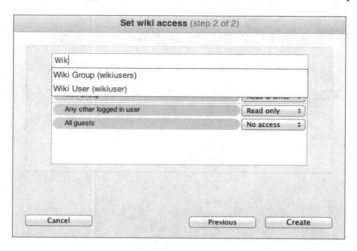

10 For the Wiki Group, choose "Read & write."

11 Change "Any other logged in user" permission to "Read only."

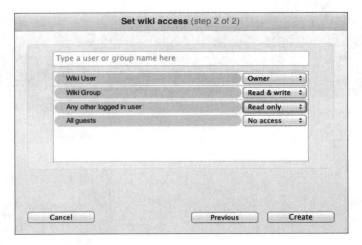

12 Leave "All guests" permission to "No access."

13 Click Create.

14 Click Go to Wiki.

15 You should see the page for the Project A wiki.

16   Click the Edit button (a pencil icon).

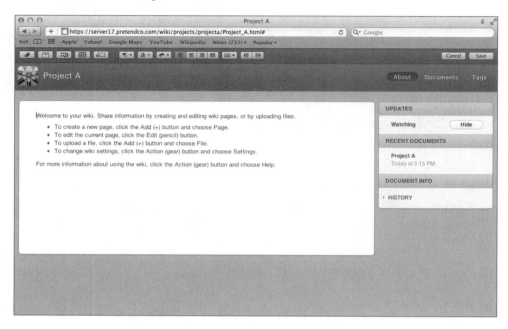

17   Click at the end of the existing text, press Return for a new line, and then click the Attachment icon (a paper clip).

18   Click Choose File, navigate to your Documents folder, select the About Stacks.pdf file, and then click Choose.

19   Click Upload to attach the file.

20   Click Save to save the edits to the page.

21   View the results of the edit. Additional media can be uploaded using the appropriate buttons in the tool bar. The media will be presented right on the webpage and won't require downloading for use by the reader.

22 To turn on the blog, click the Action pop-up menu (looks like a gear) and choose "Settings." Under the Services tab, you can toggle the blog on and click Save. Once the blog is on, you can click the Create pop-up menu (+) to add a new blog post within the wiki.

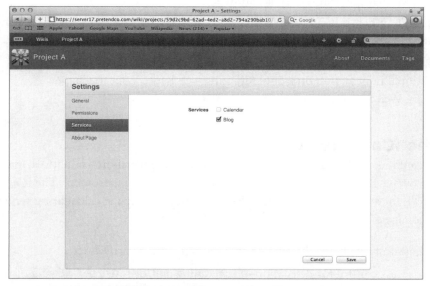

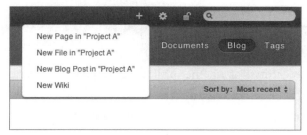

23 To delete the wiki, click on the gear menu and choose "Delete Wiki…" You will be asked to confirm your choice.

24 Click "log out," and then quit Safari.

Troubleshooting the Wiki Service

To troubleshoot the Wiki service provided by Lion Server, it helps to have a good understanding of how the Wiki service works in general. Review the sections above to make sure you understand each of the working pieces.

Here are some common problems and suggestions for rectifying them:

▶ If your users can't connect to the Wiki service on the server, check that the clients are using a DNS server that is providing the proper name resolution for the server.

▶ If users can't connect to the Wiki website, check that ports 80 and 443 are open to the server. Check that the wiki service is running.

▶ If users can't authenticate to the Wiki service, check that the users are using proper passwords. Reset if needed. Check that the users are allowed access to the service as per the access controls.

▶ For additional information on troubleshooting web issues, refer to Chapter 7, "Managing Web Services."

Using the iCal Service

Lion Server contains a calendaring service based on several open source initiatives, mainly the Calendar Server Extensions for WebDAV (CalDAV) calendaring protocol. The iCal service uses HTTP for access to all of its files. Users who want to use the calendaring service can take advantage of several handy features:

▶ Scheduling rooms or items that can be checked out, such as projectors

▶ Enabling access control for delegation of scheduling and/or restricted viewing of your calendar(s)

▶ Allowing multiple calendars per user

▶ Permitting the attachment of files to events

▶ Sending invitations to events, regardless of whether or not the recipient is a user on the iCal server

▶ Checking to see if users or meeting locations are available for a certain event

▶ Privately annotating an event with comments that only they and the event organizer can access

▶ Using Push notification to support immediate updates for computers and mobile devices

And these under-the-hood features should make administrators happy:

▶ Integration with Open Directory in Lion Server, Microsoft's Active Directory, and LDAP directory services, requires no modification to user records.

▶ Service discovery makes it easy for users to set up iCal when you choose "Create Users and Groups" or "Import Users and Groups" during your initial server setup.

▶ Server-side scheduling frees up client resources for better client performance.

▶ Optimization for the Xsan clustered file system makes it easy to add new iCal servers as the demand for calendaring services grows.

Once the iCal service is started, users can create and manipulate their events and schedules with iCal (v4.0 or higher), Calendar for iPhone and iPod touch, and wiki calendar pages. There are third-party applications that also work with the iCal service; you can locate them by doing a web search for CalDAV support.

Configuring and Starting the iCal Service

You can use the Server app to start and manage the iCal service. The parameters that you can adjust are limited to the following:

▶ Enabling or disabling of email invitations and various related settings

▶ Locations and Resources

Starting the iCal service with the Server app is very simple, but you will want to gather the email server information that you'll use with email invitations. In this exercise, you will need users called Cal Administrator (caladmin), Cal User1 (caluser1), Cal User2 (caluser2) and Cal User3 (caluser3). Create them in the Users pane of the Server app.

1 Open the Server app and select iCal in the list of services on the left.

2 Click the Allow invitations using email address box, then the Edit button next to it.

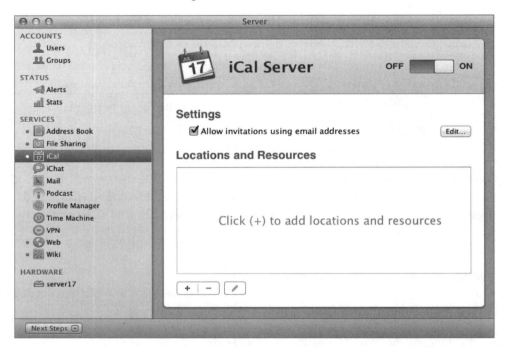

3 Enter the email address you want to use for sending email invitations, then click Next.

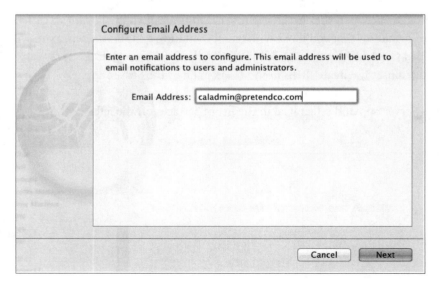

4   Enter the appropriate incoming email server information for your email server, and then click Next.

5   Enter the appropriate outgoing email server information for your email server, and then click Next.

6 Review the Mail Account Summary page and click Finish.

7 Click the iCal toggle to start the service.

8 To secure communications between the iCal service and the clients, set an SSL certificate for the service in the Server app by clicking on the server under Hardware, clicking the Settings tab, and then clicking the edit button next to SSL Certificate. Choose a certificate for iCal and Address Book service.

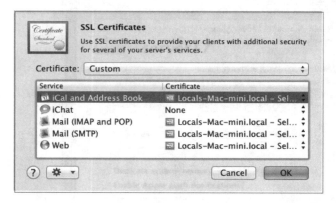

Using the Server app to Add Resources and Locations

The iCal service provides a way to create and use resources (like a projector or a set of speakers) and locations (such as a building or a meeting room). If no delegate has been set, the iCal service automatically accepts the invitation for the location or resource if it is free, and makes the free/busy information available to users. You can also define a delegate to moderate the availability of the resource or location.

Delegates can have two functions based on whether you set Automatic or With Delegates Approval. If you set Automatic, the resource will automatically accept the invitation, but the delegate can view and modify the resources calendar. If With Delegates Approval has been selected, the delegate must accept or deny the invitation. The delegate can also view and modify the resources calendar.

You add locations and resources with the Server app in the iCal pane.

To add a location and a resource with the Server app:

1 In the Server app, select the iCal service.

2 Click the Add (+) button, then choose New Location from the pop-up menu.

3 Enter and/or change the following data for your new location:

▶ The name of the Location should be Conference Room A.

▶ Accept Invitations can be set for Automatic or With Delegate Approval. Choose Automatic.

▶ Enter the name of a delegate. It should populate with choices as you type a name.

4   Click Done to save the changes to the location.

You have now added a location that will be visible when you add or modify an event on a calendar hosted by the iCal service.

5   Click the Add (+) button, and then choose New Resource from the pop-up menu.

6   Enter and/or change the following data for your new resource, then click Done:

▶   The name of the resource should be Demo iPad.

▶   Accept Invitations can be set for Automatic or With Delegate Approval. Choose Automatic.

▶   Enter the name of a delegate. It should populate with choices as you type a name. In this example we will set up Cal User 2 as the delegate who can access the Demo iPad account.

You have now added a resource that you can invite to an event.

Accessing the iCal Service as a User

Users can create and modify events with iCal, a web browser, and mobile devices. In this exercise, you will open iCal, add a network iCal account, change who can access the account as a delegate, create an event with a location and a resource, and then create one more event and access the free/busy feature.

1   On your OS X computer, open iCal (in /Applications).

2   Choose iCal > Preferences, and then click Accounts.

3   Click the Add (+) button to add an iCal service account, and enter the following data:

   ▶   For the Account type, choose Automatic.

   ▶   For the Email address, enter caluser2@server17.pretendco.com.

   ▶   For the Password, enter the user's password.

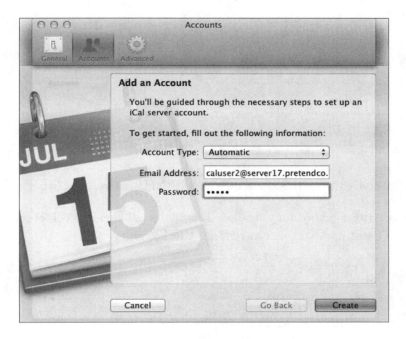

4   Click Create to add the account. You might get a certificate warning if you used a self-signed SSL certificate.

5   Delegate other users to access your calendar to edit and review your events. Click the Delegation tab. Notice that Demo iPad already is showing up in the list of accounts the user can access.

6   Click Edit.

7   Click the Add (+) button.

8 Enter Cal User1, and then choose Cal User1 from the list. Make sure you click the name to choose it.

9 Click the Add button, enter Cal User3, and then choose Cal User3 from the list.

10 Select the Allow Write checkbox for Cal User3. This allows Cal User 3 to edit events on behalf of Cal User2, and Cal User1 to view Cal User2's events.

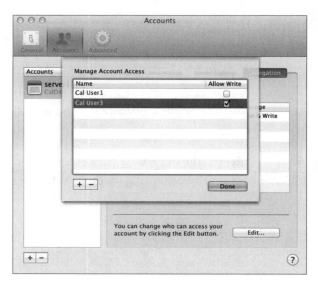

11 Click Done to close the Delegation pane.

12 Click on the General tab and choose the calendar for server17 to be your Default
Calendar.

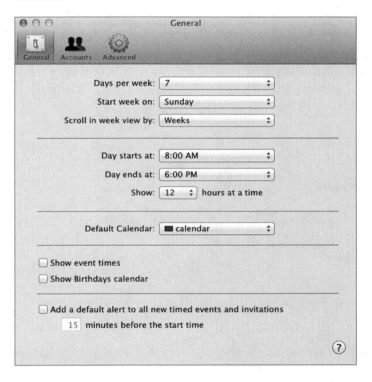

13 Close the Preferences window.

14 Choose File > New Event or click the Create Event (+) button to Create Quick Event.

15 Enter an event name such as Status Update.

16   Move to the location field, and then enter only the first few characters of Conference Room 1.

17   Click Conference Room 1 in the list that iCal displays, and then press Return to choose it.

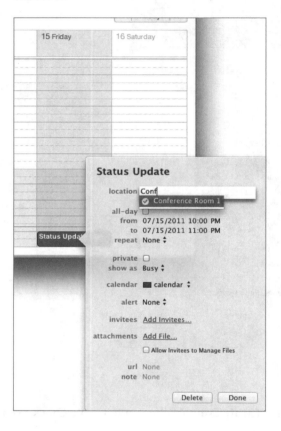

18   Click Add Invitees, and then enter only the first few characters of Cal User1.

19   Click Cal User1 in the list that iCal displays, and then press Return to choose it.

20   While still in the invitees field, enter only the first few characters of Demo iPad.

21   Click Demo iPad in the list that iCal displays, and then press Return to choose it.

22   Click Add File, navigate to your Documents folder, select About Stacks.pdf, and then click Open.

23 Click Send to save the changes to this event. This will cause Demo iPad to automatically accept the event, and Cal User1 will get an invitation to the event. The automatic accept occurred because the resource was configured to do that.

24 Click the event you just created. Choose Edit > Duplicate, which should create a new event at the same time as your original event.

25 Choose Edit > Edit Event.

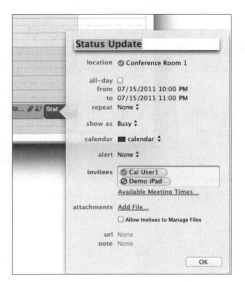

26 Note that Demo iPad has an unavailable icon, because you already scheduled an event for this time that is using the Demo iPad.

Click Available Meeting Times to choose a new meeting time that works for the location and invitees (which includes people and resources).

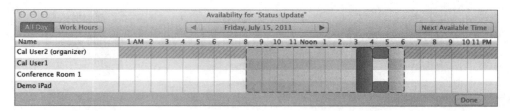

27 Note that free/busy information is listed for each participant invited to the event, including the location, people, and resources. The unavailable times are blocked out in gray, and the available times are displayed with the color assigned to your calendar.

Click Next Available Time, and note that the event moves to the next time that is not busy for each of the invitees.

28 Click Done to close the Availability window and use the new time selected.

29 Click Send to save the changes to the event and notify the invitees of the event. Locations and resources automatically accept invitations.

30 Quit iCal, or try out some of the other features.

Even though you used iCal in this exercise, you could also use the web calendar link available at the bottom of the default server home page (ie: https://server17.pretendco. com/webcal). Of course, the iCal service works with Calendar for iPhone and iPod touch through the CalDAV configuration option.

Calendars can also be added to wikis by creating a wiki, going to the Settings menu, and checking the box next to Calendar in the Services tab.

Since the iCal service relies on HTTP or HTTPS to transfer data from server to client and vice-versa, standard web troubleshooting applies such as checking for open and available ports. On a client, iCal app discovers the iCal server via DNS lookup so DNS problems could prevent iCal from working as expected.

Troubleshooting the iCal Service

To troubleshoot the iCal service provided by Lion Server it helps to have a good understanding of how the iCal Service works in general. Review the sections above to make sure you understand each of the working pieces.

Here are some common problems and potential solutions:

▶ If your users can't connect to the iCal service on the server, check that the clients are using a DNS server that is providing the proper name resolution for the server.

▶ If users can't connect to the iCal service, check that ports 8008 and 8443 are open to the server.

▶ If users can't authenticate to the iCal service, check that the users are using proper passwords. Reset if needed. Check that the users are allowed access to the service as per the service access controls.

Managing the iChat Service

iChat allows users to collaborate in real time. iChat users can use the following features to quickly share information without the delay associated with email messages and wiki posts:

▶ Exchange text messages instantly.

▶ Send files to each other.

▶ Set up an instant audio conference (using the microphone built into many Macs or an external unit).

▶ Initiate a face-to-face video conference using video cameras (including the iSight or FaceTime camera built into many Macs).

▶ Allow another iChat user to take control of their Mac (using screen sharing).

▶ Use iChat Theater to share many kinds of documents, including text files, PDFs, photos, QuickTime movies, Keynote slide shows, and iPhoto albums.

Unlike a telephone call, which you must either answer immediately or allow to go to voicemail, you can accept an instant text message but answer it when you are ready to process it.

Users who chat with each other can use the iChat service to keep those chats within their organization and control the text of the chats. Like many other services on Lion Server, the iChat service can be restricted to certain users or groups, permitting chats to be private and controlled. Chats can also be secured through encryption and logged, permitting them to be searched later. The iChat service is based on the open source Jabber project. The technical name for the protocol used is the Extensible Messaging and Presence Protocol (XMPP).

Various ports are used for the iChat service, depending on whether the service is used internal to your network or exposed to other networks. Refer to Table 6.1 for port usage information.

Table 6.1 iChat Port Usage

Port	Description
1080	SOCKS5 protocol use for file transfers
5060	iChat Session Initiation Protocol (SIP), used for audio or video chats
5190	Only required for basic Instant Messenger (IM) use
5222 TCP	Used only for TLS connections if an SSL certificate is enabled. If no SSL certificate is used, this port is used for nonencrypted connections. TLS encryption is preferred to legacy SSL connections as it is more secure.
5223 TCP	Used for legacy SSL connections when an SSL certificate is used.
5269 TCP	Used for encrypted TLS server-to-server connections, as well as nonencrypted connections. TLS encryption is preferred to legacy SSL connections as it is more secure.
5678	UDP port used by iChat to determine the user's external IP address.
5297, 5298	Used by iChat versions older than v10.5 for Bonjour IM. 10.5 and later use dynamic ports.
7777	Used by the Jabber Proxy65 module for server file transfer proxy.
16402	Used for SIP signaling in OS X 10.5 and later.
16384-16403	These ports are used by OS X 10.4 and earlier for audio or video chat using RTP and RTCP. Traffic is exchanged in .Mac (MobileMe) to determine the user's external port information.

User sessions can use standard passwords or Kerberos for authentication.

Setting Up the iChat Service

You use the Server app to enable the iChat service like most of the other services on Lion Server. Once enabled, the service is managed in a fashion similar to that of the other services.

In this exercise, you will create a folder and change the owner and group associated with that folder. If you do not have a separate volume, do not perform these steps, just read through them.

1   To protect iChat with SSL, select your server in the Server app sidebar, click Settings, and click Edit next to the SSL Certificate field. Apply a certificate to the iChat Service and click OK.

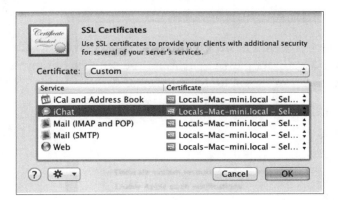

2   In the Server app, select the iChat service and click the On/Off switch.

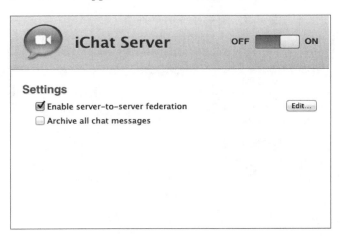

Managing iChat Service Archiving

The iChat service can be used for all sorts of purposes, among them group chatting related to projects. There may be a need to review the chat archive of a conversation, perhaps for auditing or administrative purposes. The iChat client application can archive an individual's chats for review.

The iChat service can log all chat messages. The default directory is located in /Library/Server/iChat/Data/message_archives/. Even if the communications between the iChat users are encrypted, the archives will be kept in plain text.

To enable iChat service logging:

1   Select iChat on the left side of the Server app, and then click the box next to "Archive all chat messages."

2   To view any logged messages, you must be the root user or escalate privileges and navigate to /Library/Server/iChat/Data/message_archives/. You can then use any text editor to view the log files and search them for relevant keywords.

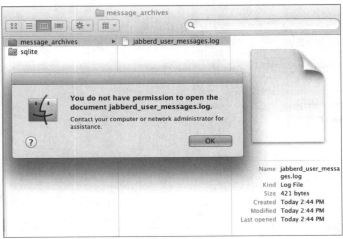

Configuring iChat Service Users

After the iChat service has been set up, you can permit users to join the iChat service (called Jabber in the interface). The iChat service account is a user's short name, the @ symbol, then an iChat service's host domain. For example, the user Chat User1 would set up the iChat application as chatuser1@server17.pretendco.com.

To enable an iChat account to use the iChat (Jabber) service:

1 On your OS X computer, select the iChat icon in your Dock and click past the introduction screen.

2 Choose Jabber from the Account Type pop-up menu.

3 Enter chatuser1@server17.pretendco.com in the Account Name field, and enter the password network in the Password field.

4 Click Continue, and then click Done.

iChat will open, and you will see your iChat (Jabber) service buddy list. In the header at the top of the window, iChat displays the full name of the user that is logged in on OS X.

You can add Jabber buddies (other users with whom you want to chat and whose names you want to appear in a list for easy access) to your buddy list as you normally would when using iChat for any other non-Jabber account. You can optionally add a buddy who exists in your Open Directory database. Be sure to include the person's full name when adding an iChat (Jabber) service buddy.

Once you add a buddy, that person receives a notification when he or she logs in to iChat (Jabber) asking if he or she would like to be added to your buddy list. If another user attempts to add chatuser2 as a buddy, you would see the following window appear.

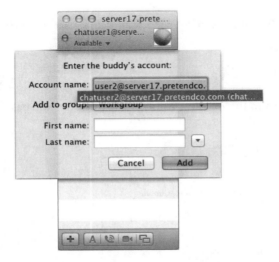

Once you have authorized the listing of your name in that person's buddy list, he or she will see you every time you log in to the iChat (Jabber) service.

You can, of course, communicate back and forth using iChat.

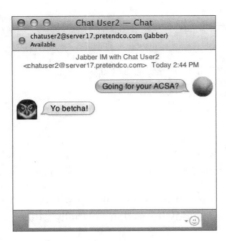

Restricting iChat Service Users

You can also restrict who is permitted to use the iChat service by using service access controls. As with many other services, you can restrict user access via the Server app.

To restrict users from chatting with others on the iChat service:

1   Open the Server App and select Users in the list of Accounts on the left.

2   Select a user and either right-click the user or choose from the Action (looks like a gear) menu below, then choose Edit Access to Services.

3   Select the iChat service and check or uncheck the box if you wish to enable or disable the user's access to iChat.

4   Click OK to save.

Using iChat Federation to Join Services

Your organization may have more than one Lion Server. If both of those servers use the iChat service, it is possible to join them together, allowing users and groups in both Open Directory masters to engage each other in instant messaging. The process of joining different iChat service servers together is called federation. Federation not only allows two Lion Servers running iChat services to join, it also allows any other XMPP chat service, such as Google Talk, to join as well. The iChat service federation is enabled by default.

> **NOTE** ▶ You can enable secure encryption for the federation if you are already using an SSL certificate. This forces all communications between the servers to be encrypted, similar to the way in which the communications between iChat and the iChat server are encrypted when using that certificate. For archiving purposes, messages are always decrypted on the server.

By default, federation is allowed with any other iChat service running on any other Lion Server or Jabber server. However, you can restrict the iChat service federation to approved iChat servers only. To do so:

1 In the Server app, choose the iChat service, make sure the "Enable server-to-server federation" box is checked, then click the edit button.

2 Select the "Restrict federation to the following domains" option and click the Add (+) button to add only those domains that you want to participate within the federation.

3 To keep communication secure between federated servers, apply an SSL certificate to the iChat service and choose the "Require secure server-to-server federation" option.

Viewing iChat Service Logs

To view the connection logs for the iChat service, use Console to view the system log. In Console, simply enter session started in the search field, and you'll see all users, dates, and times that sessions have begun.

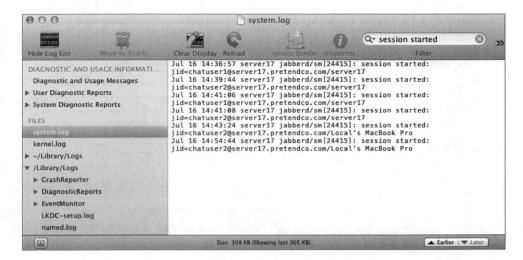

The iChat service reports in the system log can also log any errors that may occur, and you can search for them using the search field in the toolbar in a fashion similar to the way in which you locate users who have started an iChat session. Typical troubleshooting involves ensuring valid DNS entries, network configuration, Network Address Translation (if the servers are on networks with NAT), and firewall configuration. See the article "'Well known' TCP and UDP ports used by Apple software products"(link at the end of the chapter) to help troubleshoot potential firewall issues.

You must have root access to view the jabberd_user_messages.log file, which contains all the messages your users have exchanged using your server's iChat service.

Additional logs are available in the Logs section of the Server app.

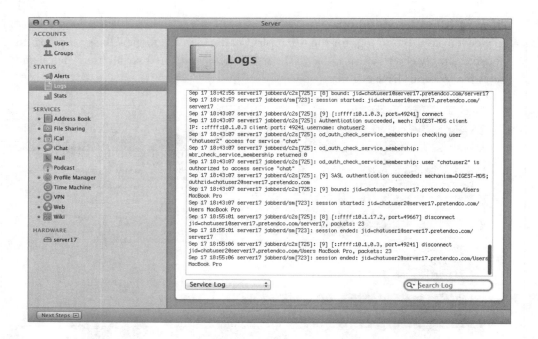

Troubleshooting the iChat Service

To troubleshoot the iChat service provided by Lion Server it helps to have a good understanding of how the iChat Service works in general. Review the sections above to make sure you understand each of the working pieces.

Here are some common problems and suggestions for rectifying them:

▶ If your users can't connect to the iChat service on the server, check that the clients are using a DNS server that is providing the proper name resolution for the server.

▶ If users can't connect to the iChat service, check that the appropriate ports are open to the server as listed in table 6.1 earlier in the section.

▶ If users can't authenticate to the iChat service, check that the users are using proper passwords. Reset if needed. Check that the users are allowed access to the service as per the service access controls.

Understanding the Address Book Service

The Address Book service enables users to store contacts on the server and to access those contacts with multiple computers and devices. The following applications in OS X are compatible with the Address Book service:

▶ Address Book

▶ Mail

▶ iChat

You can enable the Address Book service to provide LDAP searches of the directory servers that your Lion Server is bound to, so your users do not have to configure their Address Book preferences to include various LDAP servers.

The Address Book service uses open source technologies including CardDAV (an extension to WebDAV), HTTP, and HTTPS, as well as vCard (a file format for contact information). You must use Open Directory user accounts to access the Address Book service, so your server must either be an Open Directory server or be bound to one.

When you create a contact with the Address Book service, you use CardDAV, not LDAP, to copy the changes to the server.

Configuring the Address Book Service with the Server App

There is very little to configure in Address Book Service. The Server app allows you to:

▶ Turn the service on and off.

▶ Enable directory contacts for search.

In this exercise, before you start the Address Book service, you will specify an SSL certificate for the service to use.

1 To secure communications between Address Book service and the clients, set an SSL certificate for the service in the Server app by clicking on the server under Hardware, then Settings tab, and then the edit button next to SSL Certificate. Choose a certificate for the iCal and Address Book service.

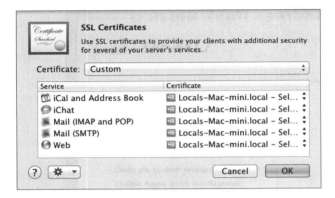

2   In the Server app, select the Address Book service.

3   Click "Include directory contacts in search."

4   Turn on the Address Book service.

5   Create a new user called Ad Book in the Server app to be used in the exercises.

Configuring OS X to Use the Address Book Service

The Address Book application in OS X is designed to work with the Address Book service on Lion Server. Before you do any configuration, perform a search for a network user's contact information, and then configure Address Book to use Ad Book's account, create a few test contacts, and perform a few searches.

> **NOTE ▶** This example has the client machine bound to Open Directory in Lion Server.

1   On your OS X computer, open Address Book (in /Applications). Click the red tab to flip the page to where it offers "On My Mac" and "Directories."

2   Select Directory Services in Address Book. This applies to all directory services to which this OS X computer is bound. In this case, your OS X computer is bound to server17.pretendco.com.

3   In the search field in the upper-right corner, enter Cal.

4 The records for all users with "cal" in their names are returned immediately. Double click Cal User1. Note that you cannot edit any information for Cal User1.

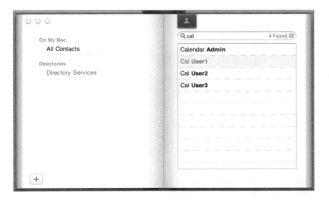

5 Choose Address Book > Preferences.

6 Click Accounts.

7 Click the Add (+) button.

8 Leave the Account type as CardDAV, as the Address Book service implements CardDAV.

9 In the User name field, enter adbook.

You must use the user's short name.

10 In the Password field, enter the proper password.

11 In the Server address field, enter server17.pretendco.com.

12 Click Create.

13 If a Verify Certificate dialog appears, click Show Certificate, select the checkbox for "Always trust," and authenticate with administrative credentials.

Of course, in a production environment, you would populate client computers to trust your known, good SSL certificates, and then train users to alert an administrator when they see an unknown-certificate message.

14 You should see the new account appear in the Accounts list.

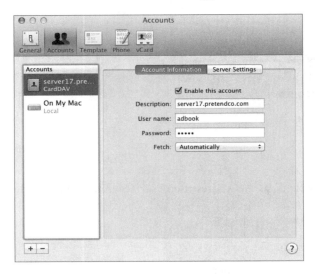

15 Select the General tab in Preferences.

16 Click the "Default account for new contacts" pop-up menu, and choose server17.pretendco.com.

Now when you create a new contact, it will automatically be created on the server.

17 Close the Preferences window.

18 Select All Contacts, then click the red tab to flip the page back.

19 Click the Add (+) button under the Name list (not the Group list) to create a new contact that will be stored on the server.

20 Enter sample information for a user, including email and Jabber addresses. You can use the following values:

First: Jet

Last: Dogg

Email (work): jet@example.com

Chat (work): jet@jabber.example.com

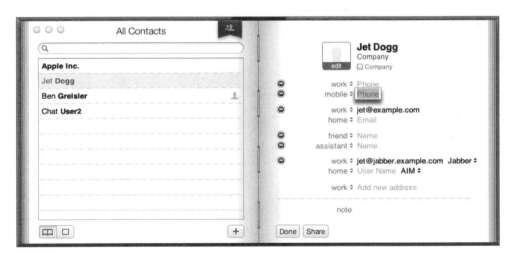

21 Click Done to save your changes.

The contact you just created is synced locally on your OS X computer for offline use, and it is also stored with the Address Book service, so you can access it from other computers and devices.

iChat also supports your Address Book Server account. Use the following steps to demonstrate that you can use your Address Book Server account with iChat. If you haven't already configured iChat with your network user account, refer to "Managing the iChat Service" in this chapter.

1 If iChat is not already running, open iChat (in /Applications).

2 If the server17 List window is not already displayed, choose Window > server17.pretendco.com List.

3 Click the Add (+) button in the lower-left corner, and choose Add Buddy.

4 Click the Disclosure button to reveal additional choices.

5 Click the entry you created (Jet Dogg).

6 Click Cancel.

In a production environment, you would click Add to add this user to your buddy list. Do not click Add now, because this would create an authorization request for the foreign Jabber server, and you are on an isolated network.

7 Quit iChat.

The contacts you create with your Address Book Server account are available to you on other OS X computers, as long as you configure Address Book with your Address Book Server account. You can also access your contacts with any application that uses CardDAV.

Troubleshooting the Address Book Service

To troubleshoot the Address Book service provided by Lion Server it helps to have a good understanding of how the Address Book Service works in general. Review the sections above to make sure you understand each of the working pieces.

Here are some common problems and how they might be rectified:

▶ If your users can't connect to the Address Book service on the server, check that the clients are using a DNS server that is providing the proper name resolution for the server.

▶ If users can't connect to the Address Book service, check that the ports 8800 and 8843 are open to the server

▶ If users can't authenticate to the Address Book service, check that the users are using proper passwords. Reset if needed. Also check that the users are allowed to use the service based on the service access controls.

Hosting Mail Services

Electronic mail, or email, is one of the fundamental services on the Internet. Lion Server includes a feature-rich email service that you can use to send, receive, and store email for your organization. Aside from the obvious reason of hosting an email server to gain an Internet identity, there are a number of other factors that make hosting your own mail service advantageous. If you have a small office with a slow Internet connection, you may find that keeping all of your email within the building rather than using external email servers makes better use of your network bandwidth. This is especially true if typical messages within your organization include large attachments. Additionally, many organizations are required to keep the information held in their email messages secure for regulatory or competitive reasons. Hosting your own email server in-house can keep confidential data from falling into the wrong hands. You may also find that various third-party email services don't offer the exact services you want. By running your own mail servers, you can customize various options to meet the needs of your organization.

The mail service in Lion Server is based on two open-source email packages:

▶ Postfix handles acceptance and delivery of individual messages.

▶ Dovecot accepts connections from individual users downloading their messages to their mail client. Dovecot is a replacement for Cyrus, found in 10.5 and earlier versions of OS X Server.

In addition to these programs, the mail service in Lion Server makes use of a number of other packages to provide features, such as webmail, spam, and virus scanning, and mailing lists. Each of these will be discussed in this chapter, but first you must learn how email works.

Understanding Mail

Although email is one of the oldest and simplest systems on the Internet, it is composed of a number of different protocols. The primary protocol is the Simple Mail Transfer Protocol (SMTP). SMTP is responsible for delivering a message from the sender to the sender's email server and between email servers. When a message is sent, the outgoing mail server first looks up the address of the destination's Mail eXchange (MX) server using DNS. A given Internet domain can have multiple MX servers to help balance the load and provide redundant services. Each MX server is assigned a priority. The highest-priority servers are assigned the lowest number and are tried first when delivering mail via SMTP.

To look up information about a domain's MX servers, you can use the Network Utility found in /Applications/Utilities on a Mac OS X computer.

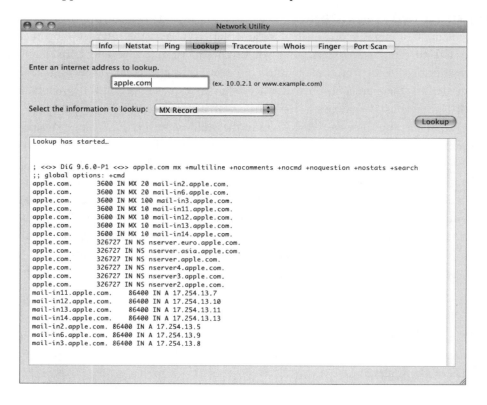

An individual email message may travel through many servers while en route to its final destination. Each server that a message passes through will tag a message with the name of the server and the time it was processed. This is done to provide a history of which servers handled a given message. To examine this trail using the Mail application, you can choose View > Message > Long Headers while viewing the message.

```
Received:  from cooper ([127.0.0.1]) by localhost (cooper.pretendco.com [127.0.0.1]) (amavisd-new, port
           10024) with ESMTP id 09379-03 for <david.pugh@pretendco.com>; Sat, 21 Sep 2002
           15:31:32 -0400 (EDT)
Received:  from mail-out4.apple.com (mail-out4.apple.com [17.254.13.23]) by cooper (Postfix) with
           ESMTP id 5D5B9B7C672 for <david.pugh@pretendco.com>; Sat, 21 Sep 2002 15:31:32
           -0400 (EDT)
Received:  from relay14.apple.com (relay14.apple.com [17.128.113.52]) by mail-out4.apple.com (Postfix)
           with ESMTP id 292BD251CA2; Sat, 21 Sep 2002 15:31:31 -0700 (PDT)
Received:  from relay14.apple.com (unknown [127.0.0.1]) by relay14.apple.com (Symantec Mail Security)
           with ESMTP id 0E96B20A4C; Sat, 21 Sep 2002 15:31:31 -0700 (PDT)
Received:  from [17.09.21.02] (sep21-2002.apple.com [17.09.21.02]) (using TLSv1 with cipher AES128-
           SHA (128/128 bits)) (No client certificate requested) by relay14.apple.com (Apple SCV relay)
           with ESMTP id E1B20A24685; Sat, 21 Sep 2002 15:31:30 -0700 (PDT)
```

Once the email message is delivered to the recipient's mail server, it will be stored there for the recepient to receive the message using either of the two available protocols:

▶ Post Office Protocol (POP) is a common email retrieval protocol used on mail servers where disk space and network connections are at a premium. POP is preferred in these environments because a mail client will connect to the server, download the email, remove it from the server, and disconnect very quickly. Although good for the server, POP mail servers are typically less user-friendly because they don't support server-side folders and may cause difficulties for a user connecting from multiple computers.

▶ Internet Message Access Protocol (IMAP) is commonly used by mail services that want to provide more features to the user. IMAP allows the storage of all email and email folders on the server, where they can be backed up. Additionally, a mail client will often remain connected to the mail server for the duration of the user session. This can result in quicker notification of new messages. The downside to using IMAP is that it puts more load on the resources of the mail server.

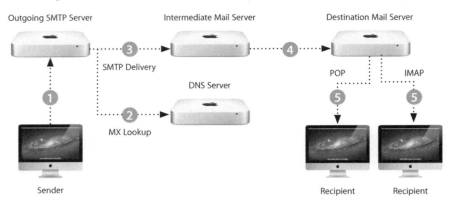

Configuring DNS for Mail

When you send an email, you'll need to ensure that DNS is configured for your domain so that mail can be delivered to the proper address. DNS can be provided by a DNS hosting company or by using your own DNS servers. While the examples here will rely on the basic DNS service provided by the Lion Server, additional DNS would be needed for a "real life" email server set up.

Specifically you will need to set up a MX record for the domain. The MX record is how the sending email server knows where to send the email. Without an MX record, the server will utilize an A record for the domain listed. Considering that often the email server will be a different server than used for hosting a domains website, this may not be a good situation, as the mail might be delivered to the wrong location.

Enabling the Mail Service

The Lion Server email service is configured using the Server app. The interface is very elegant and relatively complication-free.

1 Open the Server app and connect to your server.

2 Select the Mail service in the left column.

3 Click Edit next to "Provide mail for" and enter your domain.

4 Turn the mail service on with the toggle.

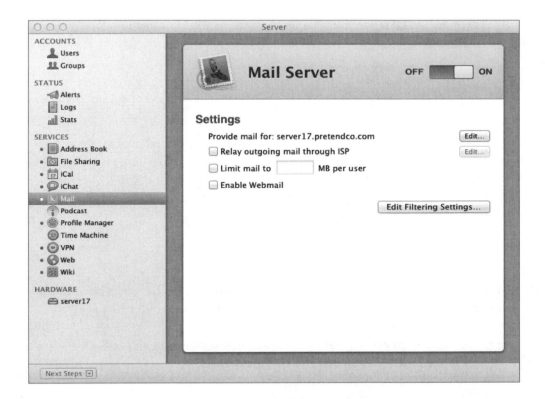

Relaying Outgoing Mail

The Lion Server email service has the option to relay outgoing email through another SMTP server. This can be important if you don't want to run your own SMTP service with the attendant issues with black lists, or if the ISP you use doesn't allow you to host your own SMTP server.

Most likely you'll need user credentials to connect to the ISP's SMTP server. If your ISP allows non-authenticated connections to the SMTP server, it will most likely be tagged an open relay at some point in the black lists. If your ISP doesn't require credentials to connect, find a new SMTP service that does to prevent problems down the line.

1 In the Mail service pane in the Server app, check the box for Relay outgoing mail through ISP.

2 Click the Edit button.

3 Fill in the SMTP server information provided by your ISP, including the user credentials and click OK.

Enabling Mail for a User

Unlike earlier versions of OS X Server, enabling email services for a user is a one step process. You simply need to provide an email address for the user in the user's record.

1 When editing an existing user or making a new user, add in an email address for the user in the Email Address box and save the change.

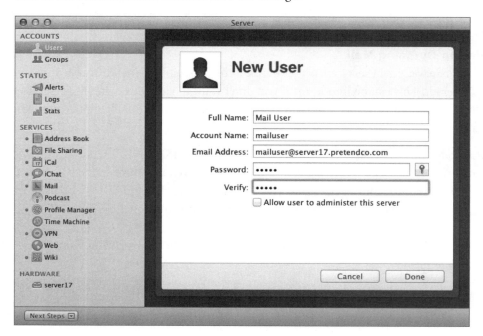

Enabling Web Mail

The Lion Server email service has the option to allow users to access their email via a web browser in addition to using a standard email client. An update to the webmail service in Lion Server is the move from Squirrelmail to Roundcube as the webmail engine. The webmail service is available even if the Web service is not running.

1 In the Mail service pane in the Server app, check the box for Enable Webmail.

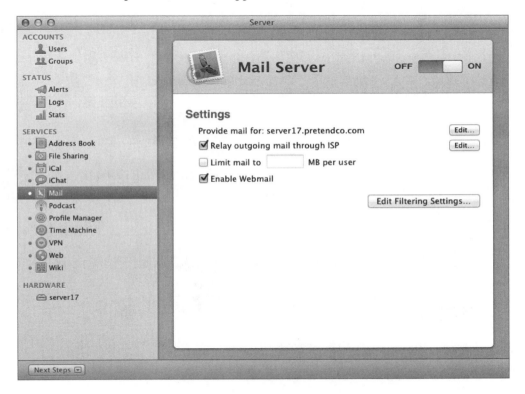

2 To protect user credentials, assign the server's self-signed SSL certificate to the Web service. Refer to Chapter 7, "Managing Web Services" for additional information.

3 Open Safari and go to https://server17.pretendco.com to access the default server web page. Click Mail at the bottom of the page.

> Mail | Calendar | Change Password | Profile Manager

4   Enter the credentials for one of the users that has an email address assigned in his or her user account.

5   The web mail interface will be presented for use. Settings and preferences for the web mail interface can be set by clicking the Settings button at the upper right to the screen.

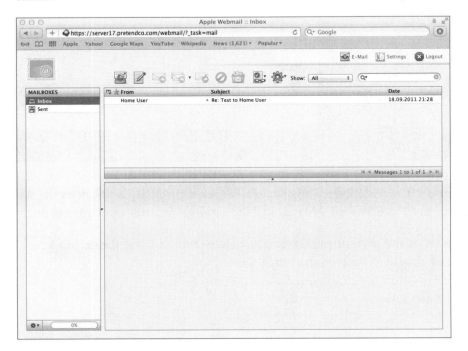

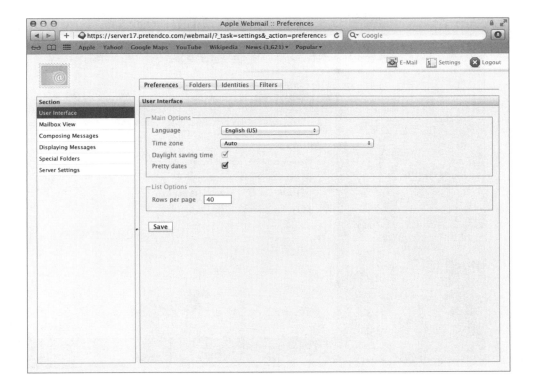

Enabling Mail Quotas for Users

To enable a mail storage quota for a user, the Server app provides a simplified management tool as compared to earlier versions of Server. A difference with Lion Server is that
the same quota is applied to all users.

A quota can be helpful to managing the amount of mail that a user can retain on the
email server, but it can also limit them if they exceed their limit and they miss email
because of full mailbox errors.

1   In the Mail service pane in the Server app, check the box for Limit mail to … MB
per user.

2   Enter a quota in MB and click out of the box to make it active.

Enabling Incoming Mail Virus Scanning

A common concern when running a mail server is how to protect your users from viruses being sent in email messages. The Lion email service uses the ClamAV virus scanning package for this purpose. The virus definitions are updated on a regular basis using a process called freshclam. Any email that has been identified as containing a virus is stored in the /var/virusmails folder and is deleted after a period of time. The user for which to whom the email was destined is notified via email.

1   In the Mail service pane in the Server app, click the Edit Filtering Settings button.

2   Check the box next to Enable virus filtering to make active.

Enabling Incoming Mail Blacklists and Junk Filtering

Blacklists are lists of domains known to host junk mail or other unwanted email servers. By subscribing to a blacklist, your email server will scan the incoming email, compare the domain from where it came, and allow it to pass or not based on whether or not that domain is listed. By default, the Lion Server email service utilizes the blacklist hosted by The Spamhaus Project. You can change this if you please to any other blacklist.

The danger of using a blacklist is that sometimes innocent domains can get listed, and thus proper and desired emails can get blocked from delivery to your users. Getting off blacklists can be daunting and may result in lost email.

The Lion Server email service can also use the SpamAssassin software package to scan incoming email and rank its likelihood of being spam. The text of the message is analyzed using a complex algorithm given a number that reflects how likely it is to be spam. This can be remarkably accurate unless the email contains terms and words commonly applied to spam. To counteract this, you can manage the service by adjusting what score is considered spam. Certain types of organizations, such as a school, might need to use higher scores, while others, like a medical office, might user a lower score.

The levels of score include:

Aggressive – The filter tolerates few signs of being junk mail.
Moderate – The filter tolerates some signs of being junk mail.
Cautious – The filter tolerates many signs of being junk mail.

Messages that are tagged as spam have the subject appended by ***JUNK MAIL*** and sent on to the recipient. The recipient can then either delete the mail, open it, or possibly configure a filter in the mail client to move it to a junk folder.

1   In the Mail service pane in the Server app, click the Edit Filtering Settings button.

2   Check the box next to Enable blacklist server filtering to make active. You can use the default zen.spamhaus.org blacklist service or replace it with another.

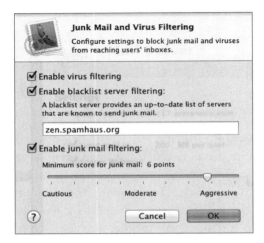

3   Check the box next to Enable junk mail filtering to make active. Move the slider to the score desired for junk mail sensitivity.

Troubleshooting Mail Services

To troubleshoot the mail service as provided by Lion Server, it helps to have a good understanding of how email works in general. Review the sections above to make sure you understand each of the working pieces.

Here are some common problems and suggestions for rectifying them:

▶ DNS problems—If the domain doesn't have proper MX records associated with it, other email servers may not be able to locate your email server to deliver the messages. You can utilize Network Utility to do a DNS lookup of your domain.

▶ Service issues—Utilize the Logs tab in the Server app to review the Mail log for clues to why the service might not start or work properly.

▶ Can't send or receive email—Review the SMTP log, for problems with users not being able to send mail, and the POP and IMAP logs, for problems with users not being able to receive mail.

▶ Too much spam being sent to the users—Increase the spam filtering rating in the filtering preferences in the Mail service in the Server app.

▶ Too many real emails being marked as spam—Decrease the spam filtering rating in the filtering preferences in the Mail service in the Server app.

▶ Webmail is being connected to via http and not https—Check that a proper SSL certificate is assigned to the default web site.

What You've Learned

▶ Setting up the wiki service involves running the Web service with at least one web server running on Lion Server.

▶ A wiki can contain files, graphics, text, and links.

▶ The iCal service is based on CalDAV, an open source initiative.

▶ The iChat service uses the XMPP protocol and is also based on an open source initiative, in this case Jabber.

▶ iChat service servers can be joined together in a process called federation.

▶ The Address Book service uses such open source technology as CardDAV, an initiative based on WebDAV; vCard; and HTTP and HTTPS.

▶ The Email service utilizes a collection of software packages including Dovecot, Postfix, ClamAV, SpamAssassin, and Roundcube.

▶ Email can be protected using blacklists.

References

The following documents provide more information about the Lion Server collaboration services. Additional resources are available at http://www.apple.com/server/macosx/resources/.

Administration Guides

Lion Server: Advanced Administration
https://help.apple.com/advancedserveradmin/mac/10.7/

URLs

Wiki site: http://www.wikipedia.org

CalConnect site: http://www.calconnect.org

CardDAV: http://datatracker.ietf.org/doc/draft-ietf-vcarddav-vcarddrev

Jabber site: http://www.jabber.org

"'Well known' TCP and UDP ports used by Apple software products":
http://support.apple.com/kb/TS1629

SpamAssassin: http://spamassassin.apache.org

The Spamhaus: http://www.spamhaus.org

ClamAV: http://www.clamav.net

Roundcube: http://www.roundcube.net

Chapter Review

1. What protocol is used for the iChat service?

2. How would you limit access to iChat service on Lion Server?

3. What tools can an administrator use to specify users that are allowed to create wikis? How does a network user specify which users and groups are allowed to edit a wiki?

4. How would you enter the iChat name for the user Jet Dogg (short name: jet) on server17.pretendco.com?

5. What application do you use to create resources and locations for use in iCal events?

6. What open source protocol does the Address Book service use?

7. What is an open relay?

8. What is an MX record?

9. What is SMTP?

10. What are the main differences between POP and IMAP?

11. What method can be used to limit the amount of disk space used on a mail server?

Answers

1. The iChat service uses the Extensible Messaging and Presence Protocol (XMPP).

2. You can limit access through Service Access Control Lists, available per user in the Server app.

3. Administrators can use the Wiki Creators list in the Wiki service settings in the Server app. When creating a wiki with a web browser, a user can specify permissions for users and groups to access and edit the wiki.

4. The iChat name format for Jet Dogg on server17.pretendco.com is jet@server17.pretendco.com.

5. The Server app is used to create resources and locations for use in iCal events.

6. The Address Book service uses CardDAV.

7. An open relay is a mail server that allows anyone on the Internet to anonymously send email messages through it. It's the primary tool used by spammers on the Internet.

8. An MX record is a DNS record that indicates the priority and host name of a domain's email server.

9. Simple Mail Transfer Protocol defines how messages travel from one computer to another on the Internet.

10. IMAP keeps a copy of the mail and it's state on the server, maintains a persistent connection between the client and server, allows folder access, and supports higher security authentication methods. POP typically stores the message only until it is downloaded by the client and requires fewer server resources than IMAP.

11. The method to control disk consumption by users is user quotas.

Index

Apple Certification
Fuel your mind.
Reach your potential.

Stand out from the crowd. Differentiate yourself and gain recognition for your expertise by earning Apple Certified Pro status to validate your OS X Lion Server skills.

This book prepares you to pass the OS X Server Essentials 10.7 Exam. This exam is available at Apple Authorized Training Centers (AATCs) worldwide. Passing this exam in addition to the OS X Support Essentials 10.7 Exam leads to Apple Certified Technical Coordinator (ACTC) certification. ACTC certification verifies a foundation in OS X and OS X Server core functionality and an ability to configure key services and perform basic troubleshooting on OS X and OS X Server.

Three Steps to Certification

1. Choose your certification path.
   More info: training.apple.com/certification.

2. All Apple Authorized Training Centers (AATCs) offer all Mac OS X and Pro Apps exams, even if they don't offer the corresponding course. To find the closest AATC, please visit training.apple.com/locations.

3. Register for and take your exam(s).

"Apple certification places you in a unique class of professionals. It not only shows that you care enough about what you do to go the extra mile to get certified, it also demonstrates that you really know your stuff."

— Brian Sheehan, Multimedia Studio Manager, MFS Investment Management

Reasons to Become an Apple Certified Pro

- **Raise your earning potential.** Studies show that certified professionals can earn more than their non-certified peers.

- **Distinguish yourself from others in your industry.** Proven mastery of an application helps you stand out from the crowd.

- **Display your Apple Certification logo.** Each certification provides a logo to display on business cards, resumes and websites.

- **Publicize your Certifications.** Publish your certifications on the Apple Certified Professionals Registry to connect with schools, clients and employers.

Training Options

Apple's comprehensive curriculum addresses your needs, whether you're an IT or creative professional, educator, or student. Hands-on training is available through a worldwide network of Apple Authorized Training Centers (AATCs). Self-paced study is available through the Apple Pro Training Series books, which are also accessible as eBooks via the iBooks app. Video training and video training apps are also available for select titles. Visit training.apple.com to view all your learning options.

Videos

The Apple Pro Video Series offers Apple-certified video training on key Apple technologies.

Apple Pro Video Series: Final Cut Pro X
9780321809629

Introducing the first Apple-Certified video on Final Cut Pro X. In this tutorial, Apple-mentor trainer Steve Martin, guides you through the new workflows, toolsets and features of Final Cut Pro X.

Apple Pro Video Series: Final Cut Pro X
9780132876308

Introducing the first Apple-Certified video on Final Cut Pro X. In this tutorial, Apple-mentor trainer Steve Martin, guides you through the new workflows, toolsets and features of Final Cut Pro X.

Apple Pro Video Training: Aperture 3
9780321749840

This Apple-certified guide to Aperture 3 includes over 3 hours of high quality video tutorials and a companion printed quick-reference guide that will get you up and running quickly, taking you step by step through Aperture's powerful editing, retouching, proofing, publishing and archiving features.

Apple Video Training: Pages for iPad, Online Video
9780321765147

In this Apple-certified guide to Pages for iPad, master trainer Rich Harrington takes you on a comprehensive tour.

Apple Video Training: Keynote for iPad, Online Video
9780132711708

In this Apple-certified guide to Keynote for iPad, master trainer Rich Harrington takes you on a comprehensive tour.

Apple Video Training: Numbers for iPad, Online Video
9780132711616

In this Apple-certified guide to Keynote for iPad, master trainer Rich Harrington takes you on a comprehensive tour.

Test your Mac skills with essential iPhone/iPad Apps

Whether you are preparing for Apple Certification exams or brushing up on your Mac skills in general, the new Test Yourself iPhone/iPad apps from Peachpit can help you prepare with confidence.

Test Yourself for Mac OS X v10.6 Server Essentials

Test Yourself for Mac OS X v10.6 Support Essentials

Test Yourself for Aperture 3 App

Introducing the Apple Pro Video iPhone/Ipad Apps

The Apple Pro Video Training iPhone and iPad Apps provide hours of high-quality video tutorials that provide a comprehensive tour of a wide variety of essential Apple topics.

Apple Pro Video Training for Aperture 3, iPhone Edition

Apple Pro Video Training for Aperture 3, iPad Edition

Video Training for Pages for iPad

Video Training for Keynote for iPad

Video Training for Numbers for iPad

WATCH
READ
CREATE

Meet Creative Edge.

A new resource of unlimited books, videos and tutorials for creatives from the world's leading experts.

Creative Edge is your one stop for inspiration, answers to technical questions and ways to stay at the top of your game so you can focus on what you do best—being creative.

All for only $24.99 per month for access—any day any time you need it.

creative
edge

creativeedge.com